# EAST EUROPEAN ECONOMIC HANDBOOK

# EAST EUROPEAN ECONOMIC HANDBOOK

EUROMONITOR PUBLICATIONS LIMITED
87-88 Turnmill Street, London EC1M 5QU

# EAST EUROPEAN ECONOMIC HANDBOOK
First edition 1985

Published by
Euromonitor Publications Limited
87-88 Turnmill Street
London EC1M 5QU

Telephone: 01-251 8024
Telex: 21120 MONREF G

ISBN 0 86338 029 8

British Library Cataloguing in Publication Data

East European economic handbook
  1.  Europe, Eastern—Economic conditions
  -1945-
  I.  Euromonitor Publications
  330.947        HC244

Phototypeset by The Fosse Bureau, Yeovil, Somerset, England
Printed by Biddles, Guildford, Surrey, England

# FOREWORD

This is the first economic handbook in a new series of economic studies to be published by Euromonitor. Each handbook will contain an economic overview of a major region of the world, its role in the world economy, its prospects for the future and an in depth analysis of the major countries in the region. Forthcoming titles in this series include the CARIBBEAN ECONOMIC HANDBOOK and the AFRICAN ECONOMIC HANDBOOK.

The main contributor to the EAST EUROPEAN ECONOMIC HANDBOOK is Alan H.Smith, Lecturer in the Economic and Social Studies of Eastern Europe at the School of Slavonic and East European Studies, University of London. Mr Smith has written the first two chapters of the book *The East European Region in a World Context* and *A Regional Overview* and also the final chapter *Outlook*. The individual country chapters have been written by a team of economic journalists.

# CONTENTS

# East Europe

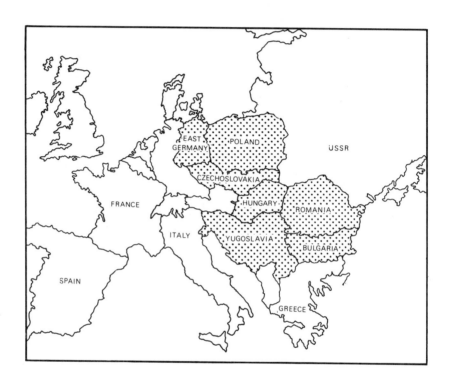

# Chapter One

# THE REGION IN A WORLD CONTEXT

## Introduction

Although this handbook is concerned with the performance and prospects of the individual economies of Eastern Europe rather than of the Soviet Union, the economic importance of the USSR as the region's major supplier of raw materials and as the major market for industrial goods means that some analysis of Soviet economic prospects and trade relations is essential to any analysis of the prospects of the region in general.

It should also be noted that although some sections of the Soviet leadership would like to see the socialist bloc reduce its trade links with the West, an expansion of trade *within* the region need not necessarily take place at the expense of trade with the West. In many cases in the past an expansion of trade within the region has been accompanied by an expansion of trade with other countries. Many schemes to develop Soviet energy and mineral resources for bloc consumption have required initial imports of capital goods from the West, while some Soviet-East European co-operation ventures have been based on East European supplies of inputs that have been initially obtained from the West.

An illustration of this process, which may be an indication of the nature of things to come, is the Orenburg pipeline. This was one of the largest Soviet-East European joint ventures undertaken in the 1970s and involved the construction of a pipeline to transmit natural gas from the Urals-Volga region in the USSR to European Russia and then on to Eastern Europe. Each participant (with the exception of Romania) was to be responsible for the supply and construction of a fixed amount of the pipeline (approximately 550 kilometres) and is repaid by imports of natural gas. John Hannigan and Carl McMillan of Carleton University, Ottowa have shown that in practice most of the participants were unable to produce the pipe themselves and had to import it from the West. As a result nearly 80% of the materials for the largest joint CMEA venture to date were in fact imported from the West. Similarly, Soviet-East European co-operation ventures in such areas as car production, animal feedstocks and chemicals involve the active participation of Western companies and Western capital and technology.

## The Role of the Region in the World Economy

*The Council of Mutual Economic Assistance (CMEA)*

Six of the East European countries that are the focus of this handbook, together with the Soviet Union and three developing countries, Mongolia, Cuba and Vietnam, are members of the Council of Mutual Economic Assistance (known by its acronym CMEA, but often referred to in the West as Comecon). Albania was a founder member of the organisation in 1949, but has played no active part in its proceedings since 1962. Yugoslavia was not a member of CMEA at its inception, as its formation was partially a response by Stalin to the rift with Tito. It was admitted as an observer from 1956-58, but did not proceed to full membership following a further round of disagreements with the Soviet leadership. Yugoslavia signed a special agreement with CMEA in 1964, allowing it to participate in certain of the organisation's activities, but is not a full member, a status that it enjoys to this day. It is difficult at the moment to foresee any closer relationship.

The CMEA is not a supranational organisation, although the USSR has made unsuccessful attempts to increase its powers in the past. It is in essence a combination of centrally-planned economies which attempt to improve their economic co-ordination (the word integration was not used officially before 1971) by drawing up joint agreements concerning industrial co-operation, specialisation in production, joint investments and attempt to co-ordinate the results through trade agreements.

CMEA decisions are implemented in the member countries by the national authorities of the countries themselves. Members need not participate in projects or proposals that they do not consider to be in their national interest. Thus a country that does not wish to join a specialisation agreement (e.g. to limit the production of steel) can simply continue to produce the commodity in question. The only sanction that other members can put in its way is to refuse to provide inputs for the item in question or to receive the outputs of the industry. Thus if the non-co-operating nation cannot supply the necessary inputs from domestic sources, or if the output of the plant exceeds domestic demand, the non-co-operating nation may be able to obtain alternative supplies or customers in world markets.

*Trade within CMEA: The Importance of Energy Supplies*

CMEA is capable of imposing less economic discipline on its members than might be expected to result from economic pressures alone and has been less capable of instituting economically rational specialisation than the EEC, the recent difficulties of the latter notwithstanding.

CMEA is in effect a trade-diverting customs union in which preference is first given to domestic suppliers and then to suppliers from other CMEA countries. The most important aspect of intra-CMEA trade is the exchange of Soviet supplies of energy and raw materials for East European machinery and equipment and agricultural produce.

As the more accessible Soviet energy sources in the European sector of the USSR have become depleted, the USSR has been forced to go eastwards into Siberia and northwards into the Arctic Circle to develop alternative sources of supply for both its own and its satellites' consumption. It is frequently difficult to comprehend the sheer scale of Siberia and the logistical problems involved in its development. Siberia itself stretches across 130 degrees from the Urals in the West to the Bering Straits in the East. The distance from the Urals to the border between Eastern and Western Europe is only half the distance from the Urals to its easternmost point.

There are therefore substantially different costs involved in developing the different sectors of Siberia, with considerable implications for the role of the region in the world economy. Construction costs in the westernmost regions of Siberia are only approximately 20-80% higher than those prevailing in the central Moscow regions, but as development moves northwards and eastwards costs escalate rapidly and can be as much as 7-8 times higher than those in the Moscow region. Consequently the capital costs of prospecting and developing East Siberia are substantially higher than those of developing West Siberia, although the richer deposits are probably located in East Siberia.

The development of the region on an optimum scale is beyond the physical capacity of the USSR alone and requires additional inputs from Eastern Europe and/or capitalist countries. Logically, however, development involved in exploiting East Siberia would necessarily involve Western suppliers and markets, but would imply a greater trade orientation towards the Pacific Coast.

In the mid 1970s the USSR proposed to develop natural gas resources in both East and West Siberia, involving importing Western equipment and technology on credit with repayment to be made in natural gas. East Siberian deposits were to be developed principally with Japanese and US participation and the products were to be piped to the Soviet east coast at Nakhodka and then shipped to Japan and the American west coast. West Siberian resources were to be developed with West European and US co-operation with the products to be piped to European Russia, Eastern Europe and then to Western Europe and even possibly to be shipped to the US East coast. The size of the projected development of East Siberia and the volume of Western capital required, made it commercially and politically risky and the project would have required official government supported credits. The Jackson-Vanik amendments to the 1974 US Trade Act limiting official Government credit support on lending to the USSR on energy projects to $40 million, prevented US co-operation in the development of East Siberia. The USSR cancelled its trade agreement with the USA and concentrated its attention on less ambitious proposals to develop West Siberian gas deposits with European and Japanese co-operation, including the construction of a pipeline from Urengoi to supply both East and West Europe.

*Scenarios for the Region in the World Economy*

Three possible scenarios for the nature of the region's relations with the world economy may be considered:

a) The region could meet less of its demand for energy and raw materials from Soviet sources, while East European countries attempt to meet a greater proportion of domestic energy consumption from the Middle East and other regions. This would require those countries either to increase their volume of exports to hard-currency sources to pay for increased imports and/or develop joint ventures and bilateral deals with suppliers of energy and raw materials. In this context the countries of the region would effectively be competing with Western producers both for markets and for sources of supply of raw materials.

b) The region could become more inward looking, seeking to balance the domestic supply and demand for energy by curtailing domestic consumption and expanding domestic output purely to meet those needs. It is unlikely that this could be achieved without considerable co-operation from the West in the short run in establishing less energy-intensive production technologies and in the development of alternative energy supplies (e.g. nuclear power, hydro-electric power, etc.).

4

c) The region could seek to expand its energy production to the maximum physically or economically possible, continuing to export energy and raw materials. This would involve continued Western co-operation and trade as in b) but also in the supply of machinery, equipment, pipelines, etc., for which the main method of repayment would either be in the form of energy products themselves, or in the form of hard currency obtained through the sale of energy products in the West. This option would therefore involve either joint production ventures with Western firms or, alternatively, direct Western lending to the region to finance the ventures concerned.

It could, however, be argued that these forms of co-operation would result in a long-term complementarity of the economic interests of the region with those of the Western industrial nations, particularly in Western Europe, with the West obtaining markets for large-scale capital ventures and supplies of fuel and materials.

## The Economic Performance of the Region compared with other Areas of the World Economy

*Background*

By most conventional economic indicators, the performance of the Soviet and East European economies in the period from the end of the Second World War to approximately the mid 1970s has been quite impressive. High rates of growth of industrial output were achieved with low or even zero rates of price inflation in state retail stores, while full employment was maintained in most sectors of the economy. In most countries a satisfactory balance of trade and payments on current account was maintained until at least the late 1960s or early 1970s.

While there is no doubt that the industrial capacity of the region expanded considerably during this period and it is probable that the material living standards of a large proportion of the working population also improved considerably, the events in Poland since 1980, and the current economic situation in Romania, suggest that official statistics give a slightly misleading impression of economic performance and of the underlying economic situation. Although economic performance in the rest of the region has not reached the crisis proportions that it has in

5

Poland and Romania, there are some indications of worsening economic performance in the early 1980s, including negative economic growth in Czechoslovakia and Hungary and a disturbing level of indebtedness in Yugoslavia, to call into question some of the apparent successes of earlier periods.

## International Comparisons of Economic Growth

Although the growth performance of the Soviet and East European economies in the period up to 1975 was quite impressive when compared with growth rates achieved in the more industrial regions of Western Europe, and in particular that of the UK, this can largely be attributed to the lower initial living standards in Eastern Europe, while comparisons with less industrialised European countries and, in particular, with Asian countries with similar per-capita income levels to those in the region, do not indicate that the region's growth performance has been exceptional.

The growth of gross domestic product in Hungary and Czechoslovakia since the Second World War has been no faster than that of Italy, while the growth of total output in Bulgaria has been broadly comparable to that of its neighbour Greece. The growth of the less developed East European states in the Balkans, Romania, Bulgaria and Yugoslavia, in the 1960s was no higher than that of Japan, South Korea or Spain.

It is striking that the rates of growth of labour productivity in both Eastern and Western Europe throughout the period up until the mid 1970s were remarkably similar and that the major differences that can be observed between their industrial growth rates can be almost entirely attributed to differences in the growth of industrial employment, involving increased employment of women in the industrial labour force and labour moving out of agriculture into industry.

Thus, although high rates of growth of industrial labour productivity and output were achieved throughout the region, there has been nothing unduly exceptional about this performance.

## The Slowdown in Economic Growth since 1978

It is clear that this growth of industrial output and national income had been subject to a secular decline and that this decline could only be

6

partially explained by the slowdown in the rate of growth of the industrial labour force. Throughout the region both labour productivity and capital productivity have also been subject to declining growth rates. Initially the slowdown in the growth of industrial output and national income was only perceptible over five-year plan periods, but in the second half of the 1970s the deceleration can be detected on an annual basis and in the period from 1978-1982 the growth performance throughout the region was exceptionally poor in comparison with preceding years. The year 1978 appears, therefore, to have marked some kind of watershed in the growth performance of the region and no country in the region has since achieved the rate of growth of gross industrial output realised in 1978, while that rate itself was below the average annual rate achieved by each country of the region in 1971-1975.

Thus the rate of growth of industrial output in the region as a whole has declined annually since 1978 and only the GDR appears to have succeeded in stabilising its industrial growth rate at just under 5% per annum. Not surprisingly in Poland, industrial output has actually declined each year since 1980, but industrial output growth was also negative in Hungary in 1980. In Bulgaria the rate of growth of gross industrial output has fallen from an annual average of around 9-10% to just under 5%, while in Czechoslovakia, Romania and (with the exception of 1979) the USSR, the growth of industrial output declined in each year from 1978-1982.

The impact of the decline in the rate of growth is more apparent when net material product (the value of all material output, excluding services, measured on a value added basis) is considered. This measure, which is the nearest East European equivalent to the Western concept of gross national product, has fallen in Poland in each year since 1980 and fell in Hungary in 1980 and in Czechoslovakia in 1981 and 1982. Net material product for the East European area as a whole (excluding the USSR) actually declined in both 1981 and 1982, although these figures were heavily influenced by the virtual collapse of the Polish economy where production levels in 1982 were only three-quarters of those achieved in 1978. The critical feature of this decline in net material product which will be of considerable importance to future output growth in the region is that it has been largely concentrated on the construction sector as the East European economies have been unable to maintain their planned levels of investment.

### The Improvement in Growth Performance in 1983

Preliminary figures indicate that growth performance for the region as a whole in 1983 was the best so far in the current five year plan. Net material product for each country in the region in 1983 was, with the exception of Yugoslavia, greater than in 1982. A more detailed analysis of the causes of the slowdown and decline in output and an assessment of whether the improved performance of 1983 can be considered as a turning point, is provided in Chapter 2.

### Recent Growth Performance in International Perspective

Many industrialised nations have experienced greater slowdowns or declines in the rate of growth of output over the same period as the Western recession has taken hold. In Eastern Europe however, the stagnation and decline in output growth has occurred at far lower levels of living standards and presents a far more serious problem for the central authorities. Furthermore, the technological level of much East European industry remains substantially below that of not just the USA, but Western Europe and Japan. There is, therefore, a clear possibility for increased growth if investment levels could be maintained and the technical level of the capital stock increased.

The slowdown in economic growth therefore bears some superficial resemblance to that experienced in Latin America and the Third World, although the scale of the problem is much smaller. The major effect of Western recession on all these countries has been to limit their potential to export to the West, simultaneously limiting their ability to purchase Western machinery and equipment. The problem has been aggravated by increased interest rates in Western financial markets in the early 1980s, which currently appear to show little sign of a permanent fall in view of US budget deficits, which have increased the cost of new capital investment and caused available hard currency earnings to be diverted to debt repayment rather than be used to purchase new equipment.

Balance of payments constraints have therefore required the East European countries (but not the USSR) to contract domestic output in the early 1980s. The contraction has not been as severe as that experienced in Latin America and although some civil unrest has been experienced (conspicuously in Poland, concealed in Romania), the

8

degree of public disturbance cannot be compared with the current situation in some Latin American countries.

*External Indebtedness in International Perspective*

Net CMEA borrowing, including the USSR and the CMEA Banks, reached $71.1 billion at the end of 1982, while Yugoslavian net indebtedness to the West stood at $18.5 billion. Alternative measures of gross debt (including credits granted but not fully taken up and not netting off holdings of East European and Soviet Banks in the West) indicate that gross debt at the end of 1982 for CMEA as a whole was $86.4 billion and for Yugoslavia was $20 billion.

The seriousness of the Polish debt situation, which at the end of 1979 stood at $20 billion (net), involving a debt service ratio in excess of 100%, resulted in the need to reschedule repayments in March 1980. In the autumn of 1981 Romania was faced with a virtually impossible cash-flow situation, aggravated by the cost of its oil imports from OPEC and a severe bunching of its scheduled repayments and also had to reschedule its repayments, while a few months later Hungary negotiated a package with a number of Western banks assisted by the IMF which enabled it to avoid an actual rescheduling. Yugoslavia did likewise in January 1983.

The inability of these three countries to meet their scheduled repayments, and the apparent reluctance of the Soviet Union to (openly) come to their assistance, appears to have caused many Western banks to lose confidence in the credit-worthiness of the region as a whole, while US banks in particular may have been influenced by political pressures following the Soviet invasion of Afghanistan. As a result, the East European countries found themselves subject to a credit squeeze and were forced to cut imports from the West in the early 1980s, although the USSR as a substantial net exporter managed to avoid this problem, it did face some cash flow problems in 1982.

Western estimates of Soviet and East European indebtedness vary, but the general consensus is that net indebtedness of the region peaked at the end of 1981 and was reduced in 1982 and 1983. The Vienna Institute for Comparative Economic Studies estimates that total CMEA net indebtedness had been reduced to $64.5 billion by the end of 1983. (Gross debt was reduced from $86.4 to 75.2 billion.)

9

In view of the increasing concern that has recently been expressed over the indebtedness position of the Latin American countries and the rumoured formation of a 'debtors club' in that region, it is important to look at this level of indebtedness in an international perspective. Total net indebtedness to the West for the region as a whole (including Yugoslavia) was $84 billion in 1983, equivalent to just over 10% of total international lending of $700 billion and approximately one-quarter of Latin American foreign borrowing. Within this total figure, the borrowing of the USSR at about $40 per head causes no grounds for concern, although at the other extreme, Yugoslavia's indebtedness at about $800 per head does give some reason for anxiety. The comparative position of the other East European countries is assessed in Chapter 2, but it may be worth noting here that the most seriously affected, Poland, had a per-capita debt of under $700 in 1983, equivalent to approximately 20% of GNP.

This position must be contrasted with that of Latin America, where two countries, Brazil ($93 billion) and Mexico ($89 billion), had levels of indebtedness larger than that of the entire region combined. These two countries do, of course, have substantially larger populations than the East European countries, but indebtedness per-capita in Brazil is still around $750 and in Mexico $1,250. Furthermore these amounts constitute over a third of GNP, while the austerity measures introduced to facilitate repayment are likely to reduce GNP more rapidly than foreign borrowing, thereby increasing the proportion. As far as the other Latin American countries are concerned, Venezuela (total indebtedness $34 billion), Argentina ($43 billion) and Chile ($18 billion) all have a per-capita indebtedness level approaching $2,000.

The position of the Latin American countries is therefore substantially worse than that of the East European countries and the latter do not really merit consideration in the same breath. Furthermore, while the so-called 'Band-Aid' solution involving new loans and further austerity measures may be of doubtful economic and social value in Latin America, the East European countries are already pursuing a programme of constraint, which if anything appears to be over-rapid.

## Trade between the Region and the Rest of the World

### *Institutional Factors Affecting the Region's Trade Relations*

The trade relations of the individual countries of the region with the non-socialist world and with each other are critically affected by the nature of the economic institutions responsible for planning the domestic economy and foreign trade. Unlike Western market economies, the functions of domestic and foreign trade are undertaken by entirely separate bodies in centrally planned economies (i.e. excluding Yugoslavia). The operation of foreign trade is exercised as a monopoly by the Ministry of Foreign Trade, while the separation of domestic and foreign trade involves entirely separate price systems in the domestic economy and the outside world and a multi-tier system of exchange rates.

### *The Foreign Trade Monopoly*

In its purest form, the state monopoly of foreign trade implies that only the state, in the form of the Ministry of Foreign Trade, not the individual consumer or enterprise, can buy goods or inputs from foreign suppliers (including other CMEA nations) or sell outputs on foreign markets. In practice the majority of East European countries conduct their foreign trade functions by means of state trading organisations which are specialised in the import or export of specific product lines and fall under the control and supervision of the Ministry of Foreign Trade. In some countries, most notably Hungary, some specially designated enterprises are authorised to participate directly in foreign trade, subject to the control of the Ministry of Foreign Trade, the Ministry of Finance and the Foreign Trade Bank. In Yugoslavia the foreign trade system is similar to that of a market economy, although enterprises may experience some difficulty in obtaining foreign exchange from the banking system.

### *Exchange Rates*

Although the currencies used in internal and external trade normally bear the same name, the functions they perform and the values attached to them are entirely separate. It is therefore impossible to compare prices designated in, say, internal roubles with those specified in external (valuta) roubles. Domestic currencies are not convertible and it is

11

normally illegal (and frequently unprofitable) to export the domestic currencies of the region. Businessmen wishing to trade with the region will, however, have to obtain domestic currency in order to meet their everyday needs while living and working in the region, while the establishment of joint ventures in the region may mean that certain costs of the venture will be specified, or estimated, in domestic prices. As a result of this multiplicity of price systems and functions there also exists a multiple system of exchange rates, of which the most important are:

## a) The Official Exchange Rate

Most dealings between countries of the region and those outside are conducted in Western (convertible) currencies at prevailing world market prices or whatever prices are negotiated between the trade partners. These dealings are subsequently converted into the currency unit of the region at the official exchange rate. This exchange rate is largely a bookkeeping device used largely for statistical purposes and its economic significance is doubtful.

## b) The Commercial Exchange Rate

The commercial exchange rate, which normally offers a better rate of exchange to the foreign businessman, is basically an average exchange rate which offers a rough approximation of domestic prices to world prices. As, however, domestic relative price ratios differ substantially from those found on world markets, the price of many commodities, when converted into Western currencies at the commercial exchange rate, may differ substantially from those prevailing on world markets. The commercial exchange rate is not, of course, determined by supply and demand conditions on world markets, but may be important to businessmen contemplating establishing joint ventures in the region, who may find that domestic production costs (e.g. labour, domestic materials, etc.) are converted into Western currencies at the commercial, not the official, exchange rate. They may also find however that some costs such as domestic labour are evaluated at some estimate of world market prices, not domestic prices.

## c) The Tourist Exchange Rate

The tourist exchange rate is the rate at which visitors to the countries of the region, organised in official tours (including package tours) and exchanges can obtain currency for their own personal use. In most cases the tourist rate offers a more favourable rate to the foreign visitor than the commercial exchange rate and nearly always offers a better rate than the official rate. This again does not really represent a market determined rate as is evidenced by the rates that prevail on the illegal black markets for foreign currency. Despite the more favourable rate of exchange that can be obtained on black markets, it is not advisable to exchange currency in those markets.

Currency remittances, e.g. from emigrés to family members or, on occasion, by employers to employees in the region made in hard currency, can often only be converted into domestic currency at the official exchange rate, thereby involving a substantial loss. In many cases visitors to the region will find it more profitable to retain hard currency which can be spent in specialised hard currency stores, restaurants, etc.

## CMEA Organisations

There is no supranational CMEA equivalent to the national ministries of foreign trade and the individual countries have exclusive powers in determining their foreign trade relations. This factor is of considerable importance in the current attempts to negotiate a treaty between the EEC and CMEA, as the powers of the CMEA to implement such a treaty are not clear. There are two CMEA banks, the International Bank for Economic Co-operation (IBEC) and the International Investment Bank (IIB). IBEC is primarily concerned with settlements in intra-CMEA trade arising from current transactions and is of little importance in East-West trade, although some of its business is conducted in convertible currencies. The IIB is primarily concerned with financing longer-term investment projects and possesses reserves of convertible currency partly raised through members' contributions and partly by borrowing in foreign markets, which can be loaned to individual countries to finance purchases for joint CMEA projects or for CMEA approved projects in the member countries.

13

## Trade Levels

If intra-CMEA trade is omitted it is apparent that most CMEA countries are not major participants in world trade. In the case of the USSR this is partly explained by the sheer size of the country and its ability to meet domestic needs from its internal sources of raw materials. The low level of East European participation in world trade is largely explained by its preference for intra-CMEA trade. As a result, in the 1970s, when East-West trade was at its highest, the CMEA countries only accounted for 3.5% of the imports of the industrial market economies and for 4-5% of the exports of those countries. Similarly CMEA countries only accounted for 5-6% of the imports of Lesser Developed Countries (LDCs) and for about 3-5% of their exports. Soviet trade with the non-socialist world accounted for about half the above. Poland alone of the East European countries (excluding Yugoslavia) accounted for more than one-half of one per-cent (0.7%) of the exports of manufactures of the industrial West.

In 1980 OECD exports to the region (excluding Albania) totalled $53.5 billion, of which the USSR accounted for $21.6 billion, the East European CMEA countries (CMEA-six) $23.7 billion and Yugoslavia $8.2 billion. This represented a two and a half fold increase in OECD exports in real terms since 1970. The fastest growing items were machinery and equipment, chemicals, foodstuffs (principally Soviet grain imports from the US), specialised steel products (including pipelines) and non-ferrous metals. OECD imports from the region did not grow as quickly as exports and only totalled $40 billion in 1979, of which the USSR accounted for $20 billion, the CMEA-six $16.2 billion and Yugoslavia $3.8 billion.

Both the USSR and the East European countries as a whole made surpluses in their trade with developing countries, while Yugoslavia incurred a deficit in this trade. The region's exports to developing countries largely comprised machinery and equipment, armaments and basic manufactured goods. Imports were largely composed of energy and raw materials, foodstuffs and non-ferrous metals. In aggregate, therefore, the region was a net importer of machinery and equipment, basic manufactured items and foodstuffs from the developed market economies during the 1970s and a net exporter of fuels (principally Soviet oil) and raw materials to industrialised countries, but was a net exporter of machinery and equipment, basic manufactures and armaments to the Third World and a net importer of fuels and raw materials and foodstuffs from the Third World. Trade surpluses with Third World countries were insufficient to offset deficits in trade with industrialised countries and the total visible trade of the region with the outside world was in deficit.

With the exception of Yugoslavia, which made a surplus on its invisible trade (amounting to $3.9 billion in 1979, the major components of which were remittances of $2.2 billion, principally from *Gastarbeiters,* and tourism $1 billion), the East European countries all incurred deficits on invisible trade and payments, influenced by the rising volume of indebtedness, were a significant proportion.

The credit squeeze in the 1980s caused the CMEA-six to reduce their imports from OECD countries from a high of $23.7 billion in 1980 to $15 billion in 1983, while Yugoslavian imports were cutback to $5.7 billion. CMEA-six exports to the OECD amounted to $16.6 billion in 1983 and Yugoslavian exports were $4.1 billion. Soviet exports were $25 billion and imports were $22.5 billion.

## The Region as a Market for Goods from Overseas

The operation of the state monopoly of foreign trade in the CMEA countries means that, with the exception of Yugoslavia, marketing to the region is quite dissimilar from marketing to Western industrialised nations and this section will be primarily concerned with the specific problems that may be encountered and the sources of advice available to businesses contemplating marketing in the area. More detailed assessments of the structure of demand for Western commodities in the individual countries and their likely evolution are provided in Chapter 2 and in the final outlook section. In addition, Western legal restrictions on the sales of items of military significance, or potential military significance combined with the renewed determination of the US administration to prevent Western Europe from becoming a conduit for the transfer of US technology to the region, have further complicated the problem of negotiating and marketing in the region.

At the risk of advising experienced traders how to suck eggs, it is essential that businesses contemplating marketing in the region for the first time ensure that they are fully conversant with the regulations and legal restrictions on both sides. Furthermore, the nature of the organisations

15

that business partners in Eastern Europe work in may mean that their perceptions of matters of importance (e.g. ensuring that a delivery is completed within a plan period) may differ from those of a Western businessman. In addition, East European regulations concerning such matters as joint ventures with Western partners differ substantially from country to country and can be subject to sudden change, presenting new trading opportunities, or closing down other potential areas of commerce.

It is therefore essential that new entrants to the market should seek up-to-date advice.

## Contacts in the Region

Contacts in the region are vital and may take some time to establish. In the first instance, businesses wishing to sell commodities to the state trading nations must deal with the appropriate department or organisation of the Ministry of Foreign Trade which will have the sole right to import the commodity in question. (In the case of Hungary some industrial enterprises may be empowered to import certain commodities directly, while Yugoslavian enterprises may deal directly with the West.) It is essential, therefore, to ascertain which foreign trade organisation is responsible for importing which particular commodity. Information of this kind is available from the East European Trade Council as well as the commercial section of East European embassies.

## How the Foreign Trade Organisation Works

In the majority of cases, hard currency allocations will be strictly rationed and the allocation to individual foreign trade organisations (FTOs) will represent the priorities already established in the five-year and annual plans. FTOs, however, may influence the allocation they receive by the requests they make to superior bodies. It is therefore the foreign trade organisation that must be persuaded either to recommend a specific item in the first place or to give its hard currency allocation to a specific company.

Taking the case where a hard currency allocation has already been made, the commodity will be one that is considered to be a high priority to the importer in the region and this will be reflected in the priorities

16

established in the five-year plans. Potential exporters will be in competition with existing Western suppliers (whether rivals are exporting to Eastern Europe will provide some indication of import priorities) and negotiators at the foreign trade organisation may be expected to possess detailed technical and commercial knowledge on the commodity in question. Potential entrants to this market will, therefore, have to provide detailed technical information about the product and the organisation of the company itself, in order to break into the market.

## The Timing of Marketing Campaigns

The method of drawing up five-year and annual plans and their foreign trade counterparts means that certain times of the year and of the five-year plan period may be critical for mounting a campaign to receive orders from funds that have been earmarked for specific imports. In the case of capital goods for example, import plans will have to be established in the five year plan, and new orders for imports of machinery and equipment may tend to be concentrated in the first two years of the five-year plan period. (In all CMEA countries five-year plans run from 1981-85, 1986-90, etc.) Similarly, plans specifying annual currency disbursements should be received during November of the preceding year and the period from November to March in each year may also see heightened activity.

Persuading a FTO to import a new commodity poses considerable difficulties. Initial contracts will have to contain substantial commercial and technical documentation, while other methods of attempting to draw the attention of the importing agency to the company or product, e.g. participation at the larger international fairs held in a number of East European cities may prove costly, however they may be essential for maintaining a presence and staying in the market in the longer term. Companies may find that the specialised industrial fairs, organised on product lines in many East European countries to be substantially more cost effective as a form of initial contact.

Even if the FTO is convinced of the desirability of importing the product it will have to persuade superior authorities to make an appropriate hard-currency allocation and will have to put the item out to competitive tender. An order may well not be placed until the next plan period (either annual or five-year depending on the nature of the product

17

and the size of the financial allocation). Initial contacts will therefore involve a considerable expenditure of both money and managerial time and expertise. It is essential that new entrants to the market budget for this and do not expect quick returns, and are willing to stay in the market even if initial signs are disappointing.

These factors have resulted in the popular view that only large companies who can withstand this initial form of expenditure and provide long term backup can operate successfully in East European markets.

Furthermore, once an order from one country in the region has been satisfactorily completed, there is a strong possibility that this will lead to further orders from other countries in the region. A large production base is therefore a considerable advantage to companies trading with the region, as it permits them to benefit more fully from the initial high overhead costs of establishing a reputation and presence in the region.

*Small and Medium Sized Firms*

In recent years the USSR and some other East European countries have started to show a special interest in establishing trade relations with small and medium sized firms in the West, especially those operating in the field of microelectronics and high technology products with a good innovational record. Once again it must be stressed that potential newcomers to this market should ascertain whether their product is subject to controls on the export of strategic items to communist countries and examine the probability of obtaining an export licence. They may also wish to consider their capability of meeting a potentially large order before entering detailed negotiations concerning technical specifications etc.

Finally, the importing authorities may act more quickly and flexibly over the import of high quality consumer goods, particularly those destined for sale in hard-currency stores or stores for senior party personnel. Exporters of such items are likely to have a high reputation in the field in question, but need not necessarily be a large company. Although the size of the order may not be large in the context of East-West trade in general, it may be significant for the individual company.

18

*Countertrade*

The shortage of hard currency has encouraged many East European foreign trade organisations to seek countertrade deals with Western manufacturers. These may range from sophisticated co-operation ventures involving 'compensation trade' or 'buyback' whereby an exporter, normally of capital goods, is paid entirely for deliveries of machinery and equipment, technical documentation etc. by the output of the plant. These operations may involve a long-term horizon stretching from 5 to 20 years and involving an element of price risk if world conditions alter more than anticipated during that period. This form of agreement may be more advantageous to integrated multinationals who may utilise components etc. elsewhere in their production process, or for ventures in the energy, raw materials and chemicals sectors where the East European produce may be more readily saleable in the West. Such ventures, however, entail something of a loss of control over production and, in particular, quality control.

A less sophisticated version is 'counter purchase' whereby a Western exporter is required to purchase commodities from a list of items made available by the East European importer and which may be entirely unrelated to the initial export and may even involve dealings with a separate foreign trade organisation in the East European country.

In both types of operation separate contracts are normally established for the purchase and sale components of the operation and this separation of contracts is a legal necessity if ECGD finance is to be obtained in the UK. Many Western exporters pass the counter-purchase half of the contract directly on to dealers with specialised expertise in that market, or to counter-traders who specialise in negotiating and selling items offered in counter-trade deals. Counter-trade dealers should be brought into negotiations at the earliest stage possible as arrangements concerning pricing, quality, discounts, etc. may considerably affect the profitability of the whole venture.

Whether an exporter will be required to enter into counter-trade dealings will depend to a considerable extent on the relative bargaining position of the two partners and the availability of hard currency to the importer. On the Eastern side, the importance of the imported commodity to the domestic economy will be the prime determinant. For commodities with low priority, for which little or no finance has been allocated in the five-year plan, counter-trade dealings covering all

19

(including interest payments) or a substantial proportion of the value, may be the only method of securing an order. Counter-trade deals are therefore the highest in the consumer goods sector and lowest in the electronics and high-technology sectors. Traditionally the USSR has been one of the highest dealers in counter-trade but this largely reflects the nature of its exports and the energy sector, where Western importers may be used to 'concessional' dealing in other parts of the globe and are prepared to accept a package that involves repayment in products. The financial problems incurred by Poland and Romania mean that those two countries also place considerable emphasis on counter-trade and that this is likely to continue for the foreseeable future. The three countries that have traditionally produced higher quality commodities and have had fewer problems marketing to the West, Hungary, Czechoslovakia and the GDR have tended to attach lower priority to counter-trade.

In the longer run however a willingness to enter counter-trade dealings may increasingly become a major selling point in Eastern Europe.

### Western Restrictions on Sales to the Region (CoCom)

CoCom is an organisation based in Paris, composed of the member countries of NATO (except Iceland), together with Japan, which controls the sale of items of potential strategic importance to communist countries. The purpose of CoCom restrictions is to prevent the transfer of technology to the communist bloc which can be utilised in the military sector. Its rationale is, therefore, entirely military and strategic, not 'moral' and it is not seen by most participants as a means for expressing disapproval of communist policies or of exerting political pressure. It is therefore argued that items to be embargoed should have a clear military use and not be easily replicable or obtainable through other channels. CoCom maintains and up-dates a list of items whose export to communist countries is controlled. The export of items on the controlled list is not automatically prohibited, but is examined on a case-by-case basis. After an export licence has been granted for such commodities it will be valid for a period of 6-12 months, during which period the item in question must be exported, or a new licence obtained.

The granting of a licence in one year does not necessarily mean it will be granted later. Many businessmen report that restrictions have grown far harder in the last five years. Even items sold in 1983 were restricted in

1984. The major problem concerns dual-use items which have a civilian use, but can also have a military application. Such items as lasers, reflecting mirrors, communications equipment, integrated circuits and items for their manufacture, such as high-pressure oxidation systems, welding alloys and even computer software, may be considered to have a military as well as peaceful purpose.

Such 'dual-use' items are likely to comprise a significant proportion of the items that CMEA nations have demonstrated an interest in purchasing from Western Europe. The distinction of whether an item is being sold for military or peaceful purposes is difficult to make and the US administration now appears more inclined to err on the side of caution and to increase the number of proscribed items. It is also far more concerned than previously to ensure that proscribed technology produced in the USA is not channelled to the communist bloc indirectly by export to a country with less restrictive legislation and then re-exported. Although the intention may be largely to entrap those who deliberately engage in such trade, it is going to make life far more difficult for businesses who legitimately trade with both the USSR and the USA and will be further assessed in the outlook section.

# Chapter Two

# REGIONAL OVERVIEW

## Regional Diversity

### Introduction

The region should not be considered as a single homogeneous unit. Two countries, Albania and Yugoslavia are not full participating members of CMEA and are not members of the Warsaw Pact. Romania, although a full member of both organisations, does not actively participate in several CMEA joint ventures and does not allow Warsaw Pact manoeuvres involving foreign troop movements on her territory, and pursues what is frequently described as an independent foreign policy, the most recent example of which was Romania's attendance at the 1984 Olympic Games.

### Living Standards

In 1979 the World Bank estimated the GNP per capita of the CMEA nations in US dollars as follows in descending order: GDR 6,430; Czechoslovakia 5,290; USSR 4,110; Hungary 3,850; Poland 3,830; Bulgaria 3,690 and Romania 1,900. Wide disparities in the distribution of income by regions in Yugoslavia mean that estimates of average income per head do not give a very meaningful indication of the living standards in the country as a whole, and the range of such measures is fairly wide. In general, most studies indicate that Yugoslavian living standards are below those of Bulgaria, while those in the southernmost Kossovo region are very similar to those in neighbouring Albania. Reliable estimates for Albania are also difficult to obtain, but one comparatively recent estimate (1976) gives a per-capita income of only $372. This figure is difficult to accept as it indicates an income level below that of some states of sub-Saharan Africa.

There are a number of difficulties involved in making such estimates and many observers have considerable difficulty in accepting the low income level estimated for Romania, which implies a per-capita income barely one-half that of Bulgaria and roughly a quarter that of the United

Kingdom, and would more readily accept a figure which would indicate a living standard closer to, but below that of Bulgaria. The Bulgarian estimate in turn seems somewhat high in Romanian statistical practices, which have been the subject of unfavourable comments by Western observers, and the low per-capita income level may have helped Romania's claim to be treated as a developing country for the purpose of obtaining trade preferences from industrialised countries. On the other hand, the estimate may have worked to Romania's disadvantage if Western commercial banks used it in assessing the debt: GNP ratio as a guide to Romania's credit-worthiness.

### The Distribution of Natural Resources

The diversity of the region is most marked by the diversity of geography and, in particular, the distribution of minerals. Most critical for the development of the individual countries of the region and for their trade relations, is the distribution of energy resources. Over 88% of CMEA's proven reserves of fossil fuels are located in the USSR, and over half the remainder are located in Poland. Poland's reserves are largely comprised of (good quality) coal, amounting to 57 billion tonnes or about 10% of Soviet proven reserves. The principal other source of energy is in Romania, but that country's reserves of oil and natural gas are being rapidly depleted and could even be exhausted at current rates of extraction by the beginning of the next decade, unless new discoveries are made in the very near future. The domestic energy base of Bulgaria, the GDR and Hungary is very poor, and all the countries of the region have been attempting to limit their dependence on imports by using domestic deposits of low-quality 'brown coal' and lignite in electricity generation. Outside CMEA, Yugoslavia is deficient in sources of fossil fuels and, although water supplies in mountainous regions make hydroelectric power technically feasible, their very remoteness makes them uneconomic at the current cost of alternative sources of supply. Albania is a marginal net exporter of energy (largely electricity to Yugoslavia) but this almost entirely results from Albania's very low living standards and consequent low level of energy consumption.

Other minerals, particularly non-ferrous metals, are distributed unevenly throughout the region (see individual country studies for more details), and the East European countries in general are deficient in domestic sources of iron ore, which initially caused them to tie their economies closely to Soviet supplies. Albania is again relatively well

23

endowed with minerals given the low level of domestic consumption and exports chromium ore.

The USSR is, therefore, the resource base for the region with 90% of the region's reserves of coal and oil and 99% of the region's reserves of natural gas. In addition, the USSR is favourably endowed with minerals and precious metals and is a significant (but not dominant) world supplier of diamonds, gold, platinum, nickel, titanium and aluminium. Although the USSR may possess a large enough share of those markets to influence world prices, the Soviet share is below 20% for all commodities and does not appear to be large enough to assist in cartel formulation.

## Comparative Economic Performance in the 1980s

### Foreign Trade and Payments

The countries of the region display considerable variation in the level of their imports from the West. In 1979 imports per-capita from the OECD nations in US dollars were as follows, in descending order: Yugoslavia 373; Hungary 279; Poland 172; Romania 171; Czechoslovakia 149; the GDR (excluding intra-German trade) 143: Bulgaria 139; the USSR 73 and Albania less than 50.

The low level of Soviet imports per-capita largely reflects Soviet ability to satisfy domestic demand from its own resources (with the notable and important exception of foodstuffs), while the low level of Albanian trade largely reflects that country's hostility to foreign contacts in general. At the other end of the spectrum, the relatively high levels displayed by Yugoslavia and Hungary, indicate those countries' greater desire to trade with the West and open their economies to foreign competition. It should be remembered that despite the low level of trade per-capita, the USSR still remains the largest single market in the region.

### The Structure of Trade with the West

The major difference between Soviet and East European imports from the West can be attributed to Soviet grain imports. Soviet grain imports vary substantially from year to year according to the level of the harvest, and foodstuffs imports have varied between 25% and 40% of all Soviet imports from non-socialist countries in recent years. East European imports of foodstuffs have normally comprised about 15% of total imports from the West. Imports of machinery and equipment account for just over a third of both Soviet and East European imports from the industrialised West, while imports of specialised steel products (particularly large-diameter pipe for use in pipeline construction) are slightly more important for the USSR (about 15%) than for Eastern Europe (10%).

The major difference between Soviet and East European trade patterns with the industrialised West lies in the structure of exports. Energy and precious metals predominate in Soviet exports to the West. In 1982 Soviet energy sales to the industrialised West amounted to $20.8 billion, or over 80% of exports to the West, of which oil sales accounted for $16.4 billion (63% of the total). Compared with this sum, exports of precious metals were relatively small, accounting for $2.2 billion. In addition, gold sales have accounted for $1.5 -2.5 billion per annum in recent years.

Whereas fuels, minerals and precious metals comprise over 90% of Soviet exports to the industrial West, they only make up 23% of East European exports, while manufactured items (54%) and foodstuffs (23%) comprise a far greater proportion.

This is not without its problems for the East European countries. In effect the poorer, more agrarian countries of south-east Europe, in particular Bulgaria, Yugoslavia and Romania, face substantial trade barriers in attempting to sell their agricultural commodities to countries in the EEC. These problems are likely to be intensified by the accession of the Mediterranean countries to EEC membership.

Furthermore, attempts to increase the volume of industrial exports to the West have not been without their difficulties. Although the GDR can gain entrance to EEC markets through the backdoor of intra-German trade, other East European countries are frequently attempting to export manufactured items to the West for which demand is in decline and which can be produced more cheaply in developing countries. Romania and Czechoslovakia, for example, are the fifth and third largest steel producers per-capita in the world and are attempting to sell lower quality steel products in Western Europe when those countries are contracting their domestic steel industries. Romania is experiencing similar problems in selling the products of its petrochemical, textile, furniture and foot-

25

wear industries in the West and has sought numerous trade preferences, largely under its claim to be a developing country.

*Energy Imports*

With the exception of Romania, the East European countries obtain the majority of their crude oil imports from the USSR. A significant proportion of this is provided at special CMEA prices, which are calculated on the basis of an average of the preceeding five years' world market prices and, until 1984, this formula represented a considerable subsidy on the world market price. It was announced in June 1984 that the formula for calculating CMEA oil prices will be altered in the future to reflect world market prices more accurately and quickly. This may still mean that East European countries will be able to obtain oil on more favourable terms inside CMEA than from Middle Eastern suppliers, as the USSR frequently accepts commodities from the East European countries in exchange that would be difficult to sell in Western markets. Furthermore, the USSR has tended to run balance of trade surpluses with the East European countries, thereby effectively advancing 'trade credit' for raw materials that would not be available from Western suppliers.

Furthermore, some East European countries also export refined oil products to the West for hard currency. In 1980, for example, Czechoslovakia imported 19.2 million tons of crude oil from the USSR out of total crude imports of 19.3 million tons, and exported 1.2 million tons of refined oil products. Similarly, Hungary imported all its 8.4 million tons of crude from the USSR in 1980 and exported 1.4 million tons of products, for the GDR the USSR supplied 19 million of imports of 21.9 million tons, while the GDR re-exported 4.1 million tons. Poland and Romania alone were substantial net importers of oil and products from Middle Eastern sources in 1980. Poland only received 13.1 million tons of its imports of 16.3 million in 1980 from the USSR, while Romania was far worse affected, importing nearly 16 million tons of oil for hard currency in 1980 at a cost of $4 billion. As a result, the *direct* effects of OPEC price increases on the East European countries, excluding Romania and Poland, have not been substantial and the majority of countries actually increased their trade surpluses with OPEC countries in the period after 1974. They have, however, suffered *indirectly* through changes in the price of Soviet oil and through the effects of the recession in Western Europe on their exports.

26

The Soviet Union announced in 1980 that it would maintain deliveries of crude oil to Eastern Europe at the levels agreed for 1980. In 1980 and 1981, actual deliveries of crude were higher than agreed (although they may have been paid for in hard currency) but in 1982 the USSR reduced the level of deliveries to Eastern Europe below those contained in agreements. The East European countries were unable to purchase alternative sources of crude, largely due to their hard-currency problems and, without exception, they were forced to cut back their oil consumption. The GDR and Czechoslovakia received the severest cut backs and their industrial growth rates were severely affected.

## *Trade Balances of the CMEA Nations with Non-Socialist Countries*

Three distinct phases can be observed in Soviet and East European trade relations with non-socialist countries, since trade relations expanded under the influence of détente. In the early 1970s, large and increasing deficits in the region's trade with developed capitalist countries were opened up, reaching a peak of $11.4 billion in 1975, of which the East European countries accounted for about $6.5 billion. Soviet trade with the West is considerably influenced by annual variations in the demand for grain, and a more detailed analysis of this is provided later. In the second stage, East European trade deficits with the industrialised West were stabilised at around $6.5 billion until the end of 1978, which represented a reduction in real terms. Surpluses in trade with the developing countries meant that total trade deficits with non-socialist countries were being gradually reduced in money terms also.

Finally, in the current stage, East European deficits with the industrialised West were first substantially reduced (1979-81) and then turned into surpluses (1982 onwards) while substantial surpluses were also made in trade with developing countries. As a result, a visible trade deficit with non-socialist countries, which had reached $11.5 billion in 1976 (for the USSR and Eastern Europe combined), was turned into a surplus of $12.2 billion in 1983. For Eastern Europe alone, a deficit of nearly $6 billion was turned into a surplus of $6.5 billion. This is equivalent to a turn round of approximately $100 per head of the population, achieved simultaneously with a deterioration in the terms of trade.

27

**Table 2.1  SOVIET AND EAST EUROPEAN TRADE BALANCES WITH NON-SOCIALIST COUNTRIES**

**Unit: million US dollars**

| | East Europe | | |
| | Industrialised | Developing | Total |
| --- | --- | --- | --- |
| 1976 | − 6,487 | +   564 | − 5,932 |
| 1978 | − 6,466 | + 1,041 | − 5,425 |
| 1980 | − 3,331 | −   315 | − 3,646 |
| 1981 | − 2,570 | + 3,363 | +   793 |
| 1982 | + 1,708 | + 3,764 | + 5,472 |
| 1983 | + 2,800 | + 3,600 | + 6,400 |
| | Soviet Union | | |
| | Industrialised | Developing | Total |
| 1976 | − 3,965 | + 1,240 | − 2,725 |
| 1978 | − 3,325 | + 4,221 | +   896 |
| 1980 | +   216 | + 2,737 | + 2,953 |
| 1981 | − 1,194 | + 1,231 | +    37 |
| 1982 | −    59 | + 4,798 | + 4,739 |
| 1983 | + 1,255 | + 4,499 | + 5,754 |

Source: CMEA Statistics, converted to dollars at official exchange rates.

East European trade surpluses with the industrialised West were achieved by reducing imports more sharply than exports. East European data indicates that imports from the developed West fell by $3.3 billion in 1981 and by a further $4.5 billion in 1982, while preliminary data indicates a further fall of around $1 billion in 1983. Exports fell by about $2 billion, but stabilised in 1982 and 1983. As a result, East European imports from the industrialised West in 1983 were only 63% of their level in 1980.

*Individual Country Profiles, Import Cuts 1981-83*

The majority of the cutback in imports from OECD countries in 1981-83 was accounted for by the two re-scheduling countries, Poland and Romania, but the generality of the situation can be seen from the fact that, with the exception of Bulgaria which only started to cut its imports in 1982, all the remaining countries in the region reduced their imports from the West in 1981, 1982 and (except GDR) 1983.

28

**Table 2.2   EAST EUROPEAN IMPORTS FROM THE OECD IN THE 1980s**

**Unit: million US dollars**

| | Imports | | | | Fall in Imports | Balance |
|---|---|---|---|---|---|---|
| | 1980 | 1981 | 1982 | 1983 | 1983/1980 | 1983 |
| Bulgaria | 1,608 | 1,848 | 1,548 | 1,560 | −   48 | −   852 |
| Czechoslovakia | 2,964 | 2,340 | 2,160 | 1,980 | −   984 | +   600 |
| GDR | 5,404 | 4,915 | 4,342 | 4,656 | −   748 | +   441 |
| Hungary | 3,276 | 3,204 | 2,868 | 2,580 | −   696 | −   276 |
| Poland | 6,504 | 4,284 | 3,264 | 2,880 | − 3,624 | +   372 |
| Romania | 3,912 | 3,048 | 1,704 | 1,308 | − 2,604 | + 1,392 |
| TOTAL | 23,668 | 19,639 | 15,886 | 14,964 | − 8,704 | + 1,677 |

Source: OECD Monthly Statistics of Foreign Trade

OECD Data (see Table 2.2) confirms that East European imports from the OECD region fell by nearly $9 billion from 1980 to 1983 and show that Polish imports were reduced by 3.6 billion and Romanian by 2.6 billion. Czechoslovakia and the GDR also cut their imports from the OECD substantially, and Czechoslovakia and the GDR were also in surplus in their visible trade with the OECD in 1983.

The stark contrast between the positions of Bulgaria and Romania at the end of 1983, shown in Table 2.2, indicates the importance of Soviet oil deliveries, not only to the East European economies, but also to East-West trade in general. Bulgaria has been able to maintain a deficit in its trade with developed capitalist nations, largely as a result of the surpluses it maintains in its trade with developing nations. It is greatly assisted in this by Soviet oil deliveries, which are larger than total domestic consumption of oil. Consequently, any additional oil imports that it can acquire through barter deals with developing countries can be exported to earn hard currency. Romania, on the other hand, has been forced to pay for all its oil imports in hard currency, and its oil import bill from the Middle East rose from $1.3 billion in 1978 to $3.8 billion in 1980. Despite reducing the tonnage of oil imports from 16 million in 1980 to 9.5 million in 1983, crude oil imports still cost Romania $2.5 billion in hard currency in both 1982 and 1983. Thus Romania is being forced to run trade surpluses with the West in order to pay for its oil imports from the Middle East. If Romanian oil imports are subtracted from Eastern

European imports from developing countries, shown in Table 2.1, East European surpluses in trade with the Third World show a steady improvement since the mid-1970s.

Similarly, Romania ($1.6 billion) and Poland ($1.1 billion) account for the greater part of the improved trade balance of $4 billion with developing countries betweeen 1980 and 1982, although Hungary, the GDR and Czechoslovakia all reduced the value of their imports from 1980-82, while increasing their exports to the Third World.

*Soviet and East European Indebtedness to the West in the 1980s*

Table 2.3 provides a summary of the major indicators concerning Soviet and East European indebtedness to the West and the effects of measures taken to rectify the problems in the 1980s. It can be seen immediately that the scale of Soviet indebtedness is not comparable with that of the East European countries and will be dealt with separately.

**TABLE 2.3   SOVIET AND EAST EUROPEAN INDEBTEDNESS WITH THE WEST**

|  | Net indebtedness (billion dollars) | | | Net indebtedness As a % of GNP | | Net indebtedness dollars per head | |
|---|---|---|---|---|---|---|---|
|  | **1980** | **1982** | **1983** | **1980** | **1983** | **1980** | **1983** |
| Bulgaria | 2.7 | 1.9 | 1.5 | 7.8 | 3.8 | 305 | 168 |
| Czechoslovakia | 3.4 | 3.4 | 3.0 | 4.1 | 3.6 | 222 | 196 |
| GDR | 11.8 | 10.4 | 9.3 | 10.5 | 7.4 | 704 | 555 |
| Hungary | 7.0 | 6.8 | 6.2 | 17.1 | 15.1 | 654 | 578 |
| Poland | 21.9 | 25.0 | 25.0 | 16.9 | 22.3 | 621 | 696 |
| Romania | 9.0 | 9.4 | 8.0 | 20.9 | 17.0 | 408 | 358 |
| **Total** | 55.8 | 56.9 | 53.0 | | | 512 | 482 |
| USSR | 9.6 | 10.6 | 7.9 | 0.9 | 0.6 | 36 | 29 |
| CMEA Banks | 4.1 | 3.6 | 3.6 | | | | |
| Total CMEA | 69.5 | 71.1 | 64.5 | | | | |

Continued...

**Table 2.3 continued...**

|  | Debt service ratio | | Net indebtedness as % exports to industrial west | |
|---|---|---|---|---|
|  | **1980** | **1982** | **1980** | **1982** |
| Bulgaria | 30 | 20 | 162 | 151 |
| Czechoslovakia | 23 | 24 | 101 | 120 |
| GDR | 36 | 29 | 260 | 173 |
| Hungary | 26 | 38 | 230 | 237 |
| Poland | 107 | 64 | 353 | 684 |
| Romania | 30 | 38 | 201 | 235 |
| USSR | 7 | 7 | 39 | 40 |

Sources: Net Indebtedness: Vienna Institute of Comparative Economic Studies; Debt
   Service Ratios: Jan Vanous, Wharton Econometrics, NATO paper 1982; other
   figures own estimates.
% GNP figure calculated on basis of World Bank estimates of GNP.

### The Indebtedness of the CMEA-six to the West in the 1980s

The visible trade surpluses achieved in 1982 and 1983 have permitted all
of the countries of the region, except Poland, to start to repay their Western loans and reduce their indebtedness to the West. Estimates by the
Vienna Institute show that the CMEA-six net indebtedness to the West
was reduced by about $4 billion in 1983, approximately half of which can
be attributed to surpluses on the current account of the balance of payments, and half of which can be attributed to the revaluation of the
dollar in terms of European currencies, which has therefore reduced the
dollar value of debt held in European currencies. Estimates of gross indebtedness made by Business Eastern Europe indicate that gross indebtedness of the CMEA-six fell from $66.2 billion at the end of 1982 to
$59.4 billion at the end of 1983.

There remain, however, substantial differences in the degree of the
seriousness of the problems facing the individual CMEA-six countries
and the measures they have currently taken to improve their external
position.

*Country Profiles of Indebtedness and Debt Reduction 1981-83*

Poland was forced to seek refinancing of its debt in 1980. It is apparent from the data in Table 2.3 that Poland's external position in 1980 was substantially worse than that prevailing elsewhere in Eastern Europe and was giving cause for concern. Although per-capita debt may have been lower than that in the GDR and Hungary, the relatively lower level of Polish exports to the industrialised West meant that the debt-service ratio (the volume of interest payments and scheduled debt repayments expressed as a percentage of hard currency earnings) was over 100% in 1980, while the level of outstanding debt was approximately 3.5 times the annual value of Polish exports to the West.

The austerity measures introduced by the Polish Government to facilitate the repayment of debt were largely instrumental in causing the strikes of July and August 1980, which had the counter-productive effect of lowering output by nearly 10% in that year, which lead to the emergence of Solidarity and the eventual imposition of martial law. The continued fall in output in 1981 and 1982 has meant that Poland has been unable to commence any readjustment measures required to start reducing its net indebtedness, although this appears to have stabilised at $25 billion in 1983, and Poland did achieve a surplus in its trade with the West in that year as well as a modest resumption of growth. By the end of 1983, however, net indebtedness was just under a quarter of GNP, per-capita debt was just under $700 and indebtedness was equivalent to nearly seven years' exports to advanced capitalist countries. This worsening of the indicators is almost entirely a result of the fall in domestic output, and there appears to be considerable justification for the arguments advanced by Jan Vanous of Wharton Econometric Associates that Poland needs only to roll over its existing debt to permit a sufficient volume of imports to stimulate a growth of output, which could in turn generate exports. This programme would permit existing interest payments to be met before a repayment programme commenced. Such a programme would appear to be conditional on social conditions in Poland, as well as an improvement in conditions in Western markets.

The second most serious problem is Romania. Romania's external indebtedness differs from that of the other CMEA nations in that it largely arises from the need to purchase Middle Eastern crude oil as a feedstock to its newly constructed refining and petrochemical complexes and, to a lesser extent, from its hard currency purchases of iron ore and coking coal for its steel industry. The doubtful profitability of these industries under favourable market conditions has all but collapsed in the recession of the early 1980s, and Romania has been forced to curtail its imports substantially. It attempted to maintain its petrochemical output in 1983 by importing gas oil directly as a feedstock, while reducing imports of crude oil. Romania first appealed to the IMF for assistance in meeting its foreign exchange crisis in 1981 and received immediate loans and standby credits to be used in each of the following three years. Repayments were again rescheduled in 1982 and in the spring of 1983. Table 2.3 indicates that Romania's per-capita debt is not severe and the apparently high ratio of debt to GNP shown there is largely a result of the World Bank's low income estimate. Romania does appear to have been squeezed somewhat more tightly than her external position might indicate, possibly as Western bank confidence may have been undermined by the paucity of adequate statistics. Currently, however, Romania appears to be embarking on an attempt to reduce its indebtedness more rapidly than may be necessary, and net indebtedness was cut by $1.4 billion in 1983. Cuts in imports and increases in exports of foodstuffs are reported to be having extremely adverse effects on domestic living standards.

Hungary appears to be the third most seriously affected, although it appears to be fairly generously regarded by Western banks who consider that the Hungarian economic mechanism may be better suited to long-term recovery. Indebtedness per-capita in 1983 was second only to Poland and indebtedness as a proportion of GNP was only just below that of Poland and Romania. The somewhat slower process of correction of external imbalance may possibly be a result of its more decentralised economic mechanism and the more stringent policies pursued in 1983 are described in greater detail in the country study.

The external position of the more centralised and pro-Soviet economies, Bulgaria, Czechoslovakia and the GDR appears to be relatively sound. The analysis of the GDR is complicated by the problem of intra-German trade. Although net indebtedness was over $700 per head in 1980, this only represented about 10% of GNP. The GDR was the only East European country to increase its exports to the West (including intra-German trade) in the 1980s, and a deficit of nearly $2 billion in 1980 had been turned into a surplus of nearly $1 billion in 1982. As a result, indebtedness was cut by $2.5 billion between 1980 and 1983 and external debt now stands at less than 8% of GNP.

Similarly, Bulgaria was heavily indebted in the late 1970s, but has achieved a substantial reduction in foreign debt as a result of its trade surpluses with developing countries, assisted possibly by its high level of crude oil imports from the Soviet Union. Although both the GDR and Bulgaria have cut their industrial growth rates below the levels realised in the 1970s, this cutback in imports has been achieved with a reasonable growth performance.

Finally, Czechoslovakia does present something of a mystery, but possibly a guide to the future. Czechoslovakia maintained a relatively conservative position in Western financial markets throughout the 1970s, which is reflected in the lowest level of net indebtedness for each indicator in Table 2.3 (except the USSR). Czechoslovakia's rundown in imports in the 1980s has resulted more from an inability or lack of desire to actually increase borrowing in the face of domestic economic problems, rather than from an unsound external position, and may be attributed to political, rather than economic, factors.

*Soviet Indebtedness to the West*

Soviet net indebtedness (excluding that of the CMEA Banks based in Moscow) was estimated by the Vienna Institute to be $7.9 billion at the end of 1983. Business Eastern Europe estimated Soviet gross indebtedness at $13.5 billion at the end of 1983, but has a somewhat lower estimate of CMEA Banks indebtedness, placing this at $2.3 billion gross, compared with the Vienna Institute's estimate of $3.6 billion net. Even taking the higher estimate of gross indebtedness, this represents only approximately 1% of GNP and $50 per-capita ($30 per head net).

The estimate of gross indebtedness includes credits granted for gas pipelines, whether drawn or not, and in view of Soviet potential for development in the energy sector and the need for capital to develop natural gas as an alternative to oil, this sum probably represents 'under-borrowing' rather than over-exposure on Western markets.

*The Role of Supplier Credit*

A further significant difference between Soviet and East European indebtedness is the role of supplier credit. Over 90% of Soviet borrowing in 1983 was accounted for by supplier credit, compared with an average of under 50% for Eastern Europe, presumably reflecting the greater proportion of Soviet borrowing that was taken up for investment in large

34

scale capital projects. There are also substantial differences between the proportion of indebtedness accounted for by supplier credit for the individual East European countries. In general, the countries with the more centralised foreign trade system, which also have a 'safer' level of foreign borrowing, are more reliant on supplier credit.

Business Eastern Europe estimates that in 1983 83% of the GDR's foreign borrowing, 67% of Czechoslovak and 65% of Bulgarian foreign debt could be attributed to supplier credit. At the other end of the spectrum, Hungary (19%) and Yugoslavia (15%), with relatively open economic systems, covered the smallest proportion of their foreign borrowing with supplier credit. Supplier credit was used to finance 48% of Polish debt and 33% of Romanian debt.

*Soviet Hard Currency Problems*

Despite its relatively low level of indebtedness to the West and the increased value of its oil sales following the OPEC price increases of 1979, the USSR has suffered from short-run cash flow problems, particularly in 1982. These problems have arisen largely from harvest failures, which have required the USSR to purchase more grain than originally anticipated and possibly, more crucially, from over-estimating world market prices for oil and precious metals. This cash flow problem also appears to have caused the USSR to cut back on its deliveries of oil to Eastern Europe. On previous occasions, the USSR appears to have been operating on the basis of a 'target' of revenue to be achieved through sales of oil and precious metals. Thus when prices have either fallen, or fallen below expectations, the USSR has responded by actually increasing the volume of sales. Thus the USSR actually increased its gold sales in September 1981 when world prices fell, and similarly increased its volume of crude oil sales to the West to meet hard currency target earnings in 1982. Whether this indicates a new trend in which Eastern Europe will receive lower priority throughout the rest of the decade as Soviet oil output slackens off, or represents a temporary adjustment, is difficult to tell.

**TABLE 2.4 SOVIET EXPORTS TO INDUSTRIALISED COUNTRIES**

Unit: million US dollars

|      | Total  | Fuel & Energy | Oil    | Precious Metals |
|------|--------|---------------|--------|-----------------|
| 1972 | 2,944  | 965           | 774    | 917             |
| 1977 | 11,973 | 7,516         | 6,092  | 1,806           |
| 1981 | 23,800 | 18,492        | 15,185 | 2,208           |
| 1982 | 26,011 | 20,838        | 16,466 | 2,280           |

Table 2.5   **SOVIET IMPORTS FROM NON-SOCIALIST COUNTRIES**

|      | Total  | Machinery & Steels | Foodstuffs | Imports from US Machinery | Foodstuffs |
|------|--------|--------------------|------------|---------------------------|------------|
| 1979 | 25,085 | 11,562             | 6,574      | 522                       | 2,870      |
| 1980 | 32,056 | 12,302             | 9,797      | 479                       | 1,256      |
| 1981 | 33,989 | 10,902             | 13,550     | 276                       | 1,577      |
| 1982 | 35,321 | 13,420             | 10,454     | 233                       | 2,120      |

Sources: All data originally derived from Soviet statistics. Precious metals estimated with the assistance of partners' data include all non-ferrous metals and diamonds but exclude gold.

*Special Features of Soviet Trade*

*a) Relations with the USA*
Soviet trade relations with the USA are noticeably different from those with Western Europe which has contributed to vastly different commercial interests in trade with the USSR on both sides of the Atlantic. Table 2.5 shows that Soviet imports of machinery and equipment from the USA have tended to be relatively small and only amounted to just over $200 million in 1982. The vast majority of Soviet imports of machinery and steel, amounting to over $13 billion in 1982, came from Western Europe and Japan, with the Federal Republic of Germany and Finland being the largest suppliers.

Similarly, Soviet exports to the USA are virtually insignificant and the majority of Soviet exports of energy are directed towards Western Europe, with Finland and West Germany the largest customers.

Soviet trade with the USA is, therefore, almost entirely uni-directional involving Soviet imports of grain and, in particular, maize, for use as an animal feedstock. Over half of Soviet imports of foodstuffs have come from the American continent (including Canada and Latin America). In the 1980s the proportion of foodstuffs (by value) in Soviet imports from non-socialist countries has increased substantially, and actually overtook imports of machinery and specialised steel in 1981. The USA did not benefit from this substantially as the increase in purchasing power was largely directed towards Latin America (particularly Argentina — the other major world exporter of maize), Canada and, to a lesser extent, the EEC, in response to President Carter's grain embargo and the rapidly deteriorating relations between the USA and the USSR in the 1980s.

### b) Relations with Developing Countries
Apart from its purchases of grain from Latin America, the USSR has maintained large surpluses in its trade with developing countries. The largest component of this has been arms deliveries, which may have been as high as $6 billion in 1982. Although the major recipients of Soviet arms are the oil-rich Middle Eastern countries, there is still considerable doubt concerning the means of payment for these deliveries and the contribution they make to Soviet hard currency earnings.

### Economic Growth 1980-1983

All the CMEA countries suffered from a decline in the rate of growth of both industrial output and net material product (the nearest equivalent to the Western concept of GNP, but which does not include the value of services) in 1981 and 1982. The effect of the virtual collapse of the Polish economy was that net material product for Eastern Europe as a whole actually declined in 1981 and again in 1982. In addition to Poland, the growth of net material product in Hungary was negative in 1980 and 1983 and in Czechoslovakia in 1981 and 1982.

The fall in economic growth can be largely attributed to the need to repay existing loans to the West and the limited availability of new credit, which has reduced the general supply of resources available to planners, and has created specific bottlenecks in the supply of components and raw materials which has had multiplied effects on output.

Net material product for the CMEA-six combined increased in 1983 for the first time since 1980 and each country recorded a positive rate of

37

growth of both industrial output and net material product. It would, however, be premature to consider that this provides a definite indication that the East European countries have turned the corner and will now be able to resume a continued upward growth trend. The fastest growth was recorded by Poland, but this only indicated a slight improvement on the very poor growth performance recorded in 1981 and 1982 and total output was still only about 75% of the 1979 level.

The economy of the GDR continued to grow at about 4.4% which, although falling below the targets originally specified in the five-year plan, was actually higher than the revised target in the annual plan, and appears to represent a creditable performance.

**TABLE 2.6   ECONOMIC GROWTH IN THE USSR AND EASTERN EUROPE 1980-1983**

| Unit: % | Net Material Product | | | | Industrial Output | | | |
|---|---|---|---|---|---|---|---|---|
| | 1980 | 1981 | 1982 | 1983 | 1980 | 1981 | 1982 | 1983 |
| Bulgaria | 5.6 | 5.1 | 4.4 | 2.9 | 4.2 | 4.9 | 4.6 | 3.9 |
| Czechoslovakia | 2.9 | -0.1 | 0.2 | 2.2 | 3.5 | 2.0 | 1.1 | 2.8 |
| Hungary | -0.7 | 2.5 | 2.6 | 0.5-1.2 | -1.8 | 2.9 | 2.2 | 0.7 |
| GDR | 4.4 | 4.8 | 2.5 | 4.4 | 4.7 | 4.7 | 3.2 | 4.1 |
| Poland | -6.0 | -11.8 | -5.5 | 5.7 | zero | -10.8 | -2.1 | 5.9 |
| Romania | 2.9 | 2.2 | 2.6 | 3.4 | 6.5 | 2.6 | 1.1 | 4.8 |
| Eastern European Average | 0.1 | -1.8 | zero | 3.4 | 3.0 | -0.6 | 1.1 | 4.6 |
| USSR | 3.9 | 3.3 | 3.9 | 4.0 | 3.6 | 3.4 | 2.9 | 4.0 |

Sources and notes: Growth rates have been subject to annual revision and estimates from different sources can differ widely. The growth rates for industrial output have been taken directly from the CMEA Statistical Handbook for 1984. Estimates for net material product are based on index numbers in the same source and the EEC Survey of Europe 1983. The figures probably underestimate the rate of inflation and consequently overestimate the real rate of growth.

Bulgaria's growth of net material product, although better than that of the UK, represents a continuation of declining growth rates. Romania's stated growth performance indicates a reversal of the annual decline in industrial growth which had continued from 1974-1982. This does, however, remain statistically suspect and is well below the five-year plan target of 7.1% per annum. It is apparent from well-informed sources that the level of consumption in Romania has declined considerably in the

1980s, and was substantially worse in 1983 than previously, with shortages of basic staple products and cutbacks in domestic electricity consumption, heating oil, etc.

Finally, Czechoslovakia's growth of 2.2% follows two years of stagnant output, leaving total output at about the same level as in 1980, while Hungary's growth was negative for the third year in the last five.

## The Non-Members of CMEA

The economic performance and, in particular, the trade relations of Albania and Yugoslavia differ substantially from those of the East European CMEA nations. It is probably most convenient to deal with those two countries' economic performance separately, particularly as the importance of Albania as a trade partner to the West is relatively insignificant and does not merit a full country study. This situation *could* alter substantially following a change in leadership which could result in the area becoming the focus of international concern.

## Albania

Albania is the smallest country in the region with a population of 2.9 million and, following its breaks with the USSR and China, is the most isolated country in Europe. It is the only remaining East European country to have been 'ruled' by a single leader, Enver Hoxha, since the war and claims to be the only pure ideological, non-revisionist Marxist nation in existence. Albania continues with an unreformed Stalinist system of administration in which all industry remains nationalised, all agriculture is collectivised or nationalised and wholesale and retail prices are fixed. Two-thirds of the population live in villages and many workers commute from the villages to work by bicycle or on foot. The most recently available figures put the industrial workforce at only 160,000 in 1973, but the workforce in industry and mining has probably been growing at around 40,000 a year under the influence of the most rapid population growth in Europe of around 2.5-3% per annum. This rapid population growth is a major contributing factor to the low growth of per-capita income.

Egalitarianism is actively fostered, the spread betweeen a worker's and a manager's wage is said to be at the maximum 2:1, while agricultural incomes have been progressively increased relative to industrial wages.

39

The country is probably best known in the West for its anti-liberal attitudes and, in particular, for its extreme chauvinism and desire to remain uncontaminated by foreign cultural influences. Foreign visitors were strongly discouraged and male visitors used to be required to have their hair cut at the border. There are some indications that these trends have been diluted recently.

The really outstanding feature of Albanian economic development, however, has been its exceedingly low level of participation in foreign trade, estimated by some to be as low as 7% of GNP. It is assisted in this regard by its favourable resource endowment and low level of development. Albania has not published systematic trade data since 1964, and estimates of trade have, therefore, to be made from partner's data. These indicate that Albania's principal exports consist of oil, chrome and other minerals and agricultural produce, while imports consist of capital goods, some fuel and raw materials and consumer goods. Albania's major trade partner in 1982 was Yugoslavia (Albanian exports were $84 million and imports $62 million) followed by Italy and West Germany. Romania and Poland have been Albania's principal trade partners in CMEA, while no trade has officially taken place with the Soviet Union since 1962.

This autarkic policy has been largely forced on Albania by its rifts with the USSR and China, and its reluctance to use Western capital. From 1947-61 Albania received aid principally in the form of direct assistance in projects to develop infrastructure from the USSR, which may have accounted for as much as 20% of domestic investment. This aid ceased after the rift with the USSR, and China became the major aid donor until the disagreement of 1975. Subsequently, Albania has received no aid from the socialist bloc, which has caused major projects to be abandoned and has caused a loss in domestic resource availability, which has been estimated to be as high as 8% of gross domestic product.

Subsequently, Hoxha has turned his back on the possibility of replacing his socialist aid donors with capital raised in Western markets. He also shows no interest in establishing joint ventures or concessions on Albanian territory for the development of natural resources. It is unlikely that this policy will be reversed in his lifetime, but it must be remembered that he is 75 and is not frequently seen in public. It is possible that a new leadership, not derived from the 'old guard' could be forced to make the country more open to foreign trade and to the West in particular. If past practice is any guide to the future, this would require a substantial input of aid, much of which would be initially required in infrastructure, which may reduce its attractiveness to Western commercial organisations unless it is undertaken by the World Bank or some similar organisation.

## *Yugoslavia*

Yugoslavia's economic system and its economic performance and trading methods differ substantially from those of the CMEA countries. This economic system is also considerably different from those obtaining in Western Europe (although the trading methods are not entirely dissimilar). In view of these difficulties, a brief account of the nature of the system of workers' self-management will be given, and the principal problem facing the Yugoslav economy in the future will be dealt with separately from those of the other countries of the region that are members of CMEA.

## *Workers' Self-Management in Yugoslavia*

Since the mid-1950s, economic activity in Yugoslavia has been directed according to the principles of workers' self-management, whereby enterprises are managed by workers' councils elected by the workers in the specific enterprise. Workers are not paid fixed wages, but receive a share of the income of the plant, which is distributed amongst the labour force according to predetermined principles, after costs and investment have been met. The enterprise operates in a market environment and workers' committees are responsible for a whole range of management decisions, including the distribution of enterprise income between ploughback and dividends to workers.

The principle of self-management means that workers' rights are far greater than those of an employee and combine, in addition, the rights of an investor, a shareholder and a member of a social group, for as long as the worker remains with the enterprise. It is, therefore, effectively impossible to reduce the labour force if demand for the product declines, although the enterprise may seek to diversify into more profitable areas of production and lower incomes may encourage some workers to seek employment elsewhere. In many cases, under these circumstances, it is the less enterprising or less productive workers who stay with the enterprise, possibly creating a vicious circle of decline.

41

Similarly, workers in more successful enterprises, or those capable of forcing up prices through monopoly powers and who are receiving relatively high incomes, will be reluctant to employ more labour, unless the newly employed labour can drive up the average level of labour productivity in the enterprise. Finally, workers are often reluctant to ploughback income into investment and vote for a high distribution of enterprise income in the form of wages, which they then lend to banks where it can be withdrawn on demand.

The system, therefore, contains many idealistic principles which the central authorities are reluctant to undermine, but also has a number of disadvantages which requires them to intervene. These are built-in tendencies towards income inequality between successful and unsuccessful enterprises which compound the severe regional income inequalities, with no automatic mechanism for labour to transfer to more successful enterprises. Surplus labour in low productivity sectors of the economy can co-exist with the output shortages, and high prices in other sectors. Investment funds tend to become concentrated in the hands of the banks, while enterprises may be reluctant to add to existing capacity.

The central authorities frequently find themselves forced to intervene to stimulate full employment and investment and to reduce income inequalities, which can be a source of tension between nationalities and a source of social instability. The methods used to achieve this have included increasing incomes to workers in less successful enterprises, encouraging enterprises to invest by offering cheap loans, and starting up new enterprises. The side effects of these policies have tended to be highly inflationary and have been accompanied by a loose monetary policy, while price controls have had to be applied to prevent monopolistic enterprises from pushing up prices.

*Economic Performance in Yugoslavia*

*a) General*
Prior to 1965, the principle of self-management was combined with a highly protectionist policy. Changes in 1965 were intended to open up enterprises to foreign competition, by allowing them to import equipment, components and raw materials and by permitting inward capital mobility including the establishment of joint ventures with capitalist firms, involving equity participation (provided the Yugoslav partner maintained the major share) and by permitting the outward

42

mobility of labour. The opening of the economy to foreign competition has not been particularly successful in eliminating the problems of unemployment and inflation and has aggravated another problem — external indebtedness.

### b) *Inflation*

Inflation in the 1960s was the highest in Europe, reaching 12.5 in 1970, while the oil price increases of 1973-4 pushed the inflation rate above 30% in the first three months of 1975. Yugoslavia imports approximately half its oil from Middle Eastern sources and does not receive CMEA preferential prices for the oil it imports from the USSR, and was affected by OPEC price increases in much the same fashion as many West European countries. Yugoslavia's policies in the mid-1970s were not dissimilar from those of the UK, although it has of course been without the benefit of domestic supplies. In the mid-1970s domestic wage and price freezes were accompanied by a gradual tightening of monetary policy, which brought some initial success in reducing the inflation rate below 10% in 1976. This had started to creep back up and reached 16% in 1979, when the second round of OPEC price increases occurred. These were fed directly into the economy and the money supply grew by 30%, and inflation rates in the 1980s have been running at just under 40%.

### c) *Foreign Trade and Payments*

In the early 1970s only 55-60% of visible imports were covered by visible exports while invisibles, principally tourism and remittances from *Gastarbeiters* working in Germany, covered the deficit on visible trade. The increased oil import bill required an increase in either visible or invisible earnings if imports were to be maintained at their previous level, without a current account deficit on the balance of payments. Neither were forthcoming in sufficient amounts and the Western recession also meant that tourist earnings stagnated and many *Gastarbeiters* were forced to return home. A relatively high level of economic growth (6-7% per annum) was maintained, however, and World Bank loans were utilised to finance investment in infrastructure, and commercial bank loans to finance investment in industry.

As a result, net foreign indebtedness had reached $14 billion by the end of 1979. Detailed statistics covering the progress of the Yugoslavian economy are provided in the country study and we may summarise at this point by indicating that indebtedness had reached $18.5 billion by the end of 1982, while debt-revising cost $4 billion a year.

43

In the 1980s some of the burden of adjustment was passed onto the consumer sector. Real wages were scheduled to fall over the 1981-85 plan period, but in practice have declined more quickly than planned, while retail sales have also fallen. Yugoslavia avoided the need to reschedule its debt repayments in 1983, largely by accepting a rescue package put together by the IMF, the World Bank and Western commercial banks, following considerable prompting by President Reagan. Consumption fell by a further 10% in 1983 and price controls that had been imposed in December 1983 had to be lifted in April 1984 as part of the package. There are considerable fears that this may result in a further round of inflationary pressures which could trigger off domestic unrest. It appears that the authorities are fearful of this outcome and Milovan Djilas was arrested and temporarily detailed after addressing a meeting on the nationalities problem in April 1984.

# Chapter Three

# BULGARIA

## Introduction

Bulgaria has experienced some of the fastest growth rates in the whole of Eastern Europe, and has been transformed from an essentially agricultural country where the industrial sector was based largely on the processing of foodstuffs, to one where machinery and engineering products make up the largest percentage of exports. Bulgaria is also likely to be the only Eastern European country to fulfill its targets in the present five-year plan (1981-85), and has also managed to keep its foreign payments situation in balance. This success can be attributed to a number of factors, including the balance the Bulgarian authorities have made between agriculture and industry in investment allocation, such that Bulgaria has a plentiful supply of food and is able to export a surplus, the emphasis on smaller projects and hence greater flexibility, and the strong links with Moscow which has resulted in a number of benefits, including low priced Soviet oil which has helped Bulgaria avoid the energy and foreign payments crisis suffered by neighbouring Romania.

The controls on the economy are gradually being relaxed, following the introduction of the New Economic Mechanism in 1982, although these are nowhere near as far-reaching as the reforms introduced in Hungary.

The standard of living is not as high in Bulgaria as in some other Eastern European countries, but this has shown a steady improvement over the years from a very low level, and the government is aiming to improve this still further.

## Economic Growth and National Income

Bulgaria has achieved one of the fastest growth rates in Eastern Europe, although it must be remembered that this growth began from a low base, as industrialisation on any scale did not begin until the formation of COMECON in 1949. During the 1976-80 five-year plan, growth averaged at an increase of 6.1% per annum, but this is planned to slow down during the present five-year plan to an annual average increase of 3.7%.

45

The results so far are an increase of 5.1% recorded in 1981 (the plan was for a 5.1% increase), and an increase of 4% in 1982 (plan was for 3.6%). For 1983 and 1984 the targets set were 3.8%.

The success of the Bulgarian growth rates has been attributed to a number of factors, including improved labour productivity, better personnel training, technological progress and a substantial amount of investment, although Bulgaria has placed less emphasis on large projects than some other Comecon countries.

A preliminary breakdown of national income in 1982 is as follows:

TABLE 3.1   STRUCTURE AND VOLUME OF NATIONAL INCOME IN 1982
(PRELIMINARY)

|  | Millions of levs | % |
| --- | --- | --- |
| Industry | 11,983 | 52.6 |
| Agriculture | 4,430 | 19.0 |
| Construction | 2,173 | 9.5 |
| TOTAL (including others) | 22,890 | 100 |

Source: National Statistics

*Economic Planning*

Economic planning is organised by the State and, as in other Comecon countries, is carried out through a series of five-year plans. The current plan runs from 1981 to 1985. The targets set for this period are lower than in the previous plan, as the emphasis is being placed more on intensive development of the economy rather than extensive development. The reasons for this change in policy are a number of constraints placed on the Bulgarian economy, including the scarcity of domestic natural resources and hence Bulgaria's dependence on the import of raw materials, plus a declining growth of the working age population. Economic growth is to be achieved through the better utilisation of existing assets and by developing new technology, which will increase labour productivity and save on the use of raw materials.

46

Investment is to grow at a lower rate than in the past, with only 30% of material investment going towards new projects, the remainder will be used to complete existing projects. Industry is expected to increase faster than national income, as it increases its share of national income, with the highest growth rates expected in mechanical engineering, electronics and chemicals. In addition, the plan proposes more development of domestic energy and raw material resources, increased productivity in arable farming and a moderate improvement in the standard of living, as Government spending for social purposes is planned to increase at an annual rate of 3.1%.

**TABLE 3.2   BASIC GROWTH INDICATORS FOR 1981-85 PLAN AND FOR 1983 (ANNUAL % INCREASE)**

|                        | 1981-85 plan | 1983 |
|------------------------|:------------:|:----:|
| National income        | 3.7          | 3.8  |
| Industrial production  | 5.1          | 4.8  |
| Agricultural production| 3.4          | 2.7  |
| Labour productivity    | 4.6          | 3.9  |
| Real per capita income | 2.8          | 2.8  |
| Foreign trade turnover | 7.0          | 8.0  |

The results for the plan so far have been encouraging and Bulgaria is probably going to be the only Eastern European country to achieve the targets set for the 1981-85 plan. This has been attributed to less emphasis on large industrial projects in Bulgaria and, therefore, greater flexibility plus relatively high earnings from agriculture, a mix which has been actively encouraged by the state, as both sectors have been considered equally important in the allocation of investment funds.

In 1981 most targets were met, many in fact exceeded, with the exception of agricultural output and the food industry. In 1982 growth was also steady with targets being met, although investment was planned to grow at a slower rate than national income. The bulk of investment that year was used in the production industries on the modernisation, reconstruction and expansion of existing facilities. The authorities have announced that the growth in national income in 1982 was achieved by increased productivity.

47

The targets set for 1983 were generally lower than those for 1982, although capital investment was planned to be higher at 7.5 billion levs.

Total capital investment for 1984 was planned to be around 8.1 billion levs, announced the Chairman of the State Planning Committee at the end of 1983. Construction of major projects such as the Kozlodui nuclear power station, the Dimitrovgrad chemical combine, the Radomin mechanical engineering enterprise and the Georgi Damyanov copper combine were to be accelerated. In addition, automation and introduction of new technology was to be increased. Industrial output was targeted to increase by 5%, with development of the mechanical engineering industry to be given priority, and more emphasis on the production of more sophisticated goods with a low metal content. Electronic components are also to be developed, while the chemical industry is expected to increase output by 8.9% with concentration on smaller volume products, plant protection agents, pharmaceuticals and cosmetics.

## The New Economic Mechanism

The New Economic Mechanism (NEM) was introduced on 1st January 1982 and follows the introduction of economic reforms a few years earlier. It is loosely based on the Hungarian system, although it will only be in force in its present form until 1985.

The main aim of the NEM is to introduce a certain amount of decentralisation into the economy and planning procedures. It was initially introduced into agriculture and then extended into the whole of industry. As a result of the NEM, enterprises will have greater independence to make their own decisions and wages and salaries will be linked to performance, thereby introducing the profit motive. State subsidies on the whole will be removed, and banks will become more involved in economic decision making. An element of competition is also being introduced into the distribution of capital investments, with those enterprises making progress receiving the best rewards. It is envisaged that the NEM will encourage the production of better quality products more efficiently.

Organisations will also have more control in making foreign purchases and will work closely with the Foreign Trade Organisation, and should respond to the demands of the international markets. Workers will also have more autonomy in the industrial enterprises, while the organisations themselves will have more independence from the economic ministries.

The reforms are one step towards more economic independence in the economy, but they are not as far-reaching as the reforms in Hungary, however. There have been few plans to increase the size of the private sector, while the central authorities still have control over the fixing of prices, the allocation of foreign exchange and of raw materials and energy.

## Population and Workforce

Bulgaria's population at the end of 1982 amounted to 8,929,000, of whom 49.8% were males and 50.2% were females. The natural birth rate that year was 13.3% live births per 1,000 inhabitants, while the death rate was 10.7% per 1,000. The natural rate of increase of the population was 2.6% per annum in 1982 and this has been steadily declining over the last few years; in 1975 the rate of increase was 6.3% and in 1980 it was 3.4%. It has been forecast that unless there is a reversal in this trend, population growth could be zero by the period 1990-95.

The population density of the country is 80.5 inhabitants per square kilometre and 64.3% of the population live in urban areas, a percentage which has increased over the years as people drifted from the countryside to the towns. The capital, Sofia, is the largest city with a population of 1,082 million, followed by Plovdiv (367,000), Varna (295,000), Rousse (179,000), Bourgas (178,000), Stara Zagora (142,000) and Pleven (136,000).

Bulgaria has a large percentage of ethnic minorities, around 1.2 million, or 13% of the population. These include Turks, Romanians, Gypsies, Jews and Armenians.

A breakdown of Bulgaria's workforce shows that over one third of all workers are employed in industry, followed by agriculture with 22%.

**TABLE 3.3   EMPLOYED PEOPLE BY BRANCHES IN 1982**

**Unit:** %

| | |
|---|---|
| Industry | 36.3 |
| Construction | 8.2 |
| Agriculture | 22.3 |
| Forestry | 0.4 |
| Transport and communications | 6.7 |
| Trade and finance | 8.2 |
| Housing and municipal services | 2.1 |
| Scientific research | 1.6 |
| Education | 5.8 |
| Culture and arts | 1.0 |
| Health, social security, sports and tourism | 4.4 |
| Administration | 1.4 |
| Other | 1.6 |
| TOTAL | 100.0 |

Source: National Statistics

The five day working week was introduced in Bulgaria in 1975. Most Bulgarians work an 8½-hour day.

Average wages in 1982 amounted to 2,365 levs per annum, although this varied from sector to sector, as seen in the following table.

**TABLE 3.4   AVERAGE ANNUAL WAGES OF WORKERS AND EMPLOYEES BY MAIN BRANCHES OF ECONOMIC ACTIVITY**

| Unit: levs | 1980 | 1982 |
|---|---|---|
| Industry | 2,288 | 2,451 |
| Construction | 2,516 | 2,750 |
| Agriculture | 1,985 | 2,212 |
| Transport | 2,494 | 2,738 |
| Science & scientific services | 2,433 | 2,637 |
| Education | 2,075 | 2,110 |
| Culture & arts | 2,081 | 2,178 |
| Public health, social insurance, sports & tourism | 2,001 | 2,085 |
| TOTAL | 2,190 | 2,365 |

Source: National Statistics

## Industrial Activities

Rapid industrialisation has taken place during the past four decades to reach the present situation where industry now accounts for over 52% of Bulgaria's national income, compared with 15% in 1939. Around 30-40% of total state investment funds have been channelled into industry during the various five-year plans, with priority being given to the following sectors: power generation, ferrous and non-ferrous metallurgy, machine building, electronics, chemicals and construction. Different results have been achieved by different sectors, machine building and chemicals have been especially successful, while in comparison, growth in metallurgy has been slower. Development of the electronics industry has been more recent, but its rapid expansion has been achieved by specialising in the production of medium-sized computers, data storage units, micro-circuits and calculators.

The Comecon joint development programme, whereby members specialise in the manufacture of different products, has also shaped Bulgaria's industry. Under the scheme, Bulgaria has been selected to specialise in certain sections of electronics and electrical engineering, and the chemical and petrochemical sectors.

During the present five-year plan (1981-85), industrial output is planned to increase by 28% or about 5.1% per annum, a more modest level than for the 1976-80 plan when a 6.8-7.7% per annum increase was planned (actual average annual increase achieved during that period was 6%). More intensive development of industry has been planned, with emphasis on development of industrial robots and computers to save labour and raw materials. During 1982, industrial output increased by 4.6%, slightly above the 4.5% planned, with the highest increases taking place in energy, mechanical engineering and electronics. For 1983, the planned increase was 4.8% and figures indicate an increase of 3.9% was achieved. For 1984 an increase of 5% was planned.

## Engineering

Engineering has been the fastest growing sector of industry and contributes nearly 30% of total industrial output and employs 25% of the industrial workforce. Among the products manufactured are mechanical handling equipment, machine tools, communication components, agricultural machinery and implements, assembly parts for the motor industry, electric and engine trucks, electric motors, telephone exchanges and apparatus, lathes, ships and marine equipment, electronic products, hydraulic and pneumatic equipment, plus complete plans for other industries.

**TABLE 3.5   OUTPUT OF CERTAIN MACHINE BUILDING PRODUCTS**

|  | 1980 | 1981 | 1982 |
|---|---|---|---|
| Machine tools ('000) | 18.9 | 18.7 | 17.9 |
| Electric motors ('000) | 1,251 | 1,234 | 1,337 |
| Automatic telephone exchanges ('000 extensions) | 337 | 388 | 406 |
| Storage batteries ('000) | 4,003 | 4,348 | 4,431 |
| Electric trucks ('000) | 43.9 | 40.7 | 39.0 |
| Telephones ('000) | 1,005 | 1,133 | 1,139 |
| Semiconductor elements (millions) | 40 | 41 | 41 |
| Engine trucks ('000) | 21.7 | 21.0 | 24.1 |
| Electric hoists ('000) | 125.3 | 125.7 | 134.4 |
| Tractors ('000) | 6.8 | 6.6 | 6.2 |
| Motor pumps ('000) | 120.8 | 131.6 | 129.3 |

Source: National Statistics

For the 1981-85 plan, the engineering sector is planned to increase by an annual average rate of 8.5%, with special emphasis on improving supplies of machinery to the energy, metallurgical, chemical and construction sectors. This will be helped by the building of three major mechanical engineering plants. One built at Hasovo is for building chemical industry equipment, one in Rousse is for constructing diesel engines for ships and equipment for the cement and mining industry, and one at Radonis is for metallurgy, ore extracting and ore-dressing equipment. Around 8,500 industrial robots and manipulators are planned to be introduced by 1985, while some machine building and electronics sectors are earmarked to expand by between 10 and 15% per annum.

The shipbuilding industry is also planned to expand, adding 300,000 tonnes of new shipping capacity for its own merchant fleet and 40 vessels, totalling more than 1 million deadweight tonnes, for other countries.

## Chemicals

The chemicals industry has been increasing its contribution to total industrial output steadily over the years from 3.7% in 1960 to 8.2% in 1982. Major complexes have been built in the past three decades at Bourgas, Vratsa, Dimitrovgrad, Vidin, Yambol and Razgrad. The country's largest complex is situated in the Devnya River valley and includes one of the world's largest soda ash plants, with a capacity of 1.2 million tonnes and one of Europe's biggest chemical fertilizer plants. New facilities have recently been introduced in Bulgaria for the production of ethylene, propylene, ethyleneglycols, carbamide, plastics, synthetic fibres, tyres and detergents.

The forecast for the current five-year plan is for an annual growth rate of 7.7% in the chemical sector, with the highest rates of increase taking place in plastics, rubber, fertilizers, perfumes and cosmetics. Half of the State's investment during 1981-85 in the chemical industry is to be spent at the Devnya, Bourgas, Dimitrovgrad, Vratsa and Yambol plants. It is hoped that the range of chemical products can be increased and that more use can be made of domestic raw materials in the chemical industry. In addition, it is planned that all basic processes will be automated and that more waste-free technology will be introduced. Already these measures are beginning to take effect, since, in 1982 alone, over 80 million levs was saved in the chemical industry from a reduction in the consumption of raw materials, fuels and power by the introduction of new technology, and by improving the technology already in use.

**TABLE 3.6   OUTPUT OF CERTAIN CHEMICAL PRODUCTS (000 TONNES)**

|  | 1980 | 1981 | 1982 |
|---|---|---|---|
| Nitrogen fertilizers (excluding urea) in 100% nitrogen | 439 | 453 | 459 |
| Phosphate fertilizers in 100% $P_2O_5$ | 217 | 258 | 239 |
| Soda ash | 1,479 | 1,469 | 1,459 |
| Sulphuric acid-monohydrate | 852 | 920 | 916 |
| Chemical fibres | 96 | 101 | 105 |
| Plastics, synthetic resins | 255 | 290 | 337 |
| Tyres ('000) | 1,532 | 1,567 | 1,577 |

Source: Bulgarian Chamber of Commerce

53

### Ferrous metallurgy

The ferrous metallurgy industry has not recorded the same impressive increases as the engineering sector, but nevertheless progress has been steady over the years. A large amount of investment was channelled into this sector during 1981 and 1982, 510 million levs in all in order to implement new technologies. A growth rate of 5.4% per annum has been targetted for this sector and the aim is for all the country's demand for high quality steel to be met, and to increase Bulgaria's exports and exchange of ferrous metals on the international market.

There are two basic iron and steel works — the 'L.Brezhnev' works in Kremikovtsi and the 'V.Lenin' in Pernik. New technology has been introduced into both plants, and in 1982 a second electric steel furnace went into operation at Pernik, with an annual capacity of half a million tonnes of steel. Another complex is being built at Bourgas, which will have a capacity of 1-1.2 million tonnes of steel sections, when finished. The first part is due on stream in 1985.

Output of rolled ferrous steel amounted to 3.25 million tonnes in 1982, a slight drop from 1981, while steel output in 1982 came to 2.58 million tonnes, compared with 2.48 million tonnes in 1981.

### Food and Beverages Industry

The food and drink industry is the oldest industrial sector in Bulgaria and before 1945 it provided the industrial base of the country. As a result of the reconstruction of agriculture and implementation of modern production methods, it has achieved a very successful growth rate, such that in 1982 it contributed over 27% of total industrial output in Bulgaria, and employed 12.2% of the industrial workforce. On a per capita basis, Bulgaria is one of the world's largest producers of wine, cigarettes and tinned vegetables. Diversification has taken place in the industry in recent years into the manufacture of new ranges of foods, such as convenience foods, children's and dietetic foods, fruit juices, meat and vegetable preserves, confectionary and drinks. Many of the products are exported.

**TABLE 3.7   PRODUCTION OF CERTAIN FOODS, DRINKS AND TOBACCO PRODUCTS**

| Unit: '000 tonnes | 1980 | 1981 | 1982 |
|---|---|---|---|
| Tinned vegetables | 313 | 314 | 315 |
| Tinned fruit | 239 | 268 | 255 |
| Meat products | 91 | 93 | 99 |
| Edible vegetable oils | 156 | 142 | 162 |
| Cheese | 109 | 117 | 124 |
| Sugar | 341 | 405 | 399 |
| Wine (million litres) | 325 | 408 | 464 |
| Tobacco products | 85 | 89 | 88 |

Source: National Statistics

## Other Industries

Another important and traditional sector is light industry and this has also received a considerable amount of investment to modernise and develop its capacity. Textiles and clothing are the largest industries, employing 177,000 people and contributing 5.8% of industrial output in 1982.

The light industry sector received about 1,000 million levs in investment during 1976-82, as the state aimed to satisfy further the demand for consumer goods in Bulgaria, and new factories were built and existing ones expanded and renovated. Another contributing factor to the increase in output and improvement in quality has been co-operation with foreign companies in introducing modern technologies and licensing the production of certain goods.

In 1982 output from textiles and clothing amounted to 367 million metres of cotton fabrics, 37 million metres of woollen cloth, 137 million knitwear garments and 19.2 million pairs of shoes.

Also included in the light industry category are glass, ceramics, building materials, cement, woodworking, furniture and paper and pulp. The large amount of construction which has taken place in industrial, transport and housing projects has created a strong demand for the building materials industry and many new plants for the production of cement, bricks, tiles, insulation materials and wooden doors and windows have been completed. The woodworking and paper and pulp industries have also been making progress, such that in 1982 65-75% of the demand for pulp, paper and cardboard in Bulgaria was met by domestic industry.

In 1982, 5.6 million tonnes of cement, 2.56 million cubic metres of reinforced concrete, 3.1 cubic metres of round timber and 354,000 tonnes of paper, were produced.

**Agriculture**

Bulgaria has one of the most efficient agricultural systems in Eastern Europe and is Comecon's second largest exporter of agricultural produce. Although within Bulgaria the agricultural sector's contribution to national income has declined in the last twenty years or so, it still plays a very important role in the economy, and the Bulgarian authorities have allocated investment funds more or less equally to both agriculture and industry in the past. In 1982, agriculture accounted for 19% of total net material product and employed 22.3% of the workforce.

Most agriculture in Bulgaria is run by the state through large agro-industrial complexes, of which there are 296, each with an average area of 13,200 hectares. These complexes have been extensively modernised and benefit from horizontal and vertical integration. The private sector is quite small, accounting for 12.5% of farmed land, although private plots of land are being offered by the Government to encourage people to stay in the rural areas, and also to increase output, while the present five-year plan envisages the development of private subsidy farming, with assistance from the agro-industrial complexes. Around one million people have small plots of land, where they grow produce for their own use and to sell in markets. The private sector provides a quarter of Bulgaria's dairy products, 38% of meat and 40% of eggs.

Of the 6.2 million hectares of agricultural land in Bulgaria, 60% is used for arable farming. Crop production is the largest sector, accounting for over half of gross agricultural output and is concentrated in the large state-run farms. Within the state-run farms themselves, workers enjoy more independence than in many other Eastern European countries, as the land is divided between small teams of 'brigades' who plan their own work and are paid according to their results.

The importance attached to agriculture by the state and the resultant flows of investment into this sector, has meant that mechanisation of state farms is widespread and modern production methods are employed. Irrigated land accounts for one quarter of all arable land. In addition, there has been an increase in the number of agriculturally trained specialists, both at university and secondary school level.

The plan for 1981-85 has been to increase grain production and to encourage its more economic use in animal nutrition. It is expected to increase grain production to 10.5 to 11 million tonnes by 1985, mostly achieved through increased yields. Livestock rearing is also planned to increase by 17% between 1981 and 1985. In addition, irrigation is to be improved and also production of fertilisers. By 1985 it has been planned that the area of irrigated land will have been extended by 85,000 hectares to 1.3 million hectares, while fertiliser production in 1985 will be double the level produced in 1980.

During 1982 agricultural output increased by 4.7%, which was more than twice the target set of 2.2%. This was largely accounted for by the increases in crop production of 6.4% and the 10 million tonnes mark was reached for the first time ever.

**TABLE 3.8   OUTPUT OF CERTAIN CROPS AND LIVESTOCK PRODUCTS IN 1982**

| Unit: '000 tonnes | 1980 | 1981 | 1982 |
|---|---|---|---|
| Wheat | 3,847 | 4,443 | 4,912 |
| Maize | 2,256 | 2,401 | 3,418 |
| Soyabeans | 107 | 105 | 116 |
| Sunflower seeds | 380 | 457 | 511 |
| Oriental tobacco | 103 | 112 | 126 |
| Sugar beet | 1,414 | 1,136 | 1,583 |
| Tomatoes | 838 | 917 | 853 |
| Apples | 394 | 433 | 426 |
| Grapes | 952 | 1,126 | 1,246 |
| Meat | 781 | 794 | 807 |
| Eggs (million) | 2,434 | 2,431 | 2,489 |

Source: PR Bulgaria

The plan for 1983 was to continue to increase grain and fodder production and for overall output to increase by 2.7%. During the summer the country was hit by a severe drought, however, and net production was less than in 1982 with lower output of wheat, sunflower seeds, sugar beet, tomatoes and grapes, although livestock production was reported to officially have risen by 3%. A compensation programme was started as a result of the drought and extensive second sowing took place, but this is not thought to have made up for the losses incurred.

## Minerals

Bulgaria has few commercial mineral deposits, the main minerals mined are iron ore, lead, zinc, copper and manganese. Iron ore is mined largely from the Chelopech mine in the Sofia district, but only in small quantities, so Bulgaria has to rely on imports of iron ore for most of its requirements. The lead and zinc deposits are found principally in southern Bulgaria, while large deposits of copper ore have been found in the Sreda Gora mountains.

## Energy Supplies

In 1982 a record output of 33.5 million tonnes of coal was mined, which is expected to have increased still further by 4.1 million tonnes in 1983. Increasing coal production is seen as one of the most important aims in expanding Bulgaria's domestic supplies of raw materials and a programme of reconstruction, modernisation and building new mines is underway. The plan is for coal production to reach 46 million tonnes by 1985, 62 million tonnes by 1990 and 78 million tonnes by the end of the century. The increase in output is being centred on the Maritsa East complex, which at present accounts for nearly two-thirds of total coal output. Two new mines are to be built at this complex with the aid of foreign co-operation and equipment. Exploration for new deposits is taking place and hard coal of very high quality has been found in the Dobrya in the south-east, although it lies at a great depth. Most of the coal found in Bulgaria is low calorie lignite, but a new system has been developed whereby this type of coal can be burned successfully in thermal power stations.

There is little in the way of domestic production of natural gas and oil, most of which has to be imported from the Soviet Union. The gas pipeline from the Soviet Union to Bulgaria is expected to be finished during the current five-year plan. In 1980 gas output only amounted to 200 cubic metres. Figures for domestic oil production are not available, but it is thought likely that production is declining. Offshore exploration attempts in the Black Sea have not proved successful so far, and co-operation from abroad is being sought.

## Electricity Production

In terms of the amount of nuclear power generated as a percentage of the total energy produced, Bulgaria is now third in the world. In 1982 around 26% of the country's electricity was generated by nuclear power. Bulgaria's first nuclear power station was built at Kozlodui with Soviet help, and came onstream in 1974. There are now four reactors at the plant, the fifth one is due to be completed in 1985 and a sixth is expected to be commissioned in 1987. Another plant is to be constructed at Belene, 100 kilometres east of Kozlodui and its first reactor is due to start working before the end of the 1980s.

Besides nuclear power, another important fuel for electricity generation is coal and this is forecast to increase its role in the future. The Maritsa East project already supplies 25% of national electricity production. Full capacity has been reached at the Maritsa East 3 thermal power station, while the Maritsa East 2 plant is being expanded and modernised. Other power stations are also being revamped.

Some electricity is also generated by hydropower. Bulgaria's largest hydro-electric power complex is at Belmeken-Sestrimo, which is in the north-eastern part of the Rila mountains. Total capacity is 755MW. Another complex is being built underground at a complex called Pavets Claira, parallel to the existing complex. Its final capacity will be 864MW.

Bulgaria is also looking into the exploitation of new forms of energy, including geothermal, solar, wind and biogas, and has entered into co-operation with Romania on this.

## Construction

A number of major projects were completed in 1983. These included the expansion of the Tryanovo-North and the Tryanovo-South pits and

59

expansion of the ammonium production facilities at Stara Zagora and the sugar refinery at Doho Mitropoliya. Reconstruction and expansion work was also carried out at the Brezhnev rolled steel plant and the sulphuric acid plant at Dimitrovgrad. In addition, 69,000 apartments were completed, together with schools, children's institutions, medical and other projects. The construction industry has had difficulty in recent years in reaching the targets set for housing, due largely to a lack of materials and a shortage of manpower. It is also claimed that many building workers work after hours and at weekends on private building work, which is booming, to the detriment of official building projects.

## Transport

Bulgaria has around 32,000 kilometres of roads and plans are for these to be improved and new roads built over the next few years. A motorway link is being built which will connect Sofia, Varna and Bourgas. The number of passengers using road public transport has increased dramatically over the past few years. Freight transport by road will also be increased, as the plan during 1981-85 is for lorry sizes to be increased and more diesel powered vehicles will be used. In addition, it is planned that there will be an increase in the amount of containerised cargo shipments. Bulgarian international road haulage, previously very successful, has been hit recently however by the disputes in the Middle East.

The total length of railway in Bulgaria amounts to about 6,465 kilometres, of which over 40% are electrified. Development of the railway system has been given priority in the transport sector and more of the railway network is to be electrified and double tracked. Completion of a double track ring linking the major cities is planned by 1985. The amount of freight transported by rail increased by 4.6% in 1982 compared with 1981, while passengers transported went up by 2.4%.

Inland river transport is declining in Bulgaria although it is planned to increase sea transport by the introduction of a ferry service between Varna and Ilyichovsk in the USSR. As part of the Comecon containerisation programme, Bulgaria is planning to increase its number of container terminals to 30 by 1990 which would quadruple existing capacity.

Air transport is increasing in importance. The state airline, Bulgarian Airlines, now has links with 40 different countries. Within Bulgaria the amount of air cargo transported increased to over 1.6 million tonnes in 1982.

## Government and Society

Chairman of the Council of State and Secretary-General of the Bulgarian Communist Party is Mr Todor Zhivkov, who has held this position since 1954. He is thought to be a popular leader and in 1981 was elected by the National Assembly for another five-year term as Head of the State Council. In early 1984, there was an extensive reshuffling of the Bulgarian Government as part of the process of accelerating economic reform which has apparently strengthened the position of Mr Zhivkov. The new economic reforms are aimed at decentralising economic management and are partly based on Hungary's successful policies. The number of economic ministries is being reduced by merging some together, while there has been a policy of promoting younger technocrats who often have gained experience or training in the West as well as in the Soviet Union.

The Bulgarian Communist party is the dominant party in Bulgaria with 826,000 members. In addition, there is the Bulgarian Agrarian Party with 120,000 members. These two parties together form the Fatherland Front.

Bulgaria has always been very close, both politically and culturally, to Moscow and there has never been any significant dissident movement. As a result, the Soviet Union has looked favourably on Bulgaria, which has benefited from Soviet assistance, especially in allocations of Soviet oil, which Bulgaria has bought at low prices and partially re-exported for hard currency.

Despite the strong links with Moscow, Bulgaria is pressing ahead with its economic reforms in advance of the Soviet Union and has also been pushing for a nuclear free zone in the Balkans. This has not been interpreted as a move against Moscow, however, rather that Bulgaria does not want to be directly involved in Warsaw Pact moves against the deployment of the US Cruise and Pershing missiles in Western Europe.

## Incomes, Consumer Expenditure and Living Standards

By Western standards, incomes in Bulgaria are low, although these have improved steadily within the country itself as it continues its long-term programme of raising general living standards. In 1982 real incomes increased by over 3% compared with 1981, following a 5.8% increase during that year. The expectation was for incomes to rise more slowly in 1983 and 1984, and the preliminiary figures for 1983 indicate an increase of 2.8%.

Within Bulgaria there are variations in the levels of incomes earned, the professions are generally poorly paid in comparison with workers engaged directly in production, while farm workers' wages are usually lower than those in the towns, although rural wage earners can often supplement their income from earnings from private plots.

Supplies of consumer goods to the population are steadily being improved, although there are still shortages of some goods and some goods are of poor quality. In 1982 around 630 million foreign exchange levs worth of consumer goods and durables were imported to improve the selection available. Retail turnover increased by 4.6% to 13,304 million levs in 1982 and personal consumption increased by 5.5% against the planned 3.5%.

Rents in Bulgaria tend to be very low and most families have two wage earners so purchasing capacity of a household can be quite high. Retail sales of consumer goods in 1982 are shown in the following table:

**TABLE 3.9   RETAIL SALES OF SELECTED COMMODITY GROUPS**

|  | 1980 | 1982 |
|---|---|---|
| Cotton fabrics (million metres) | 66 | 61 |
| Woollen fabrics (million metres) | 15 | 14 |
| Silk and rayon fabrics (million metres) | 13 | 13 |
| Cotton knitwear (million pieces) | 58 | 59 |
| Woollen knitwear (million pieces) | 21 | 20 |
| Hosiery (million pairs) | 64 | 66 |
| Footwear (million pairs) | 17 | 19 |
| Soap ('000 tonnes) | 16 | 17 |
| Wireless sets ('000) | 209 | 155 |
| TV sets ('000) | 147 | 241 |
| Washing machines ('000) | 88 | 217 |
| Refrigerators ('000) | 109 | 137 |
| Cameras ('000) | 71 | 70 |
| Watches ('000) | 1,061 | 880 |
| Sewing machines ('000) | 47 | 44 |
| Cars ('000) | 78 | 64 |
| Tobacco products ('000 tonnes) | 13 | 14 |

Source: National Statistics

Living standards have improved over the years as seen in the following table, but they started from a very low base and are still low by Eastern European standards.

**TABLE 3.10   OWNERSHIP OF DURABLES PER 100 HOUSEHOLDS**

|  | 1980 | 1982 |
|---|---|---|
| Wireless sets* | 88 | 91 |
| TV sets* | 75 | 83 |
| Refrigerators | 76 | 84 |
| Washing machines | 71 | 77 |
| Cars | 29 | 32 |
| Telephones | 24 | 30 |

* excluding transistors
Source: National Statistics

The annual per capita consumption of certain foods in 1982 was: meat and meat products 68.6 kg; eggs 220; milk and dairy products 180 litres; vegetables 109 kg.

A programme to increase the standard of living and extend social policy was introduced in February 1983. One of the objectives of this was to adjust the rise in incomes to the supply of goods in order to reduce an excess in purchasing power expected over the next few years. It is also planned to alter prices at more frequent intervals and for them to be more flexible. No recent price information is available but in 1980, according to official sources, consumer prices increased by 14% but only by 1% in 1981.

Although subsidies keep prices low for basic foodstuffs, around 42% of the average household income is spent on food, 13% on rent and 10% on clothes.

## Housing

The majority of housing in Bulgaria is privately owned and a large percentage has been built recently. Of the present 2.9 million dwellings, 1.2 million have been built since 1970, while 70% of all dwellings have been built since the end of the Second World War. This massive increase in building has been largely in urban areas, as people flowed from the rural areas into towns. Despite this impressive building record, the total demand for housing in towns has not been satisfied and targets were not met in the 1976-80 plan. The plan for 1981-85 is for 360,000 units to be built. In 1983 69,000 apartments were completed.

Figures for housing with a running water supply indicate that all towns have such a facility compared with nearly 80% of villages.

## Health

Medical care is the responsibility of the state and the service offered has steadily improved. In 1982 there were 90 hospital beds per 10,000 of the population and one doctor for 392 people.

## Education

Education is free and compulsory for all children between the ages of seven and sixteen. In 1982 there were 5,733 kindergartens with 404,000 children, while the number of students amounted to 1.49 million in 1982/83. These were divided between the various educational institutions as follows:

**TABLE 3.11   STUDENTS BY KIND OF EDUCATIONAL INSTITUTION 1982/3**

| Unit: '000 | |
|---|---:|
| Primary and secondary, labour-polytechnic schools | 1,170.4 |
| Secondary vocational-technical schools | 122.2 |
| Secondary-technical schools and art schools | 93.2 |
| Post-secondary institutions | 9.9 |
| Higher educational institutions | 83.6 |
| TOTAL (including others) | 1,498.3 |

Source: National Statistics

35% of students were studying engineering or technical subjects, followed by 23% studying mathematics, natural sciences and humanities and 15% studying economics.

## Recreation and tourism

Bulgaria has 324 sports clubs which have a total of 966,000 members. In 1982 the number of theatres numbered 63 and there were 3,302 cinemas.

There has been a steady increase in the number of visitors to Bulgaria; in 1982 there were 5.64 million visitors of whom 1.94 million were tourists, a decline from the 2.1 million in 1981. In an attempt to prevent this decline escalating and threatening a valuable source of hard currency earnings, Bulgaria has increased the premium on the official exchange rate to foreign visitors from 50% to 80%.

The largest number of visitors come from neighbouring Turkey, 2.5 million visited in 1982, followed by Yugoslavia and Czechoslovakia. From Western Europe most visitors are from West Germany and Greece. Around 551,000 Bulgarians travelled abroad in 1982, with the most popular destination the Soviet Union, followed by Romania.

Most tourism in Bulgaria is centred around the beach resorts on the Black Sea and ski resorts in the mountains where, in both places, a large amount of development has taken place.

## Foreign Trade and Payments

The bulk of Bulgaria's foreign trade is with other Comecon members; in 1982 nearly 80% of Bulgaria's trade turnover (exports + imports) was with Comecon. Although trade with Western developed countries was in deficit by nearly 600 million levs in 1982, mainly due to a fall in Bulgarian exports, this is more or less compensated for by receipts from tourism and heavy transit goods traffic and it is thought likely that the current account with the West should be in surplus. Trade with less developed countries with whom Bulgaria has a surplus has risen rapidly in recent years to around 11% of the total trade turnover in 1982.

The table below shows the breakdown between socialist countries, developed and developing countries.

**TABLE 3.12   FOREIGN TRADE TURNOVER BY GROUPS OF COUNTRIES**

Unit: million foreign exchange levs

|  | 1980 | 1981 | 1982 |
|---|---|---|---|
| *Socialist countries—total* | 12,836 | 14,320 | 16,249 |
| Exports | 6,304 | 6,811 | 7,772 |
| Imports | 6,532 | 7,509 | 8,477 |
| | | | |
| *Developed countries* | 2,833 | 3,314 | 3,062 |
| Exports | 1,407 | 1,326 | 1,237 |
| Imports | 1,426 | 1,988 | 1,825 |
| | | | |
| *Developing countries* | 1,515 | 2,183 | 2,544 |
| Exports | 1,191 | 1,723 | 1,871 |
| Imports | 324 | 460 | 673 |

Source: National Statistics

By far the largest trade partner is the Soviet Union which accounts for 53.8% of Bulgaria's overall trade in 1982, or goods worth 11,750 million foreign exchange levs.

Foreign trade turnover has been increasing steadily over the past two decades, at an average annual growth rate of 12-15%. In 1982 foreign trade increased by 10.2%, twice the annual planned target. Exports amounted to 10,880 million foreign exchange (f.e.) levs in 1982, an increase of 10.3%, while imports amounted to 10,975 million f.e. levs, an increase of 10.2%.

As can be seen by the following table, the Soviet Union is by far the most dominant customer for Bulgarian exports.

**TABLE 3.13  BULGARIAN EXPORTS**

| Unit: million foreign exchange levs | 1981 | 1982 | % 1982 |
|---|---|---|---|
| Soviet Union | 4,767.8 | 5,615.9 | 51.6 |
| GDR | 579.2 | 582.4 | 5.4 |
| Poland | 274.2 | 317.9 | 2.9 |
| Czechoslovakia | 355.3 | 413.0 | 3.8 |

continued...

| Table 3.13 continued... | 1981 | 1982 | % 1982 |
|---|---|---|---|
| Iraq | 335.6 | 495.3 | 4.6 |
| Libya | 527.6 | 515.7 | 4.7 |
| Romania | 238.4 | 220.3 | 2.0 |
| Greece | 280.5 | 217.1 | 2.0 |
| West Germany | 225.9 | 197.5 | 1.8 |
| Iran | 147.7 | 196.3 | 1.8 |
| Cuba | 174.9 | 195.7 | 1.8 |
| Switzerland | 169.4 | 183.8 | 1.7 |
| Hungary | 190.6 | 220.5 | 2.0 |
| TOTAL (including others) | 9,860.3 | 10,880.0 | |

Source: National Statistics

The largest group of commodities exported by Bulgaria in 1982 was machines and equipment, which increased considerably in 1982 to account for 46.9% of the country's exports. Some of the products exported from this group include hoisting and hauling equipment, computers, power and electrical engineering, radio, TV and communication equipment, agricultural machinery and machine tools, and ships. Bulgaria is one of Comecon's most important producers of computers and electronic equipment. Bulgaria's second largest export category is foodstuffs (16.7% of the total), followed by fuels and raw materials (12.7%).

**TABLE 3.14   EXPORTS BY COMMODITY GROUP**

| Unit: million foreign exchange levs | 1980 | 1981 | 1982 |
|---|---|---|---|
| Machinery and equipment for industrial purposes | 3,949 | 4,514 | 5,098 |
| Fuels, mineral raw materials and metals | 1,334 | 1,445 | 1,383 |
| Chemicals, fertilizers and rubber | 367 | 390 | 465 |
| Construction materials | 188 | 182 | 188 |
| Raw materials except food | 143 | 138 | 142 |
| Livestock | 5 | 5 | 3 |
| Prime materials for food/beverage industry | 432 | 393 | 522 |
| Foodstuffs | 1,592 | 1,716 | 1,824 |
| Industrial consumer durables | 787 | 912 | 1,029 |
| Other goods | 104 | 165 | 226 |
| TOTAL | 8,901 | 9,860 | 10,880 |

Source: National Statistics

The following table shows a further breakdown of exports in certain goods rather than categories. The rapid growth in machine and equipment exports has been due largely to the COMECON specialisation and co-operation scheme, a third of the value of exported machines are specialist products manufactured under this scheme. Some other products are manufactured principally for export, including electric trucks, engine trucks and electric motors, of which 90% produced are exported, 80% of lathes, 75% of soda ash and 70% of telephones and nitrogen fertilisers.

**TABLE 3.15   EXPORT OF CERTAIN GOODS**

|  | 1980 | 1981 | 1982 |
|---|---|---|---|
| Lathes | 6,184 | 5,946 | 3,804 |
| Electric motors ('000) | 1,303 | 1,468 | 745 |
| Electric hoists ('000) | 112 | 119 | 123 |
| Electric trucks ('000) | 42 | 38 | 37 |
| Engine trucks ('000) | 20 | 17 | 23 |
| Telephone sets ('000) | 548 | 672 | 617 |
| Complete plant (million levs) | 390 | 619 | 702 |
| Ships and marine equipment (million levs) | 153 | 173 | 146 |
| Soda ash ('000 tonnes) | 1,116 | 1,095 | 1,120 |
| Nitrogen fertilizers ('000 tonnes) | 242 | 193 | 237 |
| Medicines (million levs) | 172 | 229 | 267 |
| Sterilised vegetable preserves ('000 tonnes) | 276 | 258 | 257 |
| Cigarettes ('000 tonnes) | 69 | 74 | 72 |
| Table wines (million litres) | 192 | 201 | 216 |

Source: National Statistics

The Soviet Union also dominates Bulgaria's import table, accounting for 55.9% of imports in 1982.

**TABLE 3.16   BULGARIAN IMPORTS**

| Unit: million foreign exchange levs | | | % |
| --- | --- | --- | --- |
| | **1981** | **1982** | **1982** |
| Soviet Union | 5,450.6 | 6,134.2 | 55.9 |
| Poland | 370.3 | 524.0 | 4.8 |
| GDR | 551.7 | 633.7 | 5.8 |
| West Germany | 487.3 | 489.8 | 4.5 |
| Czechoslovakia | 417.8 | 424.7 | 3.9 |
| Hungary | 179.5 | 236.8 | 2.2 |
| Austria | 153.5 | 173.1 | 1.6 |
| Switzerland | 168.1 | 179.3 | 1.6 |
| Cuba | 178.0 | 163.6 | 1.5 |
| TOTAL (including others) | 9,957.9 | 10,975.9 | |

Source: Bulgarian statististical yearbook

A breakdown of Bulgarian imports shows that the largest import category is fuels, mineral raw materials and metals, accounting for 46.2% of total imports, followed by machines and equipment with 33.9%, chemicals with 5.5% and industrial consumer durables with 4.8%.

**TABLE 3.17   IMPORTS BY COMMODITY GROUPS**

| Unit: million foreign exchange levs | 1980 | 1981 | 1982 |
| --- | --- | --- | --- |
| Machinery and equipment for industrial purposes | 2,933 | 3,338 | 3,718 |
| Fuels, mineral raw materials and metals | 3,552 | 4,423 | 5,077 |
| Chemicals, fertilizers and rubber | 523 | 586 | 605 |
| Construction materials | 61 | 79 | 84 |
| Raw materials except food | 439 | 507 | 501 |
| Livestock | 6 | 7 | 7 |
| Prime materials for food/beverage industry | 251 | 375 | 280 |
| Foodstuffs | 112 | 128 | 117 |
| Industrial consumer durables | 368 | 473 | 530 |
| Other goods not included elsewhere | 38 | 43 | 57 |
| TOTAL | 8,283 | 9,958 | 10,976 |

Bulgaria has the most trade dependent economy in Eastern Europe, around 30% of its national output is for export.

Unlike some of its East European neighbours, Bulgaria has not had problems in financing its foreign trade payments or servicing foreign debt since its foreign payments position has been well balanced. Foreign debt has been declining since 1979 from nearly $4.5 billion to around $1.8 billion in mid-1983.

Bulgaria has been interested in developing trade links with Western countries in the form of co-operation agreements and joint ventures, of which there are 180 of the former and approximately 30 of the latter. This has been a disappointingly low response. It is thought that Western companies have been slow to take advantage of the relatively liberal legislation (for Eastern Europe), possibly because of the limited size of the Bulgarian market, the difficulty in selling goods in the Comecon area for convertible currency, the indifferent quality of production and slowness in decision making. The countries most interested in this have been France, Italy, Japan, Austria and West Germany. The Bulgarians are especially keen to encourage co-operation in the production of high quality metals, diesel engines, capital goods and equipment, electronics and electrical equipment, chemicals and the mining and food industries. The idea is to inject more high technology into the economy, such that Bulgaria will improve its position as a supplier of sophisticated products to Comecon.

# Chapter Four

# CZECHOSLOVAKIA

## Introduction

Since the "Prague Spring" of 1968, when eight months of political and economic liberalisation were suppressed by the Soviet Union, Czechoslovakia has been firmly entrenched in the centralised, Soviet-type routines of rigid economic planning and tight political control.

It is one of the Comecon group's most industrialised countries, supplying industrial and consumer goods on a large scale to the other members, particularly the USSR. Czechoslovakia is highly advanced, and its per capita levels of steel, cement and electricity production rival those of the US, the UK and West Germany.

Close integration with the USSR and other Comecon countries has led to problems based on import dependency. Czechoslovakia's industries rely heavily on Soviet energy and raw material supplies. The 1983 annual Comecon conference held in East Berlin, highlighted the economic dilemma the smaller satellite countries face, being so dependent on their all-powerful Soviet collaborator. Meanwhile, the continuing political and economic problems experienced in neighbouring Poland are a constant reminder of what can happen when problems grow too great.

In 1983, real economic growth was achieved, with the basic targets of increases in national income and industrial output attained. This recovery followed two years of 'negative growth', i.e. a regression in the country's national product, and a consequent decline in living standards experienced by the population. This growth was also achieved in the teeth of the international recession.

Consistent and long-term development of the Czechoslovak economy is hindered by basic inefficiencies. The industrial base is ageing, and there are serious structural deficiencies. The economy has failed to modernise and rationalise. The range of products for export has not kept up with international trends and manufacturers are not able to adapt to changing requirements. They have failed to respond to the stimulus of consumer and export demand and are slow to innovate and install new technology.

71

The high levels of investment which have been made in industry have not produced the yield expected. The economy is very energy-intensive, and its use of energy and raw materials is estimated as 40% higher than in comparable industrialised countries. Additionally, as happens elsewhere in Eastern Europe, there is a chronic labour shortage, and rationalisation is essential to mobilise workers into the more productive sectors. Labour productivity is poor and inefficiencies in industrial organisation are increasingly evident.

However, the Czechoslovaks have a generally higher standard of living than citizens of other East European countries, although the standard is tacitly admitted to be below that of Austria or West Germany. Until mid-1981, Czechoslovakia attracted other East Europeans who would come to buy the wider range of consumer goods on sale, but recently the traffic has been the other way, with neighbouring Hungary now a better source for consumer goods.

Czechoslovakia's external position has improved. Its hard currency debt in mid-1983 was estimated as between $3.2 billion and $3.7 billion, one of Comecon's smallest debts. Its foreign trade position has improved — from a record Kcs 5.6 billion deficit in 1979 to a Kcs 1.3 billion surplus in 1982.

**The Country and People**

The country has an area of 127,896 square kilometres. Czechoslovakia, 'CSSR', is a federal state formed of two republics, the Czech republic, 'CSR' and the Slovak republic 'SSR', both of which have equal rights.

Following the Second World War there were extensive population changes, with land in the east, the Sub-Carpathian Ukraine, ceded to the USSR and a large German community (which was almost one-fifth of the country's pre-1945 population) expelled. The current population is made up of 64% Czechs and 31% Slovaks, with a 600,000 Hungarian minority in Slovakia and small groups of Germans, Ukrainians, Russians, Poles and Gypsies also sharing the territory.

**TABLE 4.1   POPULATION IN 1982**

| Unit: million people | |
|---|---|
| Males | . 7.5 |
| Females | 7.9 |
| Total population | 15.4 |
| Population of working age* | 8.7 |
| Live births per 1,000 people | 15.2 |

\* 15-59 years for men, 15-54 years for women
Source: National Statistics

The working population amounts to 56.7% of the total population. There is a continuing and chronic labour shortage, so 21% of pensioners are in paid employment. Some 89% of women of working age are in paid employment.

**TABLE 4.2   LABOUR FORCE IN 1982**

| Unit: million people | |
|---|---|
| Population of working age* | 8.7 |
| Workers of retirement age | 0.7 |
| Foreign workers in Czechoslovakia | 0.03 |
| Total labour force | 9.43 |

\* 15-59 years for men, 15-54 years for women
Source: National Statistics

**TABLE 4.3 EMPLOYMENT STRUCTURE — SOCIALISED SECTOR**

| Unit: million people | 1975 | 1982 |
|---|---|---|
| *Productive activity* | 5.5 | 5.6 |
| Agriculture | 1.0 | 1.0 |
| Forestry | 0.1 | 0.1 |
| Industry | 2.7 | 2.8 |
| Construction | 0.6 | 0.6 |
| Transport and communications | 0.3 | 0.3 |
| Trade | 0.6 | 0.7 |

continued . . .

73

| Table 4.3 continued... | 1975 | 1982 |
|---|---|---|
| *Non-productive activity* | 1.6 | 1.8 |
| Education | 0.4 | 0.4 |
| Health | 0.3 | 0.3 |
| TOTAL | 7.1 | 7.4 |

Source: National Statistics

Industry is mainly located in the Czech lands, which provide 80% of Czechoslovakia's industrial output. North and south Moravia, Bohemia and the Prague area are the main concentrations. Slovakia remains less industrialised, despite heavy investment.

Czechoslovakia's main towns, with their population on lst January 1983, are: Praha (Prague) 1,185,693; Bratislava 394,644; Brno 378,722; Ostrava 323,459; Kosice 210,729; Plzen (Pilsen) 174,421; Olomouc 103,384.

Industries operating in the main towns include:

| Town | Industry | Enterprise |
|---|---|---|
| Prague | heavy engineering | CKD |
| | rolling stock | CKD-Tatra Smichov |
| | aircraft engines | Motorlet NP |
| | lorries | Praga |
| | machine tools | TOS Celakovice, Hostivar |
| Brno | heavy engineering | — |
| | textiles | — |
| | ball bearings, tractors | ZKL |
| | machine tools | Kurim |
| Bratislava | oil refining | Slovnaft (Brno is the terminal point of the 'Friendship' pipeline from the Ukraine, USSR) |
| | petrochemicals | — |
| | cables | Kablo |
| | chemicals | Dimitrov |
| Komarno | shipyards | — |
| Ostrava | coalmining | (Ostrava is the centre of the country's main coalfield, the Ostrava-Karvina field) |
| | iron and steel | Vitkovice |
| Pilsen | beer | — |
| | heavy engineering | Skoda |
| Kosice | iron and steel | East Slovak Iron & Steel Works |
| Mlada Boleslav | cars | Skoda |

## Government and Political Organisation

Czechoslovakia is a communist state. Its name was changed in the 1960 Constitution, from 'The People's Democracy of Czechoslovakia' to 'The Socialist Republic of Czechoslovakia', in order to mark a higher evolutionary stage in the constitutional theory of communism.

The President of the Republic and General Secretary of the Communist Party is Dr Gustav Husak, and the Chairman of the Council of Ministers and Prime Minister is Lubomir Strougal.

The federal assembly controls the economy, constitutional affairs, defence and foreign relations. It is a two-chamber assembly, comprising the Chamber of Nations, which has 75 Czech and 75 Slovak delegates, and the Chamber of the People, which has 137 Czech and 63 Slovak deputies.

The Communist Party is the real source of power in Czechoslovakia. Political life is organised by the National Front — this is a union of political parties, chief among which is the Communist Party of Czechoslovakia. Other smaller parties exist within the National Front, but political parties not belonging to the National Front are illegal. The Chairman of the National Front Central Committee is the General Secretary of the Communist Party.

Civil and political freedom is restricted, and open opposition to the official guidelines and laws is punished.

## Economic Growth

Historically, economic performance has been adequate to prevent disaffection among the population, but the progress made has been mainly the achievement of the country's pre-war industrial base — advanced at that time and relatively undamaged during the course of the war. Innovation was not carried out in post-war years and deficiencies became progressively more obvious. Economic difficulties were the major impetus for the consequent political turmoil. In 1968, Alexander Dubcek became First Secretary of the Communist Party, replacing Antonin Novotny, and Ludwig Svoboda became President in a new policy of the separation of political power. A programme of economic liberalisation was put into operation, but it was short-lived, and following the Soviet invasion, Dubcek was replaced by Gustav Husak in April 1969.

The rigid, centralised, planned economic structure was resumed, and with innovation stifled and change discouraged, stagnation has resulted. Economic growth was 5% per year at the end of 1960s, but then fell to 3.6% per year by the end of the 1970s. In 1981, growth was a negative -0.1%. Living standards have declined and the economy is generally in poor shape. The industrial base, competitiveness and the rate of plant renewals have fallen behind.

A limited amount of economic reform was carried out in 1978, permitting liberalisation in 12 industrial branches, comprising 150 enterprises and 9 foreign trade organisations, which together account for one-sixth of the national economy. The reforms were for an experimental period of three years. They were then to be extended to other branches of the economy, under the 1981 programme entitled ''A Set of Measures to Improve the System of Planned National Economic Management after 1980''. The aim of these measures is to make enterprises more financially aware, to improve planning operations and efficiency, to improve managerial quality and to bring in monetary and other incentives for workers to produce more. The desired result is to liberalise, to encourage enterprises into a situation of greater flexibility towards changing patterns of demand and to changing economic conditions. The key role of the central planning system is retained, and the measures are in no sense radical reforms. Subsidies and bank credits are being made available for selected 'higher production units', but these credits are only granted under particular conditions.

**TABLE 4.4   ECONOMIC INDICATORS**

Unit: % change/year

|  | 1982 planned | 1982 actual | 1983 planned |
|---|---|---|---|
| Produced national income | 0.6 | 0.0/-1.0 | 2.0 |
| Investments | -3.3 | -1.1 | -1.9 |
| Industrial production | 0.5 | 1.0 | 2.4 |
| Labour productivity in industry | 0.3 | 0.5 | 2.3-3.0 |
| Construction | 2.7 | -3.7 | 2.0 |
| Agricultural production | 3.2 | 1.1 | 2.7 |
| Retail sales, nominal | 2.8 | 2.9 | 2.0 |
| Average wages | 2.0 | 2.1 | 1.0 |

Following the poor results of 1982, when the Praesidium of the Central Committee of the Communist Party expressed its dissatisfation with the large number of enterprises which had failed in the tasks and duties allotted to them, 1983 proved considerably better. The planned growth of 2% in national income was achieved, with the expansion to have been mainly in export-related activities to improve the country's balance of payments position and reduce its indebtedness to the West.

'National income' is the main indicator of growth. National income is the country's net product — social product *less* productive consumption. National income is defined by the East European standard and excludes most services, such as banking, health, education, public administration and defence, but it does include transport.

**TABLE 4.5   NATIONAL INCOME AND SOCIAL PRODUCT 1980-1982**

|  | National income (billion Kcs at 1977 prices) | Social product |
|---|---|---|
| 1980 | 453.4 | 1,175.6 |
| 1981 | 452.9 | 1,179.2 |
| 1982 (preliminary) | 451.6 | 1,188.9 |

Source: National Statistics

'Social product' is the gross product of Czechoslovakia's economic activities.

Industry is the largest generator of social product. The state sector accounts for 95% of economic activity, but the private sector does exist, particularly in agriculture, and accounts for 5% of social product. Industrial activity is centred around the heavy engineering sectors and new steel plants, mining facilities, power plants and paper mills are among recent capital projects. Traditional activities such as textiles, wood products, timber and craft items are also important. Bohemian glassware has a world-wide reputation. Production is undertaken by 'production units' and 'higher production units', which are grouped together as 'enterprises' — enterprises operate similarly to companies in the West.

**TABLE 4.6   SOCIAL PRODUCT BY SOURCE**

| Unit: % share | 1975 | 1982 |
|---|---|---|
| Agriculture | 10.7 | 9.7 |
| Forestry | 0.6 | 0.6 |
| Industry | 67.9 | 69.2 |
| Construction | 11.5 | 9.4 |
| Transport | 2.6 | 3.0 |
| Communications | 0.3 | 0.5 |
| Trade, catering | 5.6 | 5.9 |
| Material & technical services | 0.3 | 1.1 |
| Other | 0.5 | 0.6 |

Source: National Statistics

Industrial output increased 2.8% in 1983, following a growth of only 1% — a 30-year low — in 1982. In 1982, one-sixth of enterprises had failed to reach output targets, but in 1983, targets were generally fulfilled, including a 1.4% increase in output from the construction sector, which had previously been trailing badly. In many of the energy-intensive industries, where output was to fall and restructuring to take place, plans were usually overfulfilled as enterprises resisted the planning cuts. The overall 1983 increase in industrial output was achieved without an increase in energy consumption. Personal consumption increased 2% in 1983, following a decline, which has now been officially admitted, in 1981 and 1982.

The results of 1984 and 1985 will be decisive for the final five-year plan results.

Substantial reform, which is seen as the key to lasting economic improvement, is not likely. The radical reforms which have taken place in neighbouring Hungary in recent years are not likely to be copied. The economic difficulties which exist in Czechoslovakia are seen as due to causes other than serious inherent shortcomings within the country itself.

**Economic Planning**

Five-year plans are the basis of Czechlovakia's economic organisation, but deteriorating economic conditions make it less and less easy to foresee what conditions are likely to be in the years ahead, and the planners have been forced to rethink and to adjust their original targets. Publication of the current plan was delayed and, even when it appeared, it did not give detailed information.

The 1981-85 five-year plan has been more modest than its predecessors. Higher productivity of labour is emphasised, along with energy saving, better product quality and encouragement of export-oriented industries. National income has been planned to grow 14-16% in this period, with 90-95% of the growth to be achieved by raising the social productivity of labour — in effect this means providing modest wage increases and broadcasting much exhortation and propaganda. More rational use will be made of fuel and savings will be made in the amount of raw materials consumed, and the effectiveness of that use will be increased. More electricity will be produced and nuclear power, by which Czechoslovakia sets great store, will account for 55% of the planned growth in electricity output. Energy savings will average 2% per year, while relative savings will be 12 million tonnes of standard fuel in 1985 compared with 1980. The direction in which basic funds will be spent will change, with the share of investments in renewals and in progressive modernisation increased at the expense of other investments. The investment level will remain at the 1980 average. More efficiency will be required of the planning management operating within the national economy. Agriculture is also to be encouraged; poor harvests in the early years of the plan, despite considerable efforts by farmers, will have to be compensated for. Some failure to observe agrotechnical schedules and some non-observance of sown acreage in previous years have aggravated shortfalls. Czechoslovakia's imports of grain totalled 1.5 million tonnes per year during the late 1970s and better production is essential.

The government faces very definite problems which have built up through the years, making plans difficult to formulate and achieve. In the longer term, a growth rate of 3% per year up to 1989 is aimed at and the authorities are currently working on the plan guidelines for 1986-95.

Czechoslovakia has insulated itself from economic developments in the world outside, by renouncing the discipline of market levers. The rapid rise in the price of oil and raw materials on world markets is a long-term problem with which the Czechoslovak economy has not yet grappled, cushioned as it is by supplies from the USSR, which does not charge world market prices to its Comecon customers. The economy is over extended in too many ambitious projects, while new technology has been neglected.

Western observers see long-term prosperity as being attainable by borrowing on international monetary markets, by revising growth targets downwards and imposing austerity on the population, or by wide ranging economic reform, giving individual factories the right to independence if they wish to trade with the West — but there is no sign of any change in direction. A future leadership change may bring in new policies, but meanwhile the prospects for real recovery are bleak.

## Agriculture

Farmland accounts for 54% of Czechoslovakia's territory. There were 6.8 million hectares of agricultural land in use in 1982, of which 70% was for arable use. Additionally, 36% of national territory is given over to forestry.

Most of the farmland — 95% — belongs to the socialised sector. The basic production unit is the 'unified agricultural co-operative'. These co-operatives farm an average 2,400 hectares. There were 1,708 such farms in operation in 1981 and they comprised 63% of all the socialised sector's agricultural enterprises. The co-operatives had 984,385 members, who are known as 'peasants'. The other constituent of socialised agriculture is the state farm, a large-scale government-run enterprise, farming an average 8,700 hectares. There were 204 state farms operating in 1981, with 164,304 members, who are known as 'workers'.

The private sector accounts for 5% of farmland, varying in distribution throughout Czechoslovakia from 3% of agricultural land in north Moravia to 30% in central Slovakia. There were 150,000 of these small farms operating in 1980. The private sector is being encouraged by official policies. It is gaining land, not at the expense of the socialised sector but from reclamation schemes around the cities. The private plots are for spare-time cultivation, and are not to represent a main source of income. Land which is unsuited to large-scale farming methods has been offered for private cultivation — 6,700 hectares were offered in 1981 and 70% had been taken up by March 1982. The main advantage of the private plots is that they can be most efficient as breeders of livestock and producers of fruit and vegetables, producing a high proportion of national supplies of the latter. Czechoslovakia often has chronic shortages of fresh produce, yet this is partly the fault of an inadequate distribution system. Slovakia often has gluts, while there are frequent shortages in Bohemia. Consumption of fruit and vegetables is below planned targets.

Agriculture provides 10% of Czechoslovakia's social product. It is an important sector for development, and the agricultural machinery industry will have received Kcs36 billion of investments in the 1981-85 period.

Livestock products are an important part of total agricultural output, while the main arable products are wheat, barley, potatoes, sugar beet and rye.

**TABLE 4.7   AGRICULTURAL OUTPUT BY VALUE**

**Unit: million Kcs at 1980 prices**

|  | 1980 | 1981 | 1982 |
|---|---|---|---|
| Crops | 43.5 | 41.2 | 46.9 |
| Livestock products | 60.3 | 60.0 | 58.8 |
| TOTAL | 103.8 | 101.2 | 105.7 |

Source: National Statistics

**TABLE 4.8   CROP OUTPUT BY VOLUME**

**Unit: million tonnes**

|  | 1980 | 1981 | 1982 |
|---|---|---|---|
| Grains | 10.7 | 9.4 | 10.3 |
| Wheat | 5.4 | 4.3 | 4.6 |
| Rye | 0.6 | 0.6 | 0.6 |
| Barley | 3.6 | 3.4 | 3.7 |
| Maize | 0.8 | 0.7 | 0.9 |
| Edible pulses ('000 tonnes) | 59.0 | 55.0 | 77.0 |
| Potatoes | 2.7 | 3.7 | 3.6 |
| Fodder roots | 0.9 | 0.9 | 1.2 |
| Fodder grains | 9.5 | 9.1 | 9.4 |
| Perennial fodder crops | 3.1 | 3.1 | 3.2 |
| Sugar beet | 7.3 | 7.0 | 8.2 |

Source: National Statistics

**TABLE 4.9  LIVESTOCK PRODUCTS**

| Unit: million tonnes liveweight | 1980 | 1981 | 1982 |
|---|---|---|---|
| Meat | 1.7 | 1.7 | 1.6 |
|   Beef | 0.7 | 0.7 | 0.7 |
|     Veal ('000 tonnes) | 16.8 | 12.5 | 11.6 |
|     Pork | 1.0 | 1.1 | 0.9 |
| Poultry | 0.3 | 0.3 | 0.3 |
| Milk (billion litres) | 5.7 | 5.7 | 5.8 |
| Eggs (billion units) | 4.9 | 5.0 | 5.0 |

Source: National Statistics

**TABLE 4.10  LIVESTOCK NUMBERS**

| Unit: million head | 1980 | 1981 | 1982 |
|---|---|---|---|
| Horses ('000 head) | 45 | 44 | 44 |
| Cattle | 5.0 | 5.1 | 5.1 |
|   Cows | 1.9 | 1.9 | 1.9 |
| Pigs | 7.9 | 7.3 | 7.1 |
| Sheep and rams | 0.9 | 1.0 | 1.0 |
| Poultry | 47.3 | 47.4 | 49.2 |
|   Hens | 22.4 | 22.6 | 22.9 |

Source: National Statistics

Overall agricultural output was to rise a planned 2.7% in 1983, following a growth of only 1% in 1982 (a year when animal output declined 4.2%). In many respects the 1983 plan was fulfilled or overfulfilled. The grain harvest, excluding maize, was 10.2 million tonnes, 170,000 tonnes above the plan. Good weather was able to compensate for the continuing problems farmers experienced with their machinery, particularly in the deficient supply of spare parts. However, the target for maize of 1 million tonnes was not reached, due to the excessively hot and dry weather conditions. Other crops which did not realise their targets were bulk fodder (grains and roots), fruit and vegetables, while sugar beet output fell to 7.8 million tonnes after a 17.8% increase in 1982. The country depends on grain imports (estimated as 0.7 million tonnes in the 1982/83 season) but a good harvest allows imports to be reduced.

Livestock output was good in 1983, with state purchases of meat 3.5% ahead of target. Poultry purchases were up 5.2% compared with 1982 and milk purchases were up 8.6%. Under the socialist system, the government buys produce surplus to farmers' requirements for sale on the government-run distribution network, while farmers' own consumption and produce sold outside the state distribution system are not calculated in the state purchases figure, which is thus always different from output statistics.

In 1984, meat output was expected to fall again, as a result of the reduction in fodder crops output from the 1983 season.

## Mining

Czechoslovakia's mineral resources are varied, but few ores are sufficiently plentiful for modern industrial needs. Working domestic deposits is often more expensive than buying from abroad and home output can only meet part of total demand. Reserves include hard coal, brown coal and lignite, uranium, iron ore, antimony, mercury, lead, zinc, copper, tin, gallium, bentonite, perlite and gold. There are limited oil and gas reserves. Imports, particularly from the USSR, are considerable.

**TABLE 4.11  OUTPUT AND IMPORTS OF MINERALS**

|  | output 1981 | output 1982 | imports 1981 | imports 1982 |
|---|---|---|---|---|
| Hard coal (million tonnes) | 27.0 | 27.1 | 4.4 | 5.0 |
| Brown coal (million tonnes) | 93.1 | 95.5 | 0.6 | 0.7 |
| Lignite (million tonnes) | 3.3 | 3.4 | | |
| Coking coal (million tonnes) | 10.3 | 10.6 | | |
| Metallurgical coke (million tonnes) | 8.6 | 8.7 | | |
| Crude oil (million tonnes) | 0.1 | 0.1 | 12.7 | |
| Natural gas (billion cubic metres) | 0.7 | na | 8.4 | 9.0 |
| Zinc ore ('000 tonnes) | 677.0 | 701.0 | | |
| Copper ore ('000 tonnes) | 845.0 | 880.0 | 67.0 | 59.0 |
| Iron ore (million tonnes) | 1.9 | 1.9 | 12.2 | 11.6 |
| Bauxite (million tonnes) | | | 0.5 | 0.5 |

Source: National Statistics

The 1981-85 target for coal production is to produce an average 125-128 million tonnes per year of coal of all types — no large-scale expansion from current levels of exploitation is planned. The 1983 target was 123.9 million tonnes, and this output was achieved ahead of schedule on December 20th; by the end of the year there was to have been 3.5 million tonnes 'overplan' production.

Hard coal production peaked in 1980 and while reserves will last for 50 or 60 years at current extraction rates, this will only be achieved if more difficult seams can be exploited. 86% of the country's hard coal comes from the Ostrava-Kavina coalfield in north Moravia. Expansions planned here will be at the deeper level of 1200-1500 metres. A new mine will open at Darkov, with an eventual 5 million tonnes per year capacity. Hard coal (or black coal) output will remain at 27-28 million tonnes per year to 1985.

Brown coal and lignite output will rise to 99-100 million tonnes per year by 1985, with new opencast mines coming into production and improved technology installed in old mines. Output of even this lower-grade coal is also reaching its peak and the planned expansions are relatively modest. The main reserves are in north-west Bohemia. Most of the coal is produced from opencast workings.

**TABLE 4.12   BROWN COAL PRODUCTION BY METHOD**

| Unit: million tonnes | 1981 | 1982 |
|---|---|---|
| From deep mines | 10.1 | 9.7 |
| From opencast workings | 83.0 | 85.8 |

Source: National Statistics

The worsening conditions in coal mines as seams go deeper have meant that wages and non-monetary compensations have been raised, more to counter-balance the poor conditions than to provide an incentive to higher production.

Recovery of spoil can provide substantial amounts of coal to add to conventional production and a new joint venture company is being set up, with Hungarian participation, to exploit the coal tips in Ostrava. 450,000 tonnes of spoil per year will be processed, to provide an estimated 73,000 tonnes per year of recovered coal.

The existence of uranium reserves provided the incentive for Czechoslovakia to develop nuclear power potential, with the country's first nuclear power output starting in the early 1970s. Uranium deposits are located at Hamry in north Bohemia, also at Pribram and Jachymov — the latter two deposits are almost exhausted. Production statistics are secret, but annual output is estimated as 2,000-3,000 tonnes.

Gold mining is to increase again, following years of decline as deposits became uneconomic. A new mine will be opened at Psi Hory-Celina, near Sedlcany, where estimated reserves are 5 million tonnes of ore with a gold content of 2-3 grammes of metal per tonne of ore. Production is to start in 1987.

A new mercury mine at Presov will produce 50,000 tonnes per year of mercury ores from 1985. A processing plant will also be built on the site.

**Manufacturing**

Important manufactured products are: vehicles, railway goods, aircraft, electrical goods, heavy machinery and precision equipment.

The engineering industry is the largest manufacturing sector, with output accounting for 30% of all industrial output and 30% of the country's exports. Engineering is a priority sector and output is to grow 33-35% over the five-year plan period to 1985, compared with a growth rate for industry as a whole of 18-20%.

Some speciality chemicals are to be a priority, in line with Comecon integration programmes. By contrast, energy-intensive sectors such as metallurgy, oil refining, building materials and selected chemicals, are to reduce their level of activity, since energy shortages are endemic.

Innovation and new technological installations are at a low level. The introduction of robots, which is well advanced in Czechoslovakia's neighbour East Germany, has been seriously delayed, because of concern over redeployment of labour and because of a lack of technological preparedness. There is occasional direct opposition to the installation of robots and manipulators, even where conditions of work are dangerous.

## Nuclear Plant Equipment

Among the heavy engineering sectors, of particular importance is Czechoslovakia's nuclear reactor industry. Czechoslovakia is, excluding the USSR, East Europe's only builder of heavy-duty nuclear power equipment and is the joint supplier of this machinery to the whole of the Comecon group.

By the 1990s, Czechoslovakia will produce, for its own nuclear programme, twelve 440 MW reactors and two 1000 MW reactors. For export, Czechoslovakia is to specialise in building the smaller units, while the USSR will supply the larger capacity reactors. The Czechoslovak models are the Soviet-design VVER version of the pressurised water reactor.

Reactors are built in 23 plants by 15,000 workers: Skoda builds reactor vessels, heat exchangers and heavy equipment at its Pilsen location; Vitkovice produces equipment in special steels — compensators, steam generators; Sigma produces pipes and pumps.

60% of current output goes to the domestic nuclear programme, whilst the rest is exported to Comecon countries.

## Metallurgy

**TABLE 4.13   OUTPUT OF IRON AND STEEL**

| Unit: million tonnes | 1981 | 1982 |
|---|---|---|
| Raw iron | 9.9 | 9.5 |
| Raw steel | 15.3 | 15.0 |
| Rolled steel products | 10.8 | 10.7 |
| Steel pipes | 1.5 | 1.5 |

Source: National Statistics

One of the two largest steelworks is the Klement Gottwald complex, located near Ostrava, which produces 3 million tonnes per year of pig iron, 3.7 million tonnes per year of steel and 2.5 million tonnes per year of rolled products. The other steel works is the Eastern Slovak Steel

Works, located at Kosice — here the 4.2 million tonnes per year capacity is currently being modernised. Kosice, a fast-growing industrial centre, is linked to the USSR with a broad-gauge railway for direct transport of iron ore.

Czechoslovakia also produces other metals as seen in the following table.

**TABLE 4.14   OUTPUT OF METALS**

| Unit: '000 tonnes | 1981 | 1982 |
|---|---|---|
| Tin | 0.3 | 0.3 |
| Mercury | 0.2 | 0.2 |
| Lead | 20.7 | 21.1 |
| Copper | 25.5 | 25.6 |
| Aluminium | 32.7 | 33.8 |

Source: National Statistics

**Transport Equipment**

**TABLE 4.15   OUTPUT OF TRANSPORT EQUIPMENT**

| | 1981 | 1982 |
|---|---|---|
| Cars and vans ('000 units) | 180.6 | 173.5 |
| Specialised delivery vehicles ('000 units) | 4.7 | 4.9 |
| Tractors ('000 units) | 32.1 | 33.5 |
| Construction vehicles (billion Kcs) | 2.7 | 2.8 |
| Agricultural vehicles (billion Kcs) | 2.7 | 2.9 |
| Locomotives (units) | 116 | 137 |
| Buses (units) | 382 | 282 |
| Motorcycles* ('000 units) | 139.7 | 133.7 |
| Mopeds** ('000 units) | 107.3 | 82.8 |

* over 250cc; ** up to 100cc
Source: National Statistics

Skoda is the country's main producer of passenger cars and is located at Mlada Boleslav. Tatra is the largest lorry and truck manufacturer. Tatra's lorry plant at Koprivnice is producing a new 3-axle, 15-ton, heavy-duty lorry and 66% of production will be exported to the USSR.

Czechoslovakia's largest motorcycle producer is called Jawa. It manufactures 350 units per day. A new model featuring aluminium cylinders and low petrol consumption, the 350-638 motorcycle, was to enter production in 1984.

Skoda is also Czechoslovakia's main manufacturer of electric locomotives, which are supplied in large numbers to the USSR, also of trolleybuses, many of which are again supplied to the USSR.

## Electronics

**TABLE 4.16   OUTPUT OF CONSUMER ELECTRONICS**

**Unit: '000 units**

|  | 1981 | 1982 |
| --- | --- | --- |
| Radio receivers | 248.8 | 278.7 |
| Radiograms | 30.7 | 31.1 |
| Black and white televisions | 337.7 | 320.8 |
| Colour televisions | 60.3 | 70.6 |
| Record players | 229.3 | 211.0 |
| Tape recorders* | 121.5 | 134.4 |

* including dictaphone machines
Source: National Statistics

Despite satisfactory performance overall by the key industries of the electrotechnical sector, production of consumer electronics has lagged behind output targets, particularly for colour television sets, black and white portable television sets, some types of radio and tape recorders. Quality is poor; in the first half of 1983, the quantity of damaged goods had increased 33.2% and losses from substandard production had risen by 22.4%.

**TABLE 4.17   OUTPUT OF MICROELECTRONICS**

**Unit: million Kcs**

|  | 1981 | 1982 |
|---|---|---|
| Semiconductor elements | 121 | 134 |
| Transistors | 346 | 365 |
| Monolithic circuits | 1,081 | 1,332 |
| Hybrid circuits | 8.2 | 7.8 |

Source: National Statistics

## Chemicals and Oil Products

**TABLE 4.18   OUTPUT OF CHEMICALS**

**Unit: '000 tonnes**

|  | 1981 | 1982 |
|---|---|---|
| Nitrogenous fertilisers | 539.2 | 566.0 |
| Phosphate fertilisers | 340.5 | 335.4 |
| Sulphuric acid (million tonnes) | 1.3 | 1.3 |
| Hydrochloric acid | 219.9 | 223.5 |
| Calcined soda | 118.2 | 106.4 |
| Sodium hydroxide | 331.4 | 325.1 |
| Calcium carbide | 106.3 | 89.4 |
| Methanol | 114.9 | 115.2 |
| Paints and varnishes | 133.5 | 133.4 |
| Organic pigments | 14.2 | 14.9 |
| Chemical fibres | 168.7 | 179.9 |
| Plastics | 912.9 | 956.4 |
| Phenolics | 17.9 | 17.5 |
| Aminoplasts | 2.5 | 2.4 |
| Polyvinyl chloride* | 200.5 | 198.7 |
| Cellulose derivatives | 17.4 | 16.2 |
| Polyamides | 2.4 | 2.4 |
| Polyacrylics** | 13.1 | 12.5 |
| Epoxy resins | 21.3 | 22.5 |

* includes other vinyl chloride monomer polymers; ** includes polymethyl methacrylate
Source: National Statistics

One of Czechoslovakia's largest chemical production centres is at Zaluzi, near Most. A wide range of chemicals is manufactured, based on brown coal extracts.

Czechoslovakia is to refrain from selling PVC at below-market prices in West Europe, following agreement with the European Economic Commission that the EEC will withdraw the antidumping levy which had been imposed.

**TABLE 4.19   OUTPUT OF OIL PRODUCTS**

**Unit: million tonnes**

|  | 1981 | 1982 |
|---|---|---|
| Motor oil | 4.1 | 3.8 |
| Kerosene | 0.5 | 0.3 |
| Engine oil | 0.1 | 0.1 |

Source: National Statistics

Czechoslovakia has seven oil refineries, with combined capacity of 22.75 million tonnes per year. The largest are Bratislava (9 million tonnes per year) and Zaluzi (6 million tonnes per year).

## Other manufacturing industries

**TABLE 4.20   OUTPUT OF SELECTED PRODUCTS**

|  | 1981 | 1982 |
|---|---|---|
| Cement (million tonnes) | 10.5 | 10.3 |
| Paper and board (million tonnes) | 0.9 | 0.9 |
| Newsprint ('000 tonnes) | 76.0 | 79.0 |
| Timber ('000 cubic metres without bark) | 19.1 | na |
| Steam generators (units) | 210.0 | 222.0 |
| Electric motors ('000 units) | 4.5 | 4.6 |
| Industrial robots/manipulators (units) | 784.0 | 683.0 |
| Tyres for passenger cars (million units) | 1.9 | 1.7 |

Continued...

**Table 4.20 continued...**

|  | 1981 | 1982 |
|---|---|---|
| Wall tiles (million square metres) | 6.1 | 6.2 |
| Cotton cloth (billion metres) | 574.2 | 582.9 |
| Footwear (million pairs) | 128.0 | 128.5 |
| Beer (million hectolitres) | 23.9 | 24.9 |
| Cigarettes (billion units) | 23.7 | 24.0 |
| Cameras ('000 units) | 30.1 | 29.4 |
| Wrist watches ('000 units) | 531.2 | 502.8 |
| Alarm clocks (million units) | 1.8 | 1.9 |
| Phonograph records (million units) | 13.2 | 12.9 |

Source: National Statistics

Most branches of Czechoslovak industry are well developed, producing for the home and export markets. Quality is high and Czechoslovak products are in demand. However, consumer goods' quality and variety has fallen recently, and Czechoslovakia suffers in any comparison of its consumer goods with those of the West. On the industrial goods side, Czechoslovakia is an important supplier of plant and equipment on the Comecon export market, and many complete factories — chemical plants, beer-making plants — have recently been completed by Czechoslovakia in the USSR. Success has also been achieved in the Third World.

## Construction

Among much general inefficiency in Czechoslovak industry, the building sector is the country's most disorganised industrial branch. In the 1981-85 Five-Year Plan, the construction industry has concentrated on completing the vast amount of unfinished work. Of around 30,000 industrial projects undertaken in the 1970s, only half have been completed. There was an improvement in building industry activity in 1983, with output up 1.4% compared with 1982, but there has been no progression in reducing lead times and the volume of unfinished work remained very high. (In 1981 and 1982, building industry output actually declined.) However, in the Five-Year Plan period, 550,000 new flats will be built and 40,000-50,000 modernisations carried out.

## Energy

Czechoslovakia is heavily dependent on imports for its fuel and energy supplies. Consumption is at a level of 7.5 tonnes of standard fuel per head per year, considerably higher than other industrialised countries. This is partially the result of having had plentiful supplies of energy for years from the USSR; Czechoslovakia has been a cheap-oil economy, with industries becoming more and more wasteful of energy, having no immediate incentive to carry out expensive conservation measures. The USSR sells energy, largely in the form of crude oil, to its satellite countries at less than world market prices, thereby encouraging increases in energy consumption. In the 1970s East European energy use rose from 15% of total world usage to 22%, all at the expense of the USSR. Intra-Comecon oil prices were only 50% of world market levels until recently, but have now been increased to 77% of world market levels. The Soviets are now demanding payment for the oil and other energy products in the form of higher quality manufactured goods than hitherto, and this is causing conflict between the partners. Subsidies to the consumer satellite countries are estimated to have cost the USSR some $100 billion, or $78 per inhabitant in the recipient countries between 1974 and 1978. But this generosity is becoming increasingly grudging as the rate of growth in production from the Soviet oilfields falls to 0.9% per year in the current Soviet Five-Year Plan period, compared with 4.2% per year in 1976-80 and 6.8% per year in 1971-75. Also, the Soviets need to sell oil to the West to earn hard currency, so East Europe has to make do with less.

**TABLE 4.21   CZECHOSLOVAKIA'S ENERGY AVAILABILITY**

**Unit: Petajoules**

|  | 1980 | 1981 | 1982 |
|---|---|---|---|
| Domestic resources | 2,019 | 1,992 | 2,025 |
|   Solid fuels | 1,919 | 1,888 | 1,921 |
| Imports | 1,229 | 1,189 | 1,145 |
|   Liquid fuels and gas | 1,080 | 1,058 | 1,005 |
| Exports | − 225 | − 196 | − 93 |
| Variation in stocks | − 8 | + 1 | − 17 |
| Total supplies of primary energy | 3,015 | 2,986 | 2,960 |
|   Solid fuels | 1,870 | 1,860 | 1,875 |
|   Liquid fuels | 793 | 769 | 695 |
|   Gas | 268 | 270 | 304 |
|   Primary heat and electricity | 84 | 87 | 86 |

Source: National Statistics

Effective energy conservation within Czechoslovakia is essential. Measures to rationalise energy and raw material use are a key point of the Five-Year Plan, with increases in consumption to be held to 2-3 million tonnes of oil equivalent per year. Diesel-driven buses will be replaced by electric trams, steel will be produced increasingly by oxygen converters, and energy-intensive industries will be allowed to decline.

An absolute decline in energy consumption was registered in 1979-82, but this was during a period of declining economic activity. During 1982 Czechoslovakia's socialist organisations managed to cut their oil consumption by 35% compared with the 1977 level, while generally oil's share in total energy supplies was cut from 26% of the total in 1979 to 23% in 1983.

Alternative energy research is being undertaken, and it is expected that solar, geothermal and biogas sources will provide 66,000 tonnes of standard fuel by 1985. A project to heat a 2,000-flat housing estate and the local hospital by geothermal power is being undertaken at Galanta in Slovakia, a region with promising potential.

In 1983 Czechoslovakia's import requirements were estimated as: 4.7 million tonnes of hard coal, 16.6 million tonnes of crude oil and 8.5 billion cubic metres of gas.

With its heavy reliance on solid fuel in the overall energy balance, the country is at a considerable disadvantage, since solid fuel converts to electricity much less efficiently than liquid fuel, and the outdated and inefficient machinery for conversion which is installed in Czechoslovakia's power plants hampers efficient use even further.

The energy needs for 1985 are an estimated:

**TABLE 4.22  PRIMARY ENERGY CONSUMPTION**

| Unit: million tonnes of hard coal equivalent | 1980 | 1985 |
|---|---|---|
| Coal | 64.5 | 67.8 |
| Gas | 9.9 | 12.2 |
| Oil | 28.0 | 30.1 |
| Electricity | 3.8 | 8.0 |
| Nuclear | 1.2 | 5.3 |
| Total apparent consumption | 106.2 | 118.1 |

Source: Comecon Reports

Electricity output was 74.7 TWh in 1982, compared with 73.5 TWh in 1981, and will be 80-83 TWh in 1985 according to the Five-Year Plan. Coal is and will remain the major provider of electricity. Brown coal and lignite will provide 62% of electric power in 1985, but output is now peaking and energy values are falling an average 1% per year as ash content in the coal rises. Therefore, no new thermal power plants are being built, and all future growth is to be met from nuclear power. Apart from diminishing growth in coal supplies, the burning of so much low-grade brown coal has polluted so many cities with high level sulphur dioxide emissions that there is considerable enthusiasm for the nuclear option. Also, Czechoslovakia has its own uranium deposits, and builds its own nuclear reactors. An early attempt at a nuclear power plant was completed in 1972; a heavy water gas cooled reactor, it was built over 14 years with Soviet help, and operated for 6 years. But it was decommissioned in 1978, following persistent operational problems. Since then, other plants have been opened.

**TABLE 4.23   ELECTRICITY OUTPUT BY SOURCE**

**Unit: TWh**

|  | 1981 | 1982 |
| --- | --- | --- |
| Thermal power | 64.1 | 65.1 |
| Hydroelectric power | 4.3 | 3.8 |
| Nuclear power | 5.1 | 5.8 |
| TOTAL | 73.5 | 74.7 |

Source: National Statistics

By 1990, 30% of Czechoslovakia's electric power will be generated at nuclear plants. But there have been delays in completing new nuclear facilities and the target of producing 15 TWh of power from nuclear sources in 1985 appears unrealistic, as does the 1990 target. Czechoslovakia has two 440 MW nuclear reactors operating at present, at the Jaslovske Bohunice plant in western Slovakia, while start-up of the first of the plant's two new reactors (originally planned for March 1983) was delayed to early-1984. The 1,760 MW plant being built at Dukovany in south Moravia is six months behind schedule and start-up is now estimated as 1985. Other planned nuclear facilities are: four 440 MW units to be installed by 1990 at Mochovce in western Slovakia, and four 1,000 MW units at Temelin in south Bohemia to be completed by the year 2000.

94

Hydroelectric power output will rise to 70% of the country's potential, compared with only 30% of potential currently utilised. At present there are 134 hydroelectricity generating plants working, many fewer than in previous years. Reconstruction is underway, particularly of smaller-capacity plants which will soon be providing 30% of the country's hydro-electric power. Potential power output from hydroelectric sources is estimated as 16 TWh. Czechoslovakia also imports electricity from neighbouring Romania.

Crude oil supplies from domestic sources are modest — 89,000 tonnes in 1982, 88,000 tonnes in 1981 and 93,000 tonnes in 1980. Imports come mainly from the USSR which provides 95% of Czechoslovakia's oil imports. The oil arrives via the 'Friendship' pipeline, which runs from the USSR to Czechoslovakia, Poland, Hungary and East Germany.

Natural gas production was 0.71 billion cubic metres in 1981 and 0.64 billion cubic metres in 1980. Imports from the USSR have recently been boosted by the completion of the Soviet gas pipeline, the Urengoy (in western Siberia) to Uzhgorod (on the Czechoslovak/USSR border) pipeline which is the central pivot of current Comecon energy strategy. The pipeline is reported to be working 'faultlessly' since it started deliveries in January 1984. It has been completed despite the Western embargo on equipment for its compressor stations.

**Transport, communications, tourism**

Czechoslovakia is one of Europe's major transit countries for north-to-south movement. Its transport system has many inadequacies, but improvements are taking place consistently. In 1982 there were 73,881 kilometres of major roads, 13,142 kilometres of railway and 4,144 kilometres of inland waterway.

The roads bear the largest share of freight transport in terms of volume, contributing to the country's high level of energy consumption.

The railway system is well developed. More than 20% of it is electrified, including the main east-west Friendship Railway, linking Prague with the USSR border, which forms the basis of the network.

The inland waterway system consists mainly of the rivers Danube and Elbe, but the Vltava is increasingly used and is being made more navigable. A new river port is planned for the Vltava.

**TABLE 4.24   FREIGHT TRANSPORT**

**Unit: billion ton/kilometres**

|            | 1980 | 1981 | 1982 |
|------------|------|------|------|
| Rail       | 72.6 | 72.3 | 71.6 |
| Road       | 10.3 | 11.3 | 11.3 |
| Waterways  | 3.6  | 3.8  | 3.8  |

Source: National Statistics

**TABLE 4.25   PASSENGER TRANSPORT**

**Unit: billion passenger-kilometres**

|       | 1980 | 1981 | 1982 |
|-------|------|------|------|
| Rail  | 15.4 | 13.7 | 15.1 |
| Road  | 33.8 | 34.7 | 33.7 |
| Air   | 1.8  | 1.7  | 1.2  |

Source: National Statistics

Communications facilities comprised, in 1982, 3.3 million telephone sets in use, 4.1 million licensed radios and 4.3 million licensed televisions.

Tourism facilities are limited but expansion is planned, particularly to attract more visitors from the West. Tourist numbers declined in 1981 and 1982, particularly those from Poland. Visitors from the socialist countries of East Europe form the vast majority of tourists, and outgoing Czechoslovak tourism is generally also to these countries. Travel to the West is not normally permitted and only around 20% of applications are normally granted.

**TABLE 4.26   TOURIST VISITS BY COUNTRY OF ORIGIN**

|  | 1980 | 1981 | 1982 |
|---|---|---|---|
| Socialist countries (million people) | 17.4 | 16.7 | 11.5 |
| USSR | 0.2 | 0.4 | 0.4 |
| Bulgaria | 0.2 | 0.4 | 0.3 |
| Hungary | 5.1 | 3.8 | 2.1 |
| Poland | 4.6 | 4.4 | 1.3 |
| East Germany | 6.9 | 7.0 | 6.8 |
| Romania | 0.1 | 0.2 | 0.2 |
| Yugoslavia | 0.2 | 0.4 | 0.3 |
| Nonsocialist countries ('000 people) | 1,140.7 | 1,076.3 | 992.3 |
| France | 32.4 | 27.9 | 25.9 |
| Italy | 69.6 | 52.9 | 41.9 |
| West Germany | 434.6 | 435.2 | 383.8 |
| Austria | 261.9 | 227.4 | 199.3 |
| Sweden | 33.5 | 31.7 | 29.2 |
| UK | 19.4 | 20.8 | 18.5 |
| USA | 40.9 | 30.2 | 30.5 |

Source: National Statistics

## Banking and financial services

Banking is nationalised. The Statni Banka Ceskoslovenska (the Central Bank) is the main financial institution and is the sole bank of issue. It provides credits to enterprises, deals in foreign reserves and operates the country's financial policy. The Commercial Bank of Czechoslovakia handles trade and related transactions, while the Investment Bank handles some credits. The Czech & Slovak Savings Bank provides services to the population, while the Trade Bank provides services to foreigners.

## Family life and consumer consumption

The standards of living enjoyed by the Czechoslovaks are high when compared with other East European countries, but not when compared with Western industrialised countries. Living standards declined in 1982, but improved again in 1983. The average per capita income (1983 data) is

Kcs 2,750 gross per month. Most married women work outside the home, so the typical family income exceeds Kcs 4,000 per month. The basic necessities of life are cheap, but consumer durables are very expensive.

Political freedom is restricted. The Charter 77 organisation, a civil rights group with 1,000 signatories, operates clandestinely. Dissidents are often put on trial and jailed.

Social problems exist, particularly among young people who are criticised by officialdom as degenerate. An official campaign against 'new wave' rock music is underway, on the grounds that it is a bad influence. The young are often seen to have antisocial attitudes and a low level of ideological awareness. The Communist Party aims to recruit heavily among young people, but they have not responded and some youth movement officials have felt the need to invent their own recruitment statistics in order not to be criticised for failure to attract new members. There is a graduate unemployment problem, which arises where the newly-qualified are not prepared to take their place in officially predetermined jobs.

Among all age groups there are publicly-expressed doubts about the government's 'peace policy', when Czechoslovaks see the new Soviet missiles about to be deployed in their country.

Religion is tolerated, but church activities are limited. The Roman Catholic Church, the Czech (Reformed) Church and the Orthodox Church all have substantial followings.

The state cares for the whole population with extensive welfare facilities, and the Five-Year Plan emphasises an increase in facilities for working people, families with children and older people. Some 22% of children under the age of three will have access to crèches, while an extra 7,000 places for pensioners and invalids will be provided in social care establishments.

Families generally suffer from a lack of choice in consumer goods availability, and ownership is limited compared with Western countries. The current level of car ownership is one per seven people, while telephone installations are provided at the rate of 20 telephones for 100 people. 90% of families have refrigerators and 95% own television sets. Those consumer goods which are in demand are often in short supply. The distribution system is inefficient, often due to the inadequacies of the transport infrastructure, and some parts of the country may have an abundance of one product — particularly of fresh foods — while there are simultaneous shortages elsewhere. Many Czechoslovaks have formed the habit of travelling to neighbouring East European countries in search of better goods. In 1982, consumption of consumer goods was static — variety, quality, style and technical standards were all below expectations. Car sales declined 32% in 1982, both because attractive new models are lacking and because motoring costs have increased following petrol price rises.

Consumers have unspent cash in their pockets and the level of savings has also risen. A 'parallel' or 'second' economy has found ways of providing scarce consumer goods and the government is taking steps to suppress this trade.

Entertainment facilities for the population include 2,981 cinemas, which registered 80,993 attendances, and 79 permanent theatres which registered 8,704 visitors (1981 data). Also in 1981, the country produced 7,093 new book titles and there were 1,071 periodicals in publication, including 30 daily newspapers with a combined circulation of 1.5 million copies.

Food prices have always been low in Czechoslovakia compared with world market levels. But the escalating costs of raw materials have already led to some price increases and these will become more common. Up to the early 1980s, food prices generally remained at the levels of the mid-1950s, although there were a few increases in 1966. State subsidies amount to around 40% of the average family's food. In January 1982 prices were raised substantially, with meat and meat products up 27%, fish and game up 14%, rice up 100%, cigarettes up 30%, tobacco up 39%, wine up 18% and domestic-manufacture vodka up 25%. Social security allowances were raised to compensate for the increases.

But a lack of consumer confidence can lead to 'panic buying' of essential commodities, and shortages ensue. Czechoslovaks are no longer allowed to take out of the country any of a long list of products, ranging from food to jewellery and spare parts for motor vehicles.

99

## TABLE 4.27  PER CAPITA FOOD CONSUMPTION IN 1981

**Unit: kilogrammes**

| | |
|---|---|
| Meat | 86.6 |
|    Pork | 45.1 |
|    Beef | 25.6 |
| Meat products | 23.2 |
| Poultry | 12.0 |
| Fish | 5.0 |
| Fats and oils | 22.0 |
| Milk and dairy products | 235.4 |
| Grain products | 156.4 |
| Sugar | 36.9 |
| Potatoes | 79.4 |
| Green vegetables | 66.2 |
| Fruit | 44.3 |
| Beer (litres) | 140.1 |
| Wine (litres) | 16.1 |
| Non-alcoholic drinks | 106.5 |

Source: National Statistics

## Foreign trade

Czechoslovakia carries out an enormous percentage of its foreign trade — 77.6% of the total foreign trade turnover in the first half of 1983 — with other Comecon countries. This is higher than any other Comecon country except Bulgaria.

## TABLE 4.28  FOREIGN TRADE BY COUNTRY GROUP

**Unit: billion Kcs**

| | 1980 | 1981 | 1982 | % change 1982/81 |
|---|---|---|---|---|
| *Exports* | 80.2 | 87.7 | 95.3 | + 8.7 |
| Socialist countries | 55.8 | 62.4 | 70.4 | +12.8 |
|   Comecon group | 52.2 | 58.2 | 65.4 | +12.4 |
| Non-socialist countries | 24.4 | 25.3 | 25.0 | − 1.5 |
|   Developed capitalist countries | 17.4 | 17.2 | 17.0 | − 1.4 |

Continued...

**TABLE 4.28 continued...**

|  | 1980 | 1981 | 1982 | % change 1982/81 |
|---|---|---|---|---|
| *Imports* | 81.5 | 86.3 | 94.2 | + 9.2 |
| Socialist countries | 57.2 | 62.8 | 72.2 | + 14.9 |
|   Comecon group | 53.8 | 58.6 | 67.2 | + 14.8 |
| Non-socialist countries | 24.3 | 23.5 | 22.0 | − 6.2 |
|   Developed capitalist countries | 19.9 | 19.1 | 17.9 | − 6.5 |

Source: National foreign trade statistics

The USSR is Czechoslovakia's largest individual partner, accounting for 43% of total foreign trade turnover in the first part of 1982. East Germany accounted for 9.4%, Poland for 6.1% and Western industrialised countries together for 17.8%.

**TABLE 4.29  FOREIGN TRADE WITH MAIN PARTNERS**

**Unit: billion Kcs**

|  | 1981 imports from | 1981 exports to | 1982 imports from | 1982 exports to |
|---|---|---|---|---|
| USSR | 34.5 | 33.0 | 40.9 | 38.8 |
| East Germany | 8.5 | 8.4 | 9.0 | 8.6 |
| Poland | 5.6 | 5.8 | 5.9 | 6.0 |
| Hungary | 4.8 | 4.4 | 5.1 | 5.1 |
| West Germany | 4.3 | 5.1 | 4.4 | 4.8 |
| Yugoslavia | 3.5 | 3.6 | 4.4 | 3.9 |
| Austria | 2.5 | 2.6 | 3.1 | 2.9 |
| Bulgaria | 2.1 | 2.6 | 2.6 | 2.7 |
| Romania | 2.1 | 2.2 | 2.5 | 2.4 |
| Switzerland | 2.4 | 1.3 | 2.1 | 1.5 |
| UK | 1.7 | 1.3 | 1.5 | 1.0 |
| Italy | 0.9 | 1.2 | 0.7 | 1.2 |

Source: Euromonitor, using Czechoslovak foreign trade statistics

Foreign trade operations are carried out as a state monopoly, supervised by the Ministry of Foreign Trade through a series of foreign trade organisations and other institutions. There are 40 foreign trade corporations, each responsible for the import and export of a given product range. The foreign trade corporations are independent legal entities under Czechoslovak law and have their own capital resources. Foreign companies have been allowed to set up their own sales offices within Czechoslovakia since 1976.

Foreign trade turnover (imports plus exports) is planned to expand in value to 50% of national income, compared with 33% currently. In 1985, exports are expected to have increased 43% compared with 1980, and imports 19%. This overall expansion will permit an increase in Czechoslovak trade with the Western world (trade with non-Socialist countries declined in 1982, while trade with Socialist countries increased).

**TABLE 4.30   TOTAL FOREIGN TRADE TURNOVER**

| Unit: billion Kcs | |
| --- | --- |
| 1980 | 161.7 |
| 1981 | 174.0 |
| 1982 | 189.5 |

Source: National foreign trade statistics

The trade deficit was a record Kcs 5.6 billion in 1979, but since then there has been a considerable improvement, with a Kcs 1.1 billion surplus registered in 1982. In 1982, turnover increased 9%. The 1982 surplus was achieved from trade with the non-Socialist developing world; trade with Comecon resulted in an increased deficit and trade with the developed West also was in deficit, although this was reduced from the 1981 level.

The major items in Czechoslovakia's exports are: engineering products (53.1% of all exports in 1982), including heavy plant and equipment, machine tools, tractors, passenger cars, complete technological installations; raw materials (26%), including black coal, lignite, coke, rolled steel products, timber, agricultural raw materials; consumer goods (17%), including textiles, shoes, glassware, china, ceramics and food products (3.5%).

The main imports are: raw materials (53.6% of all imports in 1982), with crude oil the largest component; plant and equipment (33%); food products (7.7%) and consumer goods (5.5%).

**TABLE 4.31   FOREIGN TRADE BY PRODUCT**

| Unit: billion Kcs | 1980 | 1981 | 1982 |
|---|---|---|---|
| *Exports* | | | |
| Machinery, equipment, tools for production | 40.2 | 45.8 | 50.6 |
| Fuels, raw materials, metals | 13.8 | 13.1 | 13.9 |
| Chemicals, fertilisers, raw rubber | 4.6 | 5.1 | 5.5 |
| Building materials | 1.8 | 2.1 | 2.2 |
| Agricultural products (excluding food) | 3.6 | 3.6 | 3.6 |
| Cattle and animals for breeding | 0.1 | 0.1 | 0.1 |
| Foodstuffs, including raw materials | 3.4 | 3.3 | 3.4 |
| Nonfood consumer goods | 12.7 | 14.7 | 16.0 |
| TOTAL EXPORTS | 80.2 | 87.7 | 95.3 |
| *Imports* | | | |
| Machinery, equipment, tools for production | 29.8 | 29.8 | 31.2 |
| Fuels, raw materials, metals | 25.8 | 31.2 | 36.9 |
| Chemicals, fertilisers, raw rubber | 7.2 | 7.2 | 6.9 |
| Building materials | 0.7 | 0.7 | 0.7 |
| Agricultural products (excluding food) | 6.0 | 6.4 | 6.1 |
| Cattle and animals for breeding | 0.1 | 0.1 | 0.1 |
| Foodstuffs, including raw materials | 7.1 | 6.3 | 7.3 |
| Nonfood consumer goods | 4.8 | 4.6 | 5.2 |
| TOTAL IMPORTS | 81.5 | 86.3 | 94.2 |

Source: National foreign trade statistics

The Brno International Engineering Fair is the most important of Czechoslovakia's international trade fairs. A very large proportion of the country's foreign trade deals are initiated and organised at this and other trade fairs. The Engineering Fair specialises in industrial machinery and equipment. Brno also hosts the International Consumer Goods Fair and the International Food Salon.

# Chapter Five

# GERMAN DEMOCRATIC REPUBLIC

## Introduction

Geographically located in the frontline of the East European Communist Bloc, the German Democratic Republic (GDR) is a well-developed industrial state, with some of the most technically advanced manufacturing facilities in East Europe.

It is considered to be the richest Comecon state, with the highest per capita income, the most passenger cars and the highest number of hospital beds. It also uses the most electricity and has the most TV sets and radios (all on a per capita basis). Progress has been remarkable, considering the devastation of industry during the Second World War, and the subsequent dismantling and removal of East German industrial establishments by the Soviet Union.

## Economic growth

Economic growth has been consistent in the past few years. GNP (gross national product) is estimated at $105 billion, or $6,300 per head for 1982. National income (also called 'net product' or 'net material product') rose 4.4% in 1983 — the target was 4.2% for the year. Industrial output, within sectors controlled by the Industrial Ministries, rose 4.5% in the first six months of 1983, with individual plan targets often exceeded. The major industrial combines produced goods in excess of targets to the value of £538 million in the six-month period.

Industry is the largest generator of national income, producing 69.8% in 1982.

**TABLE 5.1   NATIONAL INCOME VALUE BY SECTOR**

| Unit: % of total | 1981 | 1982 |
|---|---|---|
| Industry | 69.1 | 69.8 |
| Construction | 5.9 | 5.8 |
| Agriculture and forestry | 8.2 | 7.8 |
| Transport, posts, communications | 4.2 | 4.1 |
| Domestic trade | 9.6 | 9.4 |
| Other | 3.0 | 3.1 |

Source: National Statistics

The terminology which describes the GDR's total economic wealth can be confusing. GDP (gross domestic product) comprises the value contributed by all economic sectors through profits, compensation to employees and depreciation (consumption of capital). GDP is the term most familiar in the West for measurement of overall economic growth. But the 'GDP' concept is frequently not used in the centrally-planned economy countries, which prefer the 'national income' measurement. The distinction between GDP and national income can be seen in the following table:

**TABLE 5.2   CALCULATION OF GDP AND NATIONAL INCOME IN 1981**

| Unit: billion marks at 1980 prices | GDP | depreci-ation* | consump-tion** | net product |
|---|---|---|---|---|
| Industry | 403.4 | 14.5 | 245.2 | 143.7 |
| Construction | 41.7 | 1.2 | 28.2 | 12.3 |
| Agriculture and forestry | 49.7 | 3.0 | 29.6 | 17.0 |
| Transport, posts, communications | 30.2 | 3.3 | 18.3 | 8.6 |
| Domestic trade | 27.6 | 1.3 | 6.4 | 20.0 |
| Other | 11.3 | 0.7 | 4.3 | 6.3 |
| Net product of all industries | 563.9 | 24.0 | 332.1 | 207.9 |
| Adjustment for productive consumption | — | — | 11.9 | 11.9 |
| National income | 563.9 | 24.0 | 344.0 | 196.0 |

* stock depreciation and rent; ** consumption of material and productive services
Source: National Statistics

The GDR's consistent economic growth is illustrated in the following tables:

### TABLE 5.3 GROWTH OF GDP AND NATIONAL INCOME

Unit: billion marks at 1980 prices

|  | GDP | total national income | per capita national income ('000 marks) | national income per employee* ('000 marks) |
|---|---|---|---|---|
| 1977 | 481.2 | 166.0 | 9.9 | 24.6 |
| 1978 | 501.3 | 172.2 | 10.3 | 25.4 |
| 1979 | 520.3 | 179.2 | 10.7 | 26.3 |
| 1980 | 541.8 | 187.1 | 11.2 | 27.4 |
| 1981 | 563.9 | 196.0 | 11.7 | 28.7 |
| 1982 | na | 201.0 (prov.) | 12.0 (prov.) | 29.3 (prov.) |

* in productive sectors
Source: National Statistics

### TABLE 5.4 GROWTH OF GDP AND NATIONAL INCOME

Unit: 1970 = 100

|  | GDP | total national income | per capita national income | national income per employee* |
|---|---|---|---|---|
| 1977 | 144 | 141 | 144 | 139 |
| 1978 | 150 | 147 | 149 | 144 |
| 1979 | 156 | 153 | 155 | 149 |
| 1980 | 162 | 159 | 162 | 155 |
| 1981 | 169 | 167 | 170 | 162 |
| 1982 | na | 171 (prov.) | 175 (prov.) | 166 (prov.) |

* in productive sectors
Source: National Statistics

## Economic planning

The economy is centrally planned, as in other Comecon countries, and operates under an administratively developed and controlled set of plans.

The government's 'Economic Strategy for the 1980s' is a radical programme to transform the production basis of the whole economy through full exploitation of modern technology, by developing as a priority the electronic and electrical engineering industries. This will result in more effective use of the country's existing resources, including labour productivity. Structural changes are being undertaken to produce highly processed and high quality products which will improve export performance.

**TABLE 5.5   ECONOMIC PLANS 1981-85**

| Unit: %/year increases | 1981-85 plan | 1981 actual | 1982 actual | 1983 plan | 1983* actual |
|---|---|---|---|---|---|
| National income | 5.1 | 4.8 | 3.0 | 4.2 | 4.0 |
| Gross industrial output | 5.1 | 4.7 | 3.2 | 3.8 | 3.8 |
| Labour productivity in industry | 5.2 | 4.2 | 3.0 | 4.0 | 3.6 |
| Gross agricultural output | 1.1 | 1.5 (est) | − 3.6 | (net) 1.0 | na |
| Retail trade turnover** | 3.7-4.1 | 2.5 | 1.0 | 3.0 | 0.0 |
| Foreign trade turnover** | 6.3 | 10.7 | 9.2 | 13.0 | na |

* 6 months only, January-June; ** at current prices
Source: National Statistics

This plan differs from that of the 1970s, whose priority was to provide higher cultural and living standards for the population.

Success is being achieved in the present plan despite scarce resources and the adverse world economic climate. In 1982, in spite of a 10% cut in the oil supplies which the GDR receives from the USSR and despite the restrictive lending policies of international creditors, a growth rate of 3% was achieved, although the original target for the year was 4.8%. Also in 1982, industrial output rose 3.2%, with less input of material and labour than in 1981. (A severe labour shortage makes it essential for all sectors to achieve high levels of productivity and efficiency.) Energy consumption fell: the quantities of oil, heating oil, diesel fuel and coke used were respectively 30%, 25%, 13% and 11% less than in 1981. However, private consumption fell in real terms, the result of the year's gains being diverted into exports to improve the country's balance of payments position.

The GDR is the only Comecon country which has set higher targets for 1981-85 than for 1976-80, and even if it approaches these targets it will have achieved a great deal. The 1982 results were respectable by international standards, but some key areas were disappointing. The country is falling behind on the overall 1981-85 plan, and official unease is seen in the urgency with which workers and trade unions are urged and encouraged to increase productivity and to fulfil targets.

The state owns most industrial and agricultural capacity. Manufacturing facilities are organised into combines (Kombinate) or 'the people's own factories' (VEB, Volkseigene Betriebe). A combine is an amalgamation of industrial firms; there were 157 combines in operation in 1981. VEBs are separate factories, under the control of regional industry associations or local authorities; the local authorities in turn report to industrial ministries. Some 96.5% of national income is produced by the state-controlled sector.

In 1984, the government planned for higher output in all sectors — particularly of consumer goods. Continual exhortations to produce more reflect a total commitment to industrial development and expansion, and to utilising resources to the utmost. Improving 'Leistung' — general economic performance — and achieving the greatest output from the least input: these are the priorities. Labour input is to be reduced by 660 million man-hours by 1985, although it is acknowledged that productivity increases cannot be infinite. Automation, microelectronics and robotics will increasingly be able to free skilled workers for other jobs. Extensive use of these new technologies is the key to economic growth, industrial modernisation and expanding exports. The official line at the 1983 Leipzig Spring Fair was 'Programmed Efficiency through Microelectronics'.

Guidelines for the 1984 Plan were published by Neues Deutschland, the country's leading newspaper. The six main tasks were: improving the usage of energy and materials, with more extensive use being made of secondary raw materials and scrap; achieving economic growth above all by a rise in labour productivity, which is to grow faster than at present and faster than output; producing high value consumer goods at a faster rate; providing more for consumer needs, matching supply and demand through better industry/distribution links; increasing railway electrification and reducing the volume of energy-intensive road transport; advancing environmental control to reduce pollution.


## The population and workforce

There are 16.7 million East Germans living in a territorial area of 108,333 square kilometres. Population density is 154 inhabitants per square kilometre.

**TABLE 5.6   POPULATION STATISTICS**

| Unit: '000 inhabitants | male | female | total | |
|---|---|---|---|---|
| mid-1981 | 7,863.6 | 8,872.4 | 16,736.6 | |
| mid-1982 | 7,851.8 | 8,845.5 | 16,697.4 | |

| | urban | urban as % | rural | rural as % |
|---|---|---|---|---|
| mid-1981 | 12,778.2 | 76.4 | 3,957.8 | 23.6 |
| mid-1982 | 12,769.6 | 76.5 | 3,927.8 | 23.5 |

Source: National Statistics


Between 1976 and 1980, the population declined 0.1%/year. The GDR is the only European country with a continuing population drop. As well as declining, the population is imbalanced between the sexes, and it is ageing. The government has made available increased child benefit and it has eased credit facilities in an effort to encourage larger families. A modest 'baby boom' occurred during the second half of the 1970s, although the population in total still declined. In 1981, the birth rate was 14.2 per 1,000 and the death rate 13.9 per 1,000.

Workers constitute around 90% of the labour force, or about 7.6 million people. A breakdown by sector shows industry as the largest employer.

109

**TABLE 5.7  LABOUR FORCE, 1982**

Unit: %

| | |
|---|---|
| Industry | 38.0 |
| Crafts (excluding building crafts) | 3.1 |
| Construction | 7.0 |
| Agriculture, forestry | 10.6 |
| Transport | 5.8 |
| Posts, telecommunications | 1.6 |
| Trade | 10.2 |
| Other productive branches | 3.2 |
| Non-productive branches | 20.5 |

Source: National Statistics

Some 96% of workers belong to the FDGB, the Free German Trade Union Federation (Freier Deutscher Gewerkschaftsbund), which is the largest mass organisation of workers in the country.

The major cities, in order of population size, are: Berlin (the capital), Leipzig, Dresden, Karl-Marx-Stadt (formerly Chemnitz), Magdeburg, Rostock, Halle, Erfurt, Potsdam, Gera, Schwerin, Zwickau, Cottbus, Jena, Dessau and Brandenburg.

**Industrial activities**

The main industrial sectors are listed below in order of their contribution to national income in 1981:

Engineering and vehicle building
Chemicals
Food
Power and fuels
Light industry
Electrical engineering and electronics
Metallurgy

**Machinery**

The heavy machinery sector employs 330,000 workers in thirteen large combines with 227 factories. An example is the Ernst Thaelmann heavy engineering combine at Magdeburg with 28,000 workers producing 1 million tonnes per year of wire and fine and medium steel sections. The Takraf combine, set up in 1979, has 45,000 workers in 28 plants and produces goods for the power industry, mainly mining equipment, hauling machinery for opencast workings and transport and storage equipment. Bergmann-Borsig of Berlin, another important combine, was due to produce gas compressors for the USSR in 1984, part of the Comecon plan to make East Europe less vulnerable to economic sanctions from the West.

## Machine tools

The GDR is estimated as the world's fifth largest producer of machine tools, after the US, Japan, the USSR and West Germany. Some 75% of its output is exported, mainly to the USSR and other Comecon countries. In 1982, East Germany produced 6.9% of all the machine tools exported on the world market. Machine tool exports from East Germany to the UK were worth £7.5 million in 1982, and East Germany satisfies 40-50% of UK import demand in this sector. There are currently an estimated 2,500 East German boring machines operating in UK factories.

**TABLE 5.8  MACHINE TOOLS OUTPUT**

| Unit: billion marks, 1980 prices | 1980 | 1981 | 1982 |
|---|---|---|---|
| Machine tools* | 2.6 | 2.9 | na |
| Cutting type machine tools** | 2.0 | 2.2 | 2.3 |
| Numerical control machine tools (units) | 853 | 935 | 996 |
| Cold forming machine tools and shears | 0.6 | 0.7 | 0.7 |

* this is a general figure, source is Foreign Economic Trends (US Dept of Commerce)
** excluding electroplating installations, components, accessories and parts
Source: National Statistics

Machine tools are built at four combines: in Berlin (7 Oktober combine); Erfurt (Umformtechnik Herbert Warnke); Karl-Marx-Stadt (Fritz Heckert combine); and Schmalkalden.

## Electrical and electronic equipment

The sector producing electrical and electronic equipment is a major area targeted for growth in the current government plan, since development here will benefit many other industrial sectors. An increase of 9.6% per year in output is the aim, but yearly targets were set lower, at 8.9%, 7.7% and 8.5% respectively for 1981, 1982 and 1983.

**TABLE 5.9  OUTPUT OF SELECTED PRODUCTS OF THE ELECTRICAL ENGINEERING, ELECTRONICS AND PRECISION ENGINEERING SECTORS**

|  | 1980 | 1981 | 1982 |
|---|---|---|---|
| Heavy duty transformers ('000 units) | 12.3 | 13.1 | 15.7 |
| Cable & wire (billion marks) | 2.5 | 2.6 | 2.2 |
| Electrical switchgears and appliances (billion marks) | 3.2 | 3.5 | 3.7 |
| Numerical control switchgears and appliances (billion marks)* | 0.2 | 0.3 | 0.5 |
| Data processing and office equipment (billion marks) | 2.5 | 2.9 | 3.5 |
| Large typewriters ('000 units)* | 227.0 | 235.0 | 245.0 |
| Calculators and adding machines ('000 units)* | 334.5 | 407.4 | na |
| Control and monitoring devices (billion marks) | 1.3 | 1.5 | 1.6 |
| Electronic components (billion marks) | 2.3 | 2.8 | 3.3 |
| Semiconductors (billion marks)* | 1.0 | 1.3 | 1.6 |
| Integrated circuits (million units)* | 37.7 | 47.1 | 55.4 |
| AC motors (GW) | 7.6 | 7.6 | 7.5 |
| Medical-technical products (million marks) | 313.4 | 365.0 | 386.9 |

Notes: monetary units quoted are at 1980 prices; * subdivision of preceding or main category

Source: National Statistics

## Computers and data processing equipment

Output has grown consistently, and reached 3.5 billion marks (1980 prices) in 1982, compared with 2.9 billion and 2.5 billion in 1981 and 1980 respectively. The Robotron factory in Dresden is the country's sole manufacturer of these products. Its new Nova computer was launched in early 1983, just prior to the Leipzig Fair, by the Chairman of the USSR

Planning Commission, N. Baibakov. But Robotron's director has reportedly been dismissed for failure to reach production targets.

### Industrial Robots

A claimed 45,000 robots will be installed by 1985, compared with 9,000 in operation at the end of 1981. But it has been admitted that the robots referred to are in fact gripping devices, not true industrial robots. The number of freely moving, programmable robots currently installed is 370 units. This compares with 3,000 in use in West Germany, of which 300 are installed in Volkswagen factories alone.

### Motor vehicles and transport equipment

Centres of production include: passenger cars at Eisenach (where Wartburg cars are built) and Zwickau (Sachsenring cars); lorries at Karl-Marx-Stadt, Zwickau, Zittau, Ludwigsfeld, small lorries at Waltershausen, special purpose lorries in Berlin; motorcycles at Zschopau and Suhl; railway rolling stock at Halle and Goerlitz (passenger coaches), Hennigsdorf (locomotives), Dessau, Bautzen and Neisky (goods vans); shipbuilding in Warnemuende, Rostock, Wismar and Stralsund; tractors at Schoenebeck.

Some 2.8 million passenger cars were in circulation in 1982, but there remains a 10-year waiting list for potential buyers who lack black market contacts.

**TABLE 5.10  OUTPUT OF MOTOR VEHICLES AND TRANSPORT EQUIPMENT**

| Unit: '000 units | 1980 | 1981 | 1982 |
|---|---|---|---|
| Railway coaches | 1.5 | 1.6 | 1.7 |
| Passenger cars | 177.0 | 180.0 | 183.0 |
| Commercial vehicles | 37.0 | 39.4 | 38.8 |
| Mini motorcycles | 179.6 | 187.8 | 198.8 |
| Motorcycles | 80.5 | 78.8 | 81.0 |
| Bicycles | 613.6 | 627.5 | 630.9 |
| Perambulators | 532.1 | 553.4 | 530.7 |

Source: National Statistics

### Consumer goods production

Although the GDR has the highest level per head of consumer goods such as cars, TV sets and radios within the Comecon countries, general availability and ownership levels remain low compared with Western European standards. Production is deficient, and shortages of consumer goods are general and continuing, and the official economic plans have long emphasised expansion in this sector. Satisfying consumer demand with these coveted goods is seen as very relevant to raising worker productivity levels throughout industry; if the goods are in adequate supply incentives are there for workers to increase their pay packets by earning bonuses to buy the goods. Many firms are now planning to increase their output of consumer goods, and in Karl-Marx-Stadt alone, enterprises will increase production by the value of 500 million marks.

**TABLE 5.11  CONSUMER GOODS OUTPUT**

**Unit: '000 units**

|  | 1980 | 1981 | 1982 |
|---|---|---|---|
| TV sets | 578.0 | 619.0 | 652.0 |
| Colour TV sets* | 264.0 | 310.0 | 325.0 |
| Radio sets | 915.0 | 965.0 | 900.0 |
| Radio recorders* | 281.4 | 324.6 | 326.2 |
| Binoculars | 248.0 | 248.0 | 248.0 |
| Cameras | 979.0 | 955.0 | na |
| Watches (million marks, 1980 prices) | 359.3 | 421.4 | 405.2 |
| Domestic electrical appliances (billion marks, 1980 prices) | 1.7 | 1.9 | 2.0 |
| Vacuum cleaners (million units) | 1.1 | 1.2 | 1.2 |
| Water heaters, gas and electric | 607.0 | 628.0 | 635.0 |
| Domestic washing machines | 468.0 | 485.0 | 485.0 |
| Domestic refrigerators and freezers | 637.0 | 655.0 | 700.0 |
| Freezers* | 181.7 | 201.4 | 238.7 |
| Domestic sewing machines | 242.0 | 255.0 | 272.0 |
| Cookers | 167.9 | 180.6 | 196.6 |

* subdivision of preceding category
Source: National Statistics

114

## Chemicals

The chemical industry's plans complement the coal industry's strategy. Chemical components are being extracted from lignite to an ever-increasing degree. Lignite provides plastics, lubricants, solid paraffin and electrode coke. Coal gasification facilities are being intensified.

**TABLE 5.12   CHEMICAL INDUSTRY PRODUCTION**

| Unit: million tonnes | 1980 | 1981 | 1982 |
|---|---|---|---|
| Petrol | 3.3 | 3.4 | 3.9 |
| Diesel fuel | 6.1 | 5.6 | 6.1 |
| Lubricating oils | 0.4 | 0.4 | 0.4 |
| Rock salt | 3.1 | 3.1 | 3.1 |
| Sulphuric acid | 1.0 | 1.0 | 0.9 |
| Ammonia | 1.4 | 1.5 | 1.4 |
| Caustic soda | 0.6 | 0.6 | 0.7 |
| Soda ash | 0.9 | 0.9 | 0.9 |
| Caustic potash ('000 tonnes) | 48.4 | 47.6 | 50.5 |
| Hydrochloric acid ('000 tonnes) | 106.0 | 104.1 | 106.0 |
| Potash fertilisers | 3.4 | 3.5 | 3.4 |
| Nitrogenous fertilisers | 0.9 | 1.0 | 1.0 |
| Butanol ('000 tonnes) | 51.4 | 52.7 | 55.3 |
| Plastics ('000 tonnes) | 861.2 | 998.0 | 990.3 |
| High density PE ('000 tonnes) | 85.7 | 130.6 | 143.0 |
| Polyurethane ('000 tonnes) | 102.0 | 107.0 | 114.8 |
| Polyvinyl chloride ('000 tonnes)* | 256.0 | 287.0 | na |
| Tyres (million units) | 7.1 | 7.0 | 7.1 |
| Synthetic fibres ('000 tonnes) | 138.7 | 146.2 | 148.6 |
| Washing agents ('000 tonnes) | 127.9 | 128.5 | 110.1 |

* PVC figure from Foreign Economic Trends (US Dept of Commerce)
Source: National Statistics

Improvements to the country's chemical capacities include: a large crude oil processing plant under construction at Leuna; a methanol plant, also under construction at Leuna; the cracker at Swedt petrochemical combine to be enlarged; new fibre units to be built at Schwarza and Guben; and a 50,000-70,000 tonnes per year fodder protein plant almost complete at Swedt, processing diesel fuel microbiologically.

115

### Steel

Raw steel output was 7.1 million tonnes in 1982, and 7.5 million in 1981. Steel exports to the West are currently 1 million tonnes per year; 34,000 tonnes of this go to the UK.

**TABLE 5.13   STEEL OUTPUT**

| Unit: million tonnes | 1980 | 1981 | 1982 |
|---|---|---|---|
| Raw steel | 7.3 | 7.5 | 7.2 |
| Hot rolled steel | 5.1 | 5.1 | 5.0 |
| Semifinished products | 3.5 | 3.6 | 3.7 |

Source: National Statistics

The steel industry was traditionally supplied with raw materials from the Ruhr area, now in West Germany, and a result of the partition of Germany is that the East German steel industry has found alternative supply sources.

The East German Special Steels combine comprises eight plants in different locations, which together produce 4.6 million tonnes per year of crude steel. The Brandenburg steelworks is the parent plant; this was built from the ruins of the Central German Steelworks which was destroyed in the Second World War, and is now a modern plant of Western standards, except for its Siemens-Martin wire rod line which is due for closure through obsolescence.

Other improvements to the country's steel capacities include: a new cold rolling line at Ilsenburg; a new small section mill and bar steel line at Hennigsdorf and a continuous profile steel line at the Maximilian plant, with equipment supplied by Cockerill-Sambre of Belgium, and operational by the end of 1984.

Electronic equipment is being installed throughout plants to increase steel output and modernise techniques. Computer installation is well under way.

# Other industry

### TABLE 5.14   OUTPUT OF SELECTED PRODUCTS OF HEAVY INDUSTRY

|  | 1980 | 1981 | 1982 |
|---|---|---|---|
| Cast iron, malleable cold rolled and steel castings (million tonnes) | 1.3 | 1.3 | 1.3 |
| Hydraulic equipment (million marks) | 811.3 | 874.7 | 898.5 |
| Pneumatic equipment (million marks) | 53.6 | 58.7 | 61.8 |
| Lifting gear and conveyors* (billion marks) | 3.0 | 3.1 | 3.1 |
| Truck cranes ('000 units) | 1.1 | 1.2 | na |
| Railway coaches ('000 units) | 1.5 | 1.6 | 1.7 |
| Agricultural machinery (billion marks) | 4.8 | 5.2 | 5.4 |
| Tyres (million units) | 7.1 | 7.0 | 7.1 |
| Cement (million tonnes) | 12.4 | 12.2 | 11.7 |
| Plaster of Paris ('000 tonnes) | 313.0 | 303.0 | 310.0 |
| Bricks (billion units) | 1.2 | 1.2 | 1.1 |
| Wall tiles (million square metres) | 6.2 | 6.5 | 6.7 |
| Concrete products (million tonnes) | 24.6 | 22.6 | 21.7 |

* excludes excavators
Note: monetary units quoted are at 1980 prices

### TABLE 5.15   OUTPUT OF SELECTED LIGHT INDUSTRY PRODUCTS

|  | 1980 | 1981 | 1982 |
|---|---|---|---|
| Fibreboard ('000 cubic metres) | 281.0 | 280.0 | 264.2 |
| Woodpulp ('000 tonnes) | 514.0 | 506.0 | 512.0 |
| Paper ('000 tonnes) | 842.0 | 860.0 | 857.0 |
| Furniture (billion marks) | 4.6 | 4.7 | 4.9 |
| Footwear (million pairs) | 78.8 | 80.4 | 82.1 |
| Men's outerwear (billion marks) | 1.3 | 1.3 | 1.3 |
| Women's outerwear (billion marks) | 1.1 | 1.1 | 1.1 |
| Children's outerwear (billion marks) | 0.5 | 0.6 | 0.6 |
| Woven and knitted fabrics (billion square metres) | 1.2 | 1.2 | 1.2 |
| Cotton fabrics (million square metres) | 277.0 | 286.0 | 288.0 |
| Worsted and semiworsted woollen fabrics (million square metres) | 26.8 | 27.0 | 27.6 |
| Toys (billion marks) | 1.0 | 1.0 | 1.0 |
| Musical instruments (million marks) | 221.1 | 234.3 | 245.0 |

Note: monetary units quoted are at 1980 prices
Source: National Statistics

**TABLE 5.16 OUTPUT OF SELECTED FOOD INDUSTRY PRODUCTS**

|  | 1980 | 1981 | 1982 |
|---|---|---|---|
| Meat (million tonnes) | 1.6 | 1.6 | 1.6 |
| Butter ('000 tonnes) | 280.0 | 273.0 | 266.0 |
| Cheese ('000 tonnes) | 210.0 | 213.3 | 222.6 |
| White sugar ('000 tonnes) | 733.0 | 818.0 | 896.0 |
| Beer (million hectolitres) | 23.6 | 24.1 | 25.4 |
| Non-alcoholic beverages (million hl) | 13.1 | 14.0 | 14.8 |
| Cigarettes (billion units) | 26.0 | 26.0 | 25.6 |

Source: National Statistics

## Minerals

The GDR has few raw materials in plentiful supply except lignite (brown coal), copper and potash. Many other materials must be imported, and although much is supplied by the USSR and other Comecon countries, East Germany remains vulnerable to adverse terms of trade with Western 'hard currency' nations. Most high grade coal (mainly from Poland), oil (mainly from the USSR) and iron ore requirements and all the country's bauxite, chromium, manganese and phosphate needs have to be imported. Also, most chemicals, cotton, grain and lumber comes from abroad. Around 25-30% of GDP has to be allocated to paying for these imports, according to West German calculations.

Yet the country is self sufficient in many minerals — lignite and potash as well as rock salt, fluorspar, heavy spar, stone and earth for building, tin, and raw materials for glass and ceramics manufacture. It is the world's largest producer of lignite — 276 million tonnes in 1982. It also produces potash, of which it is the world's third largest producer after Canada and the USSR, with an output of 3.4 million tonnes in 1982. Rock salt output was 3.1 million tonnes in 1982. Some potash, rock salt, coal and iron is exported. Oil output is minimal — 60,000 tonnes in 1982, and exploration continues; the bulk of oil supplies, 90%, comes from the USSR, with a remaining 10% needing to be purchased as hard currency imports. A long-threatened 10% cut in Soviet oil supplies has been implemented, and East Germany now receives 17.1 million tonnes per year, compared with 19 million previously. Proven natural gas reserves were 71 billion cubic metres in 1982. Some hard coal is mined — 50,000 tonnes in 1979 — but reserves are becoming depleted. Iron ore deposits are scattered, seams are thin and the ore has only 20-35% iron content.

## Lignite

Lignite is mined in huge quantities. Reserves are estimated at 24 billion tonnes, 92% of which is suitable for mining by opencast techniques. Lignite provides 60% of East Germany's total energy requirements.

Great stress is placed on reducing fuel usage to maximise the advantages of this prolific resource. It is used, re-used, and every available calorie and component is extracted to reduce the need for fuel imports — a national priority. The volume of secondary or recycled raw materials available is increased by exhaustive lignite processing. Advanced techniques produce coke, briquettes and synthetic natural gas for chemical manufacture. Increased output of coal-chemicals, planned to rise to 11 million tonnes of oil equivalent in 1990, compared with 7 million in 1982, will increasingly substitute for the diminishing supplies of crude oil from the USSR.

There were 32 mines operating in 1981, and 21 new mines will be opened by 1990. Existing mines are located in the Cottbus, Leipzig and Halle areas.

**TABLE 5.17   OUTPUT OF LIGNITE AND LIGNITE PRODUCTS**

| Unit: million tonnes | 1980 | 1981 | 1982 |
|---|---|---|---|
| Raw lignite | 258.1 | 266.7 | 276.0 |
| Lignite briquettes | 49.7 | 49.8 | 50.0 |
| Lignite coke | 5.3 | 5.5 | 5.5 |

Source: National Statistics

**TABLE 5.18   PLANNED GROWTH IN LIGNITE OUTPUT**

| Unit: million tonnes | | |
|---|---|---|
| | 1982 | 276* |
| | 1985 | 295 |
| | 1990 | 300 |

* in 1982, the plan was overfulfilled
Sources: Various

Improved technologies are constantly being implemented. Transportation of lignite and of spoil is increasingly undertaken by conveyor as an alternative to train transport. More efficient performance of large bucket wheel excavators and improved loading of conveyors result from the introduction of computer controls. New pithead electric power stations, such as the Jaenschwalde plant, make good use of the readily available fuel. But the country pays a substantial price for all this lignite burning: a high level of atmospheric pollution.

### Energy supplies

Primary energy consumption in 1982 was 3,521 Petajoules, compared with 3,574 Petajoules in 1981. Industry continues to decrease the amount of energy it requires, using little more in total in 1982 than it did in 1975. Of the 1982 energy consumed, 2,553 Petajoules were provided by solid fuels (raw lignite provided 2,454 Petajoules).

**TABLE 5.19   COMMERCIAL PRIMARY ENERGY BALANCE IN 1981**

**Unit: million tonnes of coal equivalent**

| *Production* | | *Apparent consumption* | |
|---|---|---|---|
| Solid fuel | 80.9 | Solid fuel | 87.8 |
| Crude oil, natural gas liquids | 0.1 | Liquid fuel | 22.9 |
| Natural gas | 4.0 | Natural gas | 11.3 |
| Hydroelectric power | 0.8 | Hydroelectric power | 0.8 |
| Nuclear power | 5.2 | Nuclear power | 5.2 |
| Total production | 90.9 | Net imports of electricity | 0.7 |
| | | Total consumption | 128.8 |
| *Imports* | | *Exports* | |
| Solid fuel | 8.9 | Solid fuel | 1.9 |
| Crude petroleum | 29.8 | Petroleum products | 3.8 |
| Petroleum products | 0.5 | Natural gas | 0.3 |
| Natural gas | 7.5 | Electricity | 1.1 |
| Electricity | 1.8 | Total exports | 7.1 |
| Total imports | 48.5 | Balancing item* | 3.6 |
| *Drawdown of natural gas stocks* | | | |
| TOTAL SUPPLY | 139.5 | TOTAL DEMAND | 139.5 |

* comprises output of 930,000 tonnes of non-energy products (naphtha, lubricants etc), unidentified changes in crude stocks and statistical discrepancy
Source: UN Yearbook of World Energy Statistics

## TABLE 5.20   ELECTRICITY AND GAS OUTPUT

|  | 1980 | 1981 | 1982 |
|---|---|---|---|
| Electricity (TWh) | 98.8 | 100.7 | 102.9 |
| Manufactured gas (billion cubic metres) | 6.2 | 5.9 | 6.4 |

Source: National Statistics

Lignite provides the major part of electric power supplies — 81.5% of all power in 1982, compared with 79.3% in 1981. Oil use for power is negligible and diminishing — down to 0.7% of total power supplies in 1982, and the remaining oil-fired power stations will soon be converted to lignite or gas. However, it requires five times as much lignite (by weight) as oil to produce the same amount of heat.

## TABLE 5.21   ELECTRICITY OUTPUT BY SOURCE

|  | 1981 TWh | 1982 TWh | 1981 as % | 1982 as % |
|---|---|---|---|---|
| Lignite | 79.9 | 83.9 | 79.4 | 81.5 |
| Lignite briquettes | 0.5 | 0.5 | 0.5 | 0.5 |
| Hard coal | 0.3 | 0.3 | 0.3 | 0.3 |
| Nuclear power | 11.9 | 10.9 | 11.8 | 10.5 |
| Hydroelectric power | 1.7 | 1.8 | 1.7 | 1.7 |
| Mineral oils | 0.9 | 0.7 | 0.9 | 0.7 |
| Other | 5.4 | 4.9 | 5.4 | 4.8 |
| TOTAL | 100.6 | 102.9 | 100.0 | 100.0 |

Source: Statistical Pocketbook of the GDR, 1983

In addition to East German generation, power is imported (4.3 TWh in 1982), and also exported (3.1 TWh in 1982) under Comecon exchange arrangements. Installed generating capacity totalled 21.9 GW in 1982.

Gas supplies were provided to 35.8 million houses in 1980. Domestic production of natural gas is limited and much is imported, particularly from the USSR. In return for Soviet supplies, East Germany supplies pipeline and compressor stations for the new pipeline being built from Western Siberia to West Europe, supplying East European customers along the way. Some 235 km of this pipeline are due to be completed in East Germany by 1985, and the country will receive 650 million cubic metres per year. East Germany contributes many workers to the construction of the USSR pipeline, and has recently doubled their numbers to 10,000 — the Soviets want to complete this massive project ahead of schedule.

## Agriculture

East Germany has 4.7 million hectares of arable land and 1.25 million hectares of pasture/meadow land. There are also 2.96 million hectares of forest. The farming sector is organised with rigid specialisation, separating livestock rearing and crop growing in order to achieve maximum proficiency (although difficulties arise where transfers between these two branches are required, e.g fodder deliveries to cattle). Farms are organised into large units — LPGs, Landwirtschaftliche Producktionsgenossenschaften — which are, in effect, agricultural factories. There are 4,000 LPGs, each with around 5,000 acres. In addition to the LPGs, some 5% of agricultural land consists of small plots of less than half an acre, which are privately farmed. Despite their disproportionate size, these private plots produce up to 14% of all the country's pork supplies, 10% of beef, 40% of eggs, 30% of fruit and 11% of vegetables.

**Crops** — The 1982 grain harvest was a record 10.0 million tonnes, but despite this, overall agricultural output fell short of targets and was less than in 1981. Even grain imports were necessary.

Sugar beet yields are low, and 20% of needs are met by imports from Cuba, for which precious hard currency is not necessary since Cuba is a member of Comecon.

Fodder production frequently results in supply deficiencies, and 25.3% of needs are imported. The government aims at self-sufficiency in fodder supplies by 1985, but achieving this is likely to prove difficult; an agreement has been signed with Canada to buy 1 million tonnes per year of fodder to 1986. Supplies will be boosted by the 50,000-70,000 tonnes per year fodder protein plant in Swedt, producing protein manufactured microbiologically from diesel fuel.

**TABLE 5.22    NET OUTPUT OF CROPS**

| Unit: million tonnes | 1980 | 1981 | 1982 |
|---|---|---|---|
| Cereals | 9.6 | 8.9 | 10.0 |
| Wheat | 3.1 | 2.9 | 2.7 |
| Rye | 1.9 | 1.8 | 2.1 |
| Barley | 4.0 | 3.5 | 4.1 |
| Oats | 0.6 | 0.6 | 0.9 |
| Fodder root crops | 1.5 | 1.9 | 2.0 |
| Field fodder crops (excluding maize) | 24.5 | 25.2 | 20.3 |
| Maize, green and silage (as main crop) | 11.4 | 13.4 | 10.4 |
| Oilseeds | 0.3 | 0.3 | 0.3 |
| Potatoes | 9.2 | 10.4 | 8.9 |
| Sugar beet | 7.0 | 8.0 | 7.2 |
| Vegetables under glass ('000 tonnes)* | 64.0 | 69.0 | 78.0 |
| Vegetables (outdoor)* | 1.1 | 1.3 | 1.1 |

* from Socialist enterprises
Source: National Statistics

**TABLE 5.23    FARM MACHINERY IN USE IN 1982**

| Unit: '000 units | |
|---|---|
| Tractors | 149.5 |
| Lorries | 53.5 |
| Trailers | 266.4 |
| Combine harvesters/threshers | 14.5 |
| Potato harvesters | 8.0 |
| Beet harvesters | 2.6 |

Source: National Statistics

**Livestock, animal products** — liveweight slaughterings totalled 2.4 million tonnes in 1982, of which 1.5 million was pigmeat, 0.7 million was cattle and calves and 0.2 million was poultry and rabbit. This compares with 2.6 million tonnes total slaughterings in 1981 and 2.5 million in 1980. Also in 1982, milk output was 7.8 million tonnes, egg production 5.7 billion units and honey from bees 7,225 tonnes. Yields registered were 3,626 kilogrammes of milk per cow, 214 eggs per hen and 18.3 kg of honey per bee colony.

**TABLE 5.24   ESTIMATED OUTPUT OF ANIMAL PRODUCTS IN 1982**

| | |
|---|---|
| Meat (carcass weight), million tonnes | 1.8 |
| Milk, million tonnes | 6.7 |
| Eggs, billion units | 5.7 |

Source: UN Economic Survey of Europe, using GDR data

## Government and society

The GDR is a Socialist state where all power is held by the Socialist Unity Party, the SED, Sozialistiche Einheitspartei Deutschlands. Erich Honecker is Head of State and First Secretary of the Party. Relations with the USSR are of great importance — illustrated by the visit to the USSR by Honecker in early 1983. He was the first visiting Comecon leader to be met personally at Moscow airport by the late Soviet head of state Andropov, after the latter had become General Secretary of the USSR Communist Party.

The GDR is very much a part of the Eastern Bloc, politically and economically. Due to the country's reliance on Comecon for its raw materials, trends within the Soviet Bloc have a great influence on its overall development. The Socialist ethic is all-pervading, and the state participates in all aspects of life. Through the central planning mechanism, economic and social life is channelled into set patterns. One of the benefits of a centrally-planned economy is that unemployment need not exist — in fact, East Germany, in common with many Comecon countries, has an acute labour shortage.

Official emigration is virtually unknown. The border with West Germany is closed and intensively guarded, denying free access to the Western world. The Berlin Wall was constructed in 1961 and completed the sealing of the border. East Germans are not permitted to live abroad, although some citizens do find ways of transferring themselves into West Germany, sometimes via the transit roads running from West Berlin to the West German border with the use of falsified papers or other devices.

Good citizenship is encouraged. One illustration of this, frequently commented upon by visitors to East Germany, is the lack of litter in the streets. Pride in the appearance of their cities goes with pride in their achievements. If the border were reopened tomorrow, there is no evidence to suggest that there would be a mass exodus of discontented East Germans seeking a better life elsewhere.

### Family life and consumer goods availability

Large families are encouraged by the policies of a government worried by the continual population decline (although small families remain very much the norm). Generous child benefits and easier credit facilities aim to make living more comfortable.

Working women are highly regarded, since work is seen as a social responsibility and a right. Most married women work outside the home, and children are catered for in official crêches. Single parenthood is officially discouraged, although it is widespread — almost 25% of births in 1981 were to single mothers. Many women choose to live like this. They get priority access to crêches and nursery schools and more time off work (paid) if children are sick. Currently an extremely high 88% of women of working age are either working or studying.

In 1982 there were 6,926 crêches operating, providing 314,554 places for children under 3.

Although housing is still in short supply, the government expects to provide sufficient accommodation for everyone by 1990.

Consumer goods ownership is high by East European standards, although not by those of the West. East Germans own, on a per capita basis, the highest level of cars, TV sets and radios within the East European bloc.

**TABLE 5.25   CONSUMER GOODS DISTRIBUTION**

| Unit: units per 100 households | 1980 | 1981 | 1982 |
|---|---|---|---|
| Passenger cars | 36.8 | 39.0 | 40.0 |
| Motorcycles and scooters | 18.4 | 18.4 | 18.4 |
| Refrigerators and freezers | 99.0 | 99.0 | 99.0 |
| Washing machines | 80.4 | 83.4 | 83.8 |
| Radio licences | 99.0 | 99.0 | 99.0 |
| TV licences | 88.1 | 89.2 | 89.7 |

Source: National Statistics

Average monthly net income was 1,490 marks in 1980.

**TABLE 5.26 CONSUMER EXPENDITURE IN 1982**

**Unit: % spent on each sector**

| | |
|---|---|
| *Consumption of goods and services* | *83.1* |
| Goods | 70.1 |
|    Food, drink, tobacco | 34.7 |
|      Food | 24.8 |
|      Drink and tobacco | 9.9 |
|    Industrial goods | 35.4 |
|      Shoes, leather goods | 2.5 |
|      Textiles, clothing | 9.8 |
|      Other | 23.1 |
| | |
| Paid services | 13.0 |
|    Transport | 1.2 |
|    Rents | 2.8 |
|    Electricity, water, etc. | 1.5 |
|    Repairs | 1.9 |
|    Education, entertainment, recreation | 3.6 |
| | |
| *Other* | *16.9* |
| (taxes, fees, increases in monetary stocks and accounts) | |
| | |
|    TOTAL | 100.0 |

Source: National Statistics

**TABLE 5.27 PER CAPITA CONSUMPTION OF FOOD, DRINK AND TOBACCO**

**Unit: kilogrammes**

| | 1980 | 1981 | 1982 |
|---|---|---|---|
| Meat | 89.5 | 90.7 | 91.0 |
| Beef and veal* | 22.8 | 23.7 | 24.8 |
| Pork* | 57.8 | 58.0 | 55.8 |
| Poultry* | 8.9 | 9.0 | 10.3 |
| Fish and fish products | 7.4 | 7.4 | 7.4 |
| Eggs and egg products (units) | 289.0 | 288.0 | 301.0 |
| Edible fats | 33.0 | 32.9 | 33.4 |

continued...

**Table 5.27 continued...**

|  | 1980 | 1981 | 1982 |
|---|---|---|---|
| Milk (litres) | 98.7 | 99.2 | 100.9 |
| Cheese | 7.5 | 7.8 | 7.9 |
| Flour, cereals | 94.5 | 95.0 | 97.1 |
| Vegetables | 93.8 | 93.1 | 95.6 |
| Fresh vegetables* | 64.3 | 59.2 | 63.4 |
| Fruit | 71.1 | 60.4 | 70.2 |
| Fresh fruit* | 37.1 | 27.9 | 31.8 |
| Sugar and sugar products (white sugar equivalent) | 40.6 | 40.8 | 44.0 |
| Coffee | 2.8 | 2.9 | 3.2 |
| Tea (grammes) | 99.0 | 103.0 | 129.0 |
| Cigarettes ('000 units) | 1.7 | 1.7 | 1.8 |
| Tobacco (grammes) | 27.0 | 24.0 | 26.0 |
| Beer (litres) | 139.1 | 140.7 | 147.0 |

* subdivision of preceding main category
Source: National Statistics

## Construction

The government has aimed at a 3.4%/year growth to 1985 in the construction industry's output and it expects to have solved the country's housing problem by 1990. Some 940,000 new or modernised flats will have been completed during the current five-year plan. In 1982, the target was overfulfilled with a 4.2% growth rate registered.

## The transport system

The GDR had 14,232 kilometres of railway operational in 1982. Some 1,934 km of this was electrified. A further 730-750 km will be electrified in the 1981-85 plan, with 140 km completed in 1982 and 200 km to be finished in 1983.

The country has 47,461 km of roads; 13,121 km are classified as state roads (including 1,818 km of motorway) and 34,340 km are classified as district roads (1982 figures).

There are 2,319 km of inland waterways, and 566 km of canals.

There were 120,523 km of airways in 1982, with 60 different internal routes operating. Some 34 million km were flown.

In accordance with the government's energy-saving policies, it is planned to transfer an ever-greater proportion of freight traffic to the railways in order to save fuel. In 1982 the railways carried 323 million tonnes of freight, up 4% compared with 1981. In the same year, motor transport carried 608 million tonnes, the inland waterways 17 million and maritime transport 11 million. Civil aviation carried 28,000 tonnes. As regards passenger transport, in 1982 the railways provided for 623 million passenger-journeys, motor transport 3.4 billion, inland waterways 7 million and air transport 1.3 million. The main seaports are Rostock, Wismar and Stralsund; freight handled through these in 1982 totalled 20.2 million tonnes (15.4 million tonnes of which went through Rostock).

The telecommunications system consists of 3.3 million telephones in use, and 14,200 telex stations.

## Health

East Germany considers the health service a priority. In 1982 there were: 171,280 hospital beds available (103 per 10,000 head of population); 35,377 doctors (21.2 per 10,000 head of population); 10,512 dentists (6.3 per 10,000 head of population); and 3,564 pharmacists (2.1 per 10,000 head of population).

## Education

Schooling begins at 6 years and the curriculum emphasises science and mathematics. The ten-year educational programme includes, in the latter years, practical experience to bridge the gap between school and work. When students have completed the programme, most begin vocational training as apprentices in local factories. Further education is well developed.

In 1982 there were 5,865 comprehensive schools, providing education for 2.1 million pupils. The average number of pupils per class was 20.6.

Some 130,442 students were enrolled in East Germany's 54 universities and colleges in 1982. The most popular faculty was engineering and technology, with 39,513 students.

## Sport and recreation

Vital to the GDR's world prestige is its performance in the field of sports. For a country of its modest size, performance is extraordinarily brilliant. Sportsmen and women are trained from an early age and given all the official encouragement and help possible.

A network of sports facilities encourages the nation's interest. In 1982 there were: 329 sports stadiums; 1,173 sports grounds; 9,854 small sports fields; 5,246 gymnasiums over 180 square metres in area; 187 gymnasiums with spectator capacity; 192 indoor swimming pools; 694 swimming stadiums; and 9,659 sports clubs with combined membership of 3.3 million people.

Cinema admissions are falling. In 1982 there were 832 cinemas operating, compared with 1,369 in 1960. Admissions in 1982 totalled 72.4 million, compared with 76.5 million in 1981, 79.5 million in 1980 and 84 million in 1977. Theatre admissions are also declining; theatre-goers numbered 10 million in 1982, and there were 178 theatres operating.

## Tourism

There has been a recent easing of the exchange regulations for Western visitors and revenues from 'hard currency' countries are of vital importance to help East Germany's balance of payments position. East European tourists to East Germany number around 800,000 per year. Reiseburo, the state tourist office, promotes the country's attractions, which are considerable and have a wide appeal to those interested in cultural activities. There are 31 Interhotel establishments, which provide 15,077 beds. A five-star hotel, with 550 beds, will be opened in Dresden in 1985. As regards outgoing tourism, some 809,335 East Germans travelled abroad in 1982, mainly to other East European countries.

## Foreign trade

Trade with the West is generally in deficit, as is trade with the USSR, a major trading partner. East Germany has been increasing its oil imports from the West as Soviet supplies have declined, and this has had an adverse effect on its hard currency trading account.

Improving its international financial position is of supreme importance and the current five-year plan aims to raise the volume of foreign trade turnover by an average 6.3%/year.

The GDR's own trade figures do not show a complete picture. Its deficit with Comecon trebled in 1981, but a full assessment is hampered by incomplete statistics.

The official East German figures show trade turnover up to 145 billion valuta marks (based on current prices) in 1982, of which 95 billion valuta marks was with Socialist countries — 55.2 billion with the USSR alone. Trade with industrialised capitalist countries totalled 40.8 billion valuta marks, and with the developing world 8.4 billion. Of the total turnover figure, exports represented 75 billion valuta marks and imports 69.9 billion. Machinery and equipment and means of transport accounted for 48.5% of East German exports, with fuels and minerals accounting for 18.5% and chemicals and allied products for 11.9%. Fuels and minerals were the largest import sector, accounting for 39.9%. Machinery and equipment and means of transport accounted for 32% of imports.

**TABLE 5.28   EAST GERMAN FOREIGN TRADE**

**Unit: billion valuta marks**

|      | Exports | Imports | Total turnover |
|------|---------|---------|----------------|
| 1980 | 57.1    | 63.0    | 120.1          |
| 1981 | 65.9    | 67.0    | 132.9          |
| 1982 | 75.2    | 69.9    | 145.1          |

Source: National Statistics

Foreign trade statistics are given in valuta marks (VM). The 1981 conversion rate was $1 = 3.34 VM. The East German mark (sometimes shown as 'M', 'EM' or 'OM' to distinguish it from the DM) is a nonconvertible currency officially pegged at 1:1 with West Germany's Deutsch Mark (DM).

The government does not elaborate on its current account position, but it is estimated that foreign debts are around $13 billion.

Trade with the USSR rose 7% to reach 11.5 billion roubles in 1982, according to East German sources. Imports into East Germany totalled 6.4 billion roubles, of which 2.4 billion were petroleum and petroleum products. Exports from East Germany to the USSR totalled 5.8 billion roubles, predominantly machinery for heavy industry.

Trade with West Germany has increased substantially, up 13% in 1982 to a record DM14 billion (£3.7 billion). West Germany is East Germany's largest trading partner in the West.

**TABLE 5.29   INTER-GERMAN TRADE**

| **Unit: billion DM)** | **1980** | **1981** | **% change** |
|---|---|---|---|
| Total trade | 12.50 | 14.10 | + 13 |
| East German exports | 6.35 | 6.99 | + 10 |
| West German exports | 6.13 | 7.08 | + 16 |
| East German balance (including services) | 0.22 | − 0.09 | |

Source: Economist Intelligence Unit (West German figures)

Trade with the EEC and with EFTA in 1982 fell substantially, according to Western sources. Trade with the US in 1982 comprised imports to the value of $222.7 million (including foodstuffs worth $203 million) and exports to the value of $53.9 billion (including machinery worth $14 billion).

Trade with the OECD (excluding West Germany) in 1982 resulted in a first-time surplus for East Germany.

**TABLE 5.30   EAST GERMANY'S TRADE WITH THE OECD***

| **Unit: US $million** | **1982** | **% rise vs 1981** | **1983 Jan-June** | **% rise vs Jan-June 1982** |
|---|---|---|---|---|
| OECD imports from East Germany | 2,388 | + 9.3 | 1,293 | + 10.3 |
| OECD exports to East Germany | 1,716 | − 29.9 | 976 | + 6.6 |
| Balance for OECD | − 672 | — | − 317 | — |

* excluding West Germany
Source: OECD Statistics for Foreign Trade

131

East Germany is particularly interested in trading with countries able to produce advanced technology (robots, electronics). Equipment which will enable the economy to improve its energy and fodder supply situations is especially sought after. If credit is supplied on easy terms and the exporter country will buy East German goods in return, much official support is forthcoming.

The East German Chamber of Foreign Trade stresses that, when doing business with East Germany, partners are invited to participate in the March and September Leipzig fairs, which are held regularly every year. These fairs provide the main 'shop windows' through which trade deals take place. An ever-increasing number of businessmen from all parts of the world travel to Leipzig to strengthen and extend their commercial ties. Taking part in technical seminars and organising symposia are also recommended as methods which can provide regular contacts. The Leipzig Spring Fair is the larger of the two fairs, and it focusses on heavy industry (metallurgy, heavy machinery and machine tools), materials handling equipment, electronics, telecommunications and data processing equipment, agricultural machinery, precision instruments and laboratory equipment, ventilation and air conditioning equipment. The Leipzig Autumn Fair specialises in chemicals, plastics, textiles, printing, automotive products, medical equipment and light industry.

Western companies need to adapt their techniques and expectations when planning to enter the East German market, adjusting to the central planning system and the Foreign Trade Enterprise's monopoly of foreign trade. The government sets the value of trade, the composition of imports and exports and the geographical distribution of trade. Buying and selling operations are conducted by some 51 specialised Foreign Trade Enterprises, known as FTEs. An indication of potential market sectors can be obtained by looking at the priorities assigned in the official plan to particular economic sectors.

Some major East German exporters are:

Textima            which produces plant and equipment for the textile industry

Polygraph          which produces printing machinery

| | |
|---|---|
| Elektrotechnik | which represents electronic and microelectronic machinery manufacturers Elektromaschinenbau, Nachrichtenelektronik, and other combines — goods are sold under VEM brand name |
| WMW | which represents the country's four machine tools combines |
| VEB Schwermaschinen-baukombinat Takraf | which produces hoisting and conveying equipment |
| VEB Kombinat Baukema | which produces construction and roadbuilding machinery, representing 3 specialist combines |
| Ernst Thaelmann Magdeburg (SKET) | which makes industrial plant for the metals sector |
| Chemieanlagen | which makes chemical P & E, from specialist units to complete chemical works |
| Fortschritt Nagema | which makes plant and equipment for the food industry |
| VEB Carl Zeiss Jena | which makes precision optical instruments |
| Robotron | which makes data processing and office equipment |
| VEB Kombinat Medizin-& Labortechnik Leipzig | which makes medical and laboratory equipment — affiliated to Foreign Trade Enterprise Intermed. |

# Chapter Six

# HUNGARY

## Introduction

Hungary has often been described in the West as the showcase of Eastern Europe because of the progress which has been made with economic reform and its policy of decentralization. It is the most outward looking of all the Comecon countries, keen to develop its overseas trade links and as a member of the IMF and the World Bank has successfully negotiated several loans.

The economic reforms began in 1968 when the New Economic Mechanism was introduced by the government. Greater freedom was given to enterprises to decide production schedules, where to purchase equipment and raw materials and how to market their products, while profits could be retained to increase incentives for the workforce. As a result consumers benefited from the greater competition created and the improved flexibility of enterprises to changes in demand. Standards of living improved and growth increased steadily. The state maintained overall macro-economic control through party officials, the State Bank and its influence on investment and hard currency restrictions while Hungarian enterprises were still cushioned from the full impact of the market-place with subsidies and temporary protective measures. Nevertheless Hungary has been the first country in Eastern Europe to break away from the traditional communist economic model and has achieved this without incurring the disapproval of Moscow. It even seems likely that some other Comecon countries are considering applying some of Hungary's policies to their own economies.

Hungary officially acknowledges its private sector known as the 'second economy', which is largely service orientated. It is estimated that up to 70% of workers are involved in the second economy. Most of these are workers who already have first jobs in the state sector but who legally 'moonlight' in their spare time, plus 150,000 workers who have left manufacturing in the past five years to work full-time in the service industries.

The government has encouraged the development of many small industrial co-operatives and 'economic partnerships' in order to fill the gaps in the market left by the larger enterprises. Even within the larger companies workers can now negotiate with factory managers to lease plant equipment and facilities after normal working hours to do special contract work either for themselves or for the company.

To improve its competitiveness on world markets, Hungary has introduced new measures within its economy. The exchange rate for the forint was unified in 1981 and is now aligned with world currency by adjusting its value against a trade weighted basket of Western currencies. In addition Hungarian companies with more than a small share of their sales accounted for by exports must now fix their domestic prices in line with foreign prices. Hungary has also suggested reforms within Comecon itself, in particular the creation of a multilateral Eastern European currency and better specialisation within the area.

Yet despite all the progress achieved care must be taken not to over-emphasise the nature of the reforms. Economic policies are still controlled centrally by the State and Hungary is still very much a part of Comecon especially with regard to political and foreign policy.

**Economic growth and national income**

A deterioration in Hungary's terms of trade with the West between 1974 and 1978 and a surge in imports and a slowdown in exports meant that improving Hungary's balance of payments position became the main priority in economic policy during the late 1970s to the detriment of economic growth.

Deflationary policies to reduce consumption and investment were introduced, the effects of which became most apparent in 1980 when net material product fell by 0.7%. By 1981, however, the situation had improved and net material product increased by 2.5% with industrial production growing by 2.8% and agricultural production by 1%, although gross fixed investment fell by 6%.

In 1982 net material product amounted to 696.4 billion forints — an increase of over 2%. Net material product is roughly equivalent to national income, it is the method of calculation used by socialist countries. By definition net material product is the total of goods and services relating to physical production, transport and distribution. Banking, health, education, public administration and defence are excluded.

135

**TABLE 6.1   NATIONAL PRODUCT 1981-1983**

**Unit: billion forints**

|  | 1981 | 1982 | 1983 |
|---|---|---|---|
| Net national product | 683.6 | 746.8 | 795.0 |
| National income (net material product) | 634.9 | 696.4 | 744.0 |
| Surplus of imports ( + ), exports ( − ) respectively | + 8.2 | − 6.8 | − 17.6 |
| Domestic use of national income | 643.1 | 689.6 | 726.4 |
| Material consumption of population | 439.4 | 474.8 | 512.2 |
| Material consumption for collective needs | 68.7 | 74.1 | 78.6 |
| Material consumption | 508.1 | 548.9 | 590.6 |
| Net capital formation | 135.0 | 112.8 | 113.5 |

The following breakdown shows the various components making up national income in 1982.

**TABLE 6.2   DISTRIBUTION OF NATIONAL INCOME (NET MATERIAL PRODUCT) BY ACTIVITIES (AT CONSTANT PRICES)**

**Unit: %**

|  | 1980 | 1981 | 1982 |
|---|---|---|---|
| Industry | 44.2 | 44.7 | 45.1 |
| Construction industry | 12.4 | 12.3 | 12.0 |
| Agriculture and forestry | 18.6 | 18.0 | 18.8 |
| Transport and communications | 9.4 | 9.5 | 9.2 |
| Trade | 14.3 | 14.5 | 14.0 |
| Water works and supply | 0.7 | 0.5 | 0.4 |
| Other material branches | 0.4 | 0.5 | 0.5 |
| TOTAL | 100.0 | 100.0 | 100.0 |

Continued...

**Table 6.2 continued...**

**NATIONAL INCOME (NET MATERIAL PRODUCT) BY SOCIAL SECTORS**

| Unit: % | 1980 | 1981 | 1982 |
|---|---|---|---|
| Socialist sectors | 97.4 | 96.3 | 95.8 |
| of which: | | | |
| State | 70.7 | 69.0 | 68.4 |
| Co-operative | 23.6 | 23.6 | 23.6 |
| Auxiliary farms of persons employed | 3.1 | 3.7 | 3.8 |
| Private sector | 2.6 | 3.7 | 4.2 |

Source: National Statistics

## Economic planning

The State is responsible for all macro-economic policy which it implements through a series of five year plans. The Sixth Five Year Plan runs for the period 1981 to 1985. This plan is intended to be more of a blue print than a statement of intent. The main objectives of the plan are:

i National income to grow by 14-17%, but real wages to increase by only 1-2% per annum.

ii To maintain living standards but only by reducing investment.

iii Continuing emphasis to be placed on export and import substitution industries. Foreign trade with the West to increase by 25-30%. Trade with Comecon countries to remain around 50% of the total.

iv The development of energy resources and a policy of energy conservation.

v Greater independence of enterprises, with more use of the profit motive and less state support for the ineffective. Labour mobility should be increased.

Of the proposed increase in national income it is estimated that about 5% of this will be needed to offset the worsening terms of trade, while 5% would be needed to improve efficiency of the export industry and about 5% would be left for domestic distribution. Any rise in the standard of living would come from improved public services. The severe housing shortage is expected to remain a major social problem despite plans for new building and modernisation. Per capita incomes are expected to increase by 6-7% during the plan, a five-day week introduced and the level of social benefits maintained.

On the question of energy it is proposed that energy consumption will not grow by more than 10-11% over the period. The introduction of nuclear power is expected to reduce energy requirements supplied by hydrocarbons from 63-64% in 1980 to 56-60% in 1985. Production of crude oil is to be maintained while output of natural gas will increase to 10,000 million cubic metres a year by 1985. The plan foresees that electricity consumption will not exceed 38,000 million kW by 1985.

The plan will give more responsibility to individual managers and encourage them to use their initiative in running their enterprises and to increase worker participation. The profitability of an enterprise will be reflected in wage levels.

Economic decisions will only be made by the government directly on the following:

a)   the achievement of central development and other programmes for the period 1981-85;
b)   state investment;
c)   measures affecting the standard of living;
d)   economic management.

The targets for the 1981-85 plan and individual years are given below:

**TABLE 6.3   TARGETS FOR SIXTH FIVE YEAR PLAN**

Unit: % change over previous year

| | 1982 Planned | Actual | 1983 Planned | 1981-85 Planned |
|---|---|---|---|---|
| National income | 1.0/1.5 | 2.6 | 0.5/1.0 | 2.7/3.2 |
| Industrial production | 2.0/2.5 | 2.2 | 1.0/2.0 | 3.5/4.1 |
| Agricultural production | 4.0/4.5 | 5.0 | 1.0/2.0 | 2.3/2.8 |
| Domestic consumption | −1.0/−2.0 | −2.0 | −3.0/−4.0 | 0.6/0.9 |
| Per capita real income | 0.0/0.5 | 0.5 | −1.5/−2.0 | 2.3/2.8 |
| Exports | 6.0/8.0 | 8.4 | 7.0 | 6.5/6.8 |
| Imports | 2.0/3.0 | 3.3 | 0.0 | 3.4/3.5 |

Source: various

According to the draft economic plan economic growth in 1984 was expected to continue at a slow rate. National income was to expand by 1.5 to 2.0%, industrial production was planned to increase by 1.5-2.0%

138

the same as planned for 1983 although the actual achievement for the ten months to the end of October 1983 was a growth rate of only 1.3%. After the disappointing results for agricultural output in 1983 because of the drought, the plan for 1984 was for farm output to remain at 1982's level or an increase of 1%. The level of personal consumption for 1984 was expected to remain at 1983's level which should have declined but in fact rose because of earnings in the second economy.

## The population and workforce

Hungary has a total land area of 93,000 square kilometres and on 1st January 1983 its population amounted to 10.7 million. Population density is 115 inhabitants per square kilometre, with Pest county the most heavily populated district. There has been a slight fall in population since 1981; in 1982 the natural rate of decrease was 0.1% as the death rate (13.5 per 1,000) exceeded the birth rate (12.5 per 1,000). The surplus of females in Hungary are all in the older age groups.

**TABLE 6.4   POPULATION LEVELS AT 1st JANUARY**

| Unit: '000s | Males | Females | Total |
|---|---|---|---|
| 1982 | 5,185 | 5,526 | 10,711 |
| 1983 | 5,177 | 5,523 | 10,700 |
| 1984 | 5,164 | 5,515 | 10,679 |

Source: National Statistics

The capital, Budapest, is by far the largest city with a population of 2.06 million or 19.3% of the total population of Hungary. Of the remainder nearly 35% of people live in other towns and 45.8% in villages. There has been a drift of population towards the towns from the villages in the last twenty years or so especially among the younger generations but this has slowed down recently as agricultural incomes kept pace with those in the towns.

After Budapest the largest cities are: Miskolc (210,000); Debreca (198,000); Pécs (173,000); Szeged (174,000); Gyor (127,000); Nyiregyhaza (113,000) and Szekesfehervar (108,000).

Hungary has a workforce of just over 5 million who are employed as follows:

**TABLE 6.5   LABOUR FORCE IN 1981**

Unit: %

| | |
|---|---|
| Industry | 32.4 |
| Construction industry | 7.7 |
| Agriculture and forestry | 21.1 |
| Transport and telecommunications | 7.9 |
| Trade | 9.8 |
| Water works and supply | 1.5 |
| Personal and social services | 3.9 |
| Sanitary, social and cultural services | 11.0 |
| Public administration and other services | 4.7 |
| TOTAL | 100 |

Source: National Statistics

More than 96% of the total workforce belong to trade unions. The average wage in Hungary in 1982 was 4,396 forints per month, although the average earnings level was higher at 4,624 forints largely due to over-time working. Workers in the construction industry enjoyed the highest wages as illustrated below.

**TABLE 6.6   AVERAGE WAGES AND EARNINGS IN THE SOCIALIST SECTOR 1982**

| Unit: forints per month | Wages | Earnings |
|---|---|---|
| Industry | 4,512 | 4,692 |
| Construction industry | 4,808 | 4,965 |
| Agriculture | 4,056 | 4,339 |
| Forestry | 4,228 | 4,394 |
| Transport and communications | 4,765 | 5,048 |
| Trade | 3,917 | 4,129 |
| Water works and supply | 4,494 | 4,830 |
| Other material branches | 4,114 | 4,430 |
| Non-material branches | 4,445 | 4,703 |
| AVERAGE | 4,396 | 4,624 |

140

A large proportion of Hungarians, estimates have put this as high as 70%, also have second jobs, moonlighting in the 'second economy' and this provides additional income which is considered necessary for many families.

In November 1983 the government decreed that some factories could cut their employees' working week to 40 hours provided this did not affect production. Most Hungarians work more than 40 hours a week mainly because of overtime and weekend working requirements.

**Industrial activities**

Industry is the largest single contributor to the Hungarian economy accounting for nearly 45% of net material product in 1981. The most important sectors are the engineering, metallurgical, chemical and food processing industries. Emphasis has been focussed on certain industries under Comecon's joint co-operation and specialisation scheme. These are bus manufacture, chemicals and pharmaceuticals, data processing equipment and aluminium.

During 1982 gross industrial production increased by 2% compared with the previous year, yet output until the end of October 1983 had increased by only 1.3% falling well short of the 3.5-4.1% per annum increase proposed under the Five Year Plan. Other objectives set for industry for 1983 were increasing exports to convertible-currency countries, increasing its share of the domestic market, reducing convertible-currency imports needed for industrial production and fulfilling Comecon contractural obligations.

The poor industrial performance in 1983 has been blamed on a number of reasons. One was the difficulty in making sales in all major markets of the world as the recession continued together with slow modernisation of the productive structure, sluggish attempts to improve its competitiveness and organisational short-comings. Productivity is still lower than expected at only 80% of the level achieved in the GDR.

The machine tool industry is very export-orientated, over 75% of its output is sold abroad. Hungary has been one of the few countries to have increased output in recent years despite the general recession.

The domestic demand for television sets is completely met by home production and a sizeable proportion is exported. Other consumer products exported are refrigerators, tape recorders, and incandescent and fluorescent lamps.

**TABLE 6.7   OUTPUT OF THE VEHICLE AND TRANSPORT INDUSTRY 1982**

|  | **Production** | **Exports** | **Imports** |
|---|---|---|---|
| Tractors | 300 | — | 4,984 |
| Diesel motors for vehicles | 23,925 | 9,312 | — |
| Trucks | 928 | 673 | 17,320 |
| Buses | 11,819 | 10,516 | — |
| Bicycles | 271 | 11 | 212 |
| Passenger cars | — | — | 96,374 |
| Motorcycles | — | — | 98,435 |

**TABLE 6.8   OUTPUT OF CONSUMER GOODS IN THE ENGINEERING SECTOR 1982**

| **Unit: '000s** | **Production** | **Exports** |
|---|---|---|
| Refrigerators | 442 | 278 |
| Washing machines | 253 | — |
| Radios | 121 | 715 |
| Television sets | 351 | 117 |
| Tape recorders | 552 | 475 |
| Incandescent lamps (millions) | 432 | 380 |
| Fluorescent lamps (millions) | 18 | 18 |
| Electric boilers | 201 | 61 |
| Cookers and stoves | 328 | — |

Source: National Statistics

## Chemicals

Within the chemical industry petroleum processing accounted for 40.4% of total chemical production in 1982, although only 7.8% of its sales were exported. This sector is expected to receive a high priority in the future and development is taking place with the Soviet Union from whom Hungary imports most of its oil in exchange for ethylene.

142

In terms of exports the leading chemical sector is pharmaceuticals. Hungary is often called the pharmacy of Eastern Europe. It supplies 40% of the Soviet Union's drug imports and is making determined efforts to infiltrate Western markets. Hungary is planning to expand its pharmaceutical industry at twice the rate of the rest of the chemical industry with priority being given to animal drugs and plant protection chemicals for Hungarian agriculture and export, as well as turn-key projects.

The rubber industry and synthetic fibres are also important exporters.

**TABLE 6.9   BREAKDOWN OF THE CHEMICAL INDUSTRY 1982**

|  | % of total production | % of sales exported |
|---|---|---|
| Crude petroleum processing | 40.4 | 7.8 |
| Gas production and distribution | 10.1 | 0.2 |
| Organic and inorganic chemicals | 12.0 | 20.1 |
| Fertilizers and plant protectives | 11.4 | 19.0 |
| Synthetic fibres and materials | 5.1 | 24.1 |
| Synthetic material processing | 4.4 | 7.9 |
| Rubber | 3.8 | 36.7 |
| Pharmaceuticals | 11.4 | 58.6 |

Source: National Statistics

## Metallurgy

The metallurgy industry centres around the processing of iron ore and aluminium. The aluminium is produced from Hungary's own bauxite reserves and most is exported. In 1982, 745,000 tonnes were produced of which 540,000 tonnes were exported. Most of the aluminium is destined for the Soviet Union whereby under the 1962 Hungarian-Soviet agreement, which expires at the end of 1985, Hungary delivers 330,000 tonnes of aluminium to the Soviet Union in return for 165,000 tonnes of aluminium bars. The renewed extended agreement for the 1986-1990 period calls for the delivery by Hungary of 530,000 tonnes of aluminium and 5,000 tonnes of semi-finished aluminium products in return for 205,000 tonnes of bars.

Most of the iron ore and coke used in crude iron production in Hungary has to be imported; an annual 4 million tonnes of iron ore is bought in from the Soviet Union. 10-12% of Hungary's demand for iron ore is met

143

by domestic production (450,000 tonnes per annum). In order to increase efficiency in this sector a development programme has been introduced which includes the construction of high efficiency converter plants at the Lenin metallurgic factory and the Duna Iron Works.

## Other industries

Hungary has a large food processing industry which is able to supply both domestic needs and contribute appreciably to exports. In 1982 processed food products to the value of 50,300 forints were exported, around 25% of exports and 37% of convertible currency exports providing a valuable contribution to the balance of payments. The industry has recently been restructured in order to increase flexibility and decentralization. In 1982 the industry recorded a 4.4% increase in production with rises in the meat, poultry, egg processing and vegetable oil industries.

Light industry covers the production of textiles, clothing, leather and shoes, timber processing, paper-making and handicrafts. Around 130,000 million forints worth of goods are produced each year from this sector, of which about a third is sold on the domestic market and the remainder exported. A slight decline in output in 1982 of 1.6% was experienced and a fall in numbers employed by 3% which is expected to fall still further as this industry aims to improve its technology and organisation and therefore increase labour productivity. Its share of total output has been declining in recent years.

One industry in which Hungary lags behind other Comecon countries is electronics and plans have been made to remedy this situation. A development programme covering the period up to 1990 has been introduced and about 10 billion forints is to be spent on research and development and production plant in order to manufacture sophisticated microelectronic components in small production runs. The programme is already behind schedule however.

## Agriculture

Hungary is essentially a flat country and 72% of the land is cultivated, while 17% is covered by forests and only 11% is uncultivated.

144

The agricultural sector is largely controlled by the state through state farms and co-operatives, although there is a small private sector. Around 70% of gross agricultural output is produced by co-operatives, 20% by the state farms and 10% by private farmers. About a quarter of the private farm plots are owned by members of co-operatives who are each entitled to their own plot of land and who often buy fodder or hire equipment on a contract basis from the co-operatives and either sell livestock back to the co-operatives or at town markets. These plots can as much as double the incomes of co-operative members. The remaining private plots are owned by 'hobby gardeners' from the towns who grow food for their own consumption and for sale. It is estimated that about 50% of Hungary's pork, 40% of poultry and most fruit and vegetables are produced by private plots, something which is encouraged by the authorities.

**TABLE 6.10   CULTIVATED AREA BY SECTOR 1982**

**Unit:** %

| | |
|---|---|
| State sector | 26.4 |
| State farms, complex farms | 11.2 |
| Co-operative sector | 68.1 |
| Collective farms | 62.1 |
| Household plots | 3.9 |
| Auxiliary farms of employed people | 4.4 |
| SOCIALIST SECTOR | 98.9 |
| Private sector | 1.1 |
| TOTAL | 100.0 |

Most state farms are on average twice as large as the co-operatives although there are exceptions. There are 130 state farms which cultivate 11% of the arable land specialising largely in the production of wheat and maize. High grain yields are achieved both on state farms and the co-operatives and in terms of per hectare yields Hungary is among the world's top five large-scale producers of wheat and maize.

State farms are run by managers appointed by the Ministry of Agriculture who can decide which crops are to be grown. Workers on state farms receive wages whatever the crop results, only their bonuses will be affected if there is a poor harvest. Co-operative members' wages depend

145

entirely on the co-op's profits and vary according to farm output and marketing skills. Co-operatives which run into financial difficulty have to resort to borrowing from the bank but under the latest reforms consistent failures unable to pay back loans will cease to exist. Besides cultivating the land most co-operatives also engage in small-scale manufacturing producing a wide variety of products which can be an important supplement to incomes, especially in those areas with less favourable growing conditions.

Agricultural production in Hungary has increased steadily over the years, which can be attributed partly to the thriving private sector. The country produces 30% more food than it consumes, with the surplus going for export. A large proportion of its exports (73% in 1982) are in convertible currencies to make agriculture Hungary's leading hard currency earner.

**TABLE 6.11   HARVEST RESULTS OF FIELD CROPS 1982**

**Unit: '000 tonnes**

| | |
|---|---|
| Wheat | 5,747 |
| Rye | 116 |
| Barley | 865 |
| Oats | 123 |
| Maize | 7,730 |
| Rice | 48 |
| Sugar beet | 5,363 |
| Sunflowers | 577 |
| Potatoes | 975 |
| Silage maize | 6,093 |
| Hay | 1,988 |

After a successful year in 1982 when agricultural production increased by 5%, a record grain harvest was achieved and total food exports increased by 10%, a similar year was predicted for 1983. A severe drought hit the country during the summer, however, and agricultural production fell dramatically. It is estimated that the cereal harvest was 2 million tonnes short of the expected 14.5 million tonnes for the year. For other important crops such as sugar beet, sunflowers and potatoes the shortfall is expected to have been in the region of 15 to 30% of the total. Problems in the supply of fodder were expected and the harvest shortfall hit production in the food industry during the second half of 1983 and the beginning of

146

1984. It has been estimated that Hungary may have lost about $200 million in export earnings as a result of the drought.

**TABLE 6.12   ANIMALS FOR SLAUGHTER AND OTHER ANIMAL PRODUCTS 1982**

**Unit: '000 tonnes**

| | |
|---|---|
| Cattle | 333 |
| Pigs | 1,219 |
| Sheep | 49 |
| Poultry | 527 |
| Rabbits | 42 |
| Other | 8 |
| TOTAL | 2,178 |
| Milk (million litres) | 2,639 |
| Eggs (million) | 4,440 |
| Fish (thousand tonnes) | 25 |
| Raw wool (thousand tonnes) | 12 |

Source: National Statistics

## Minerals

Hungary does not have vast resources of minerals or raw materials. Bauxite is the most important mineral mined. In 1982 2.6 million tonnes of bauxite was mined, about 10% less than in 1981, and 467,000 tonnes was exported. Hungary's bauxite reserves are expected to last another thirty years but extraction is becoming increasingly expensive. Nevertheless investment is being channelled into bauxite mining and aluminium processing to encourage production.

Domestic production of iron ore amounted to 467,000 tonnes in 1982, not enough to satisfy domestic demand so a further 3.76 million tonnes had to be imported, mainly from the Soviet Union.

Hungary also has small deposits of lead and zinc ores, which are mined. A study is underway to establish the economic feasibility of exploiting the estimated 150 million tonnes of copper at Recsk. Abundant supplies of non-metallic minerals such as dolomite, limestone and quartz sand are present, some of which are exported.

### Energy supplies

Hungary possesses coal, oil and natural gas reserves but these are insufficient to satisfy domestic demand so imports of all three fuels have to be made. In terms of output, coal is Hungary's most important energy resource. In 1982 26.08 million tonnes were produced, but most of this was low calorific brown coal and lignite. About 2 million tonnes of coal have to be imported annually.

**TABLE 6.13   COAL PRODUCTION IN 1982**

**Unit: '000 tonnes**

|           |        |
|-----------|--------|
| Hard coal | 3,039  |
| Brown coal| 14,754 |
| Lignite   | 8,286  |
| TOTAL     | 26,079 |

There has been little change in coal output since the mid-1970s despite a massive amount of investment made under the country's energy saving programmes. New mines and machinery are being introduced under the 'Eocine' programme throughout the country's two black and six brown coal mining districts. Two new mines have been opened recently.

The use of coal as a proportion of total energy has declined in the past twenty years from 50% to 27% but it is still considered to be an important energy reserve.

Domestic oil production in 1982 amounted to 2.03 million tonnes accounting for about one fifth of total energy consumption and, as in the case of coal, oil's share of total energy use has declined in recent years as natural gas has increased in importance. In order to supplement domestic supplies of oil, Hungary has to import supplies. In 1982 7.7 million tonnes of oil were imported, the bulk of which was from the USSR. The import figure for 1982 represents a drop of around two million tonnes in imports of oil since 1979, just before the Soviet Union cut back its exports of oil to its Comecon partners.

The share of natural gas in total energy consumption has doubled since 1970, it now accounts for over a quarter of all Hungary's energy use. In 1982 domestic natural gas production increased by more than 10% to 6,600 million cubic metres and the target for 1983 was a similar level. 4,000 million cubic metres of gas is imported annually from the Soviet Union and there are plans for this to be increased to reach an annual level of 11,000 million cubic metres by 1985. Domestic production is planned to remain stable during the Five Year Plan at over 6,000 million cubic metres and, although a new gas field will be put into operation, the increase in consumption as many sectors of the economy change from oil to gas will be met by the expansion in Soviet imports.

The energy saving programme mentioned earlier was introduced in 1980 and was given extra impetus when at the end of 1981 the Soviet Union asked its Comecon partners to accept a 10% cut in the level of Soviet crude oil deliveries under the clearing trade agreement for 1980-85. The fall in Hungarian oil imports of 20% has been achieved by decreasing the petrochemical industry output and eliminating wastage. One of the objectives of the energy programme is to maximise domestic production of coal, oil and gas, and for the Soviet Union to become Hungary's only foreign supplier of oil. In addition the programme aims for a maximum increase in primary energy consumption of 2% per year, a maximum increase in electricity consumption of 3.5% per year and a cut in the share of hydro-carbons in total energy use from 64% in 1980 to 59% in 1985.

**Electricity supplies**

Production of electricity amounted to 24.5 million kilowatt hours during 1982. About half of the electricity generated in Hungary comes from coal while 38% comes from gas and 12% from oil. Not enough electricity can be generated domestically, so over 10.6 million kWh have to be imported although 2.6 million kWh are exported. Electricity is imported direct from the Soviet Union via a 750 kW line from the Comecon unified power system, while electricity is obtained from Austria under a 15-year exchange agreement. During wet periods of the year Austria supplies Hungary with electricity generated from hydro power while during dry periods Hungary supplies Austria with electricity derived from thermal stations. This results in a 10% gain for Hungary equivalent to about 8 billion kW a year.

Production of electrical energy is expected to be changed during the present Five Year Plan as coal and gas gain in importance to the detriment

149

of oil. Two coal-fuelled power stations are in the planning stages. Another development will be the coming onstream of Hungary's first nuclear power station at Paks. The plant is due to be completed in 1986 and will supply 17% of the country's electricity.

## Construction

During the first half of the 1970s the construction industry expanded at an annual average rate of 7.4% but growth has declined since then and the industry has contracted during the 1980s. Two of the largest construction projects underway are the Paks nuclear power station and part of the Budapest underground railway.

Despite the downturn in domestic work the Hungarian construction industry is currently involved in a number of projects abroad both as main contractor and as a sub-contractor.

## Transport

Investment worth Ft 113-114 billion is to be channelled into transport during the current Five Year Plan as Hungary continues developing its transport network.

In 1982 the country had 7,758 kilometres of railway track, of which about 1,500 kilometres was electrified. In terms of volume, rail transports about a third of freight, although in terms of freight/tonne per kilometre the percentage increases to 56%. Investment on the railways will be spent on the modernisation of track, the reconstruction of several stations, increasing containerisation and constructing Budapest's underground railway system.

Hungary has nearly 30,000 kilometres of roads, most of which are metalled or paved. Nearly half of transport investment is to go into the development of and maintenance of the road network, as road transport gains in popularity both for freight and passenger traffic. Air transport and waterways account for a tiny proportion of the total traffic.

## Government and society

Hungary's only political party is the Hungarian Socialist Workers' Party which has over 850,000 members. The party elects the Central Committee which in turn elects the Political Committee to direct government policy. The First Secretary of the Central Committee is Mr Janos Kadar, who has been in power since 1956.

Hungary has been described as a latently pluralist society — formally a socialist block but informally a collection of pressure groups and lobbies trying to influence political decisions, e.g. the farmers' lobby, trade union lobby, heavy industry lobby.

An official policy of equality of the sexes has been pursued since the post-war years, in what is still a traditional society. Nearly 90% of women go out to work and the state has eased the burden on working mothers by providing generous maternity leave and then the option for either parent to stay at home for up to three years with a state allowance and still be able to return to their previous jobs. Women tend to work in the lower paid sectors and on average earn 70-80% of the average male income. The responsibility for running the home is still firmly placed with women and this heavy burden is considered to be a significant factor behind the high divorce rate.

As from 1st July 1983 a new ruling has allowed Hungarians to work in the West as private employees of Western firms, the only Comecon country to allow this. The only conditions are that there are no political objections to this move, the employee has a job to go to and that they send back 20% of their hard currency earnings to be converted into Hungarian forints at the official rate.

## Housing

Hungary has a large privately owned and privately financed stock of housing and funding for new dwellings from state and co-operative sources is actually declining. State finance is available for assistance in the building of housing principally through loans from the National Savings Bank which provides over 95% of loans for housing construction.

**TABLE 6.14   OCCUPIED DWELLINGS BY OWNERSHIP IN 1980**

**Unit:** %

| | |
|---|---|
| Family house | 64.4 |
| Block of owner-occupier dwellings | 6.2 |
| Privately owned dwellings built by home-building co-ops | 5.4 |
| State dwellings | 23.8 |
| Other dwellings | 0.2 |

Source: National Statistics

Family houses are especially numerous in the villages. Most houses are supplied with electricity but other facilities are not so widespread. The percentage of dwellings with electricity in 1983 was 97.7%, those with a water conduit 66.6%, those with gas (both piped and bottle) 74.5% and the percentage with a flush toilet 55.9%.

The economic plan for 1981-85 aims for the construction of between 370,000 and 390,000 dwellings of which 240,000 are expected to be in the form of small blocks of owner-occupied apartments and 150,000 family houses. 270,000 of these dwellings will be financed privately. Housing construction has fallen since 1976 and Hungary has a chronic shortage of housing.

**Health**

Public health care has improved during the last decade, and hospitals and the health service have been made a priority area during the 1981-85 plan. An extra 7,000 hospital beds are to be created and better facilities provided for the handicapped and the increasing number of aged. In 1982 there were 32,476 doctors in Hungary (30.4 per 10,000 inhabitants) and 98,535 hospital beds (92.1 per 10,000).

**Education**

Compulsory schooling starts at the age of six but 92% of three to six year olds already attend nursery school. There are 539 secondary schools catering for different vocations and abilities. The general grammar schools offering an academic education and industrial vocational and technical schools are the most numerous, although there has been a trend recently away from the grammar schools towards the vocational secondary schools. In 1982 there were 56 higher-education institutions and 100,564 students. By far the most popular subject studied was engineering.

## Recreation and tourism

Hungary has nearly 4,000 sports clubs with over 1.2 million members. The most popular sport is football. The number of television licence holders is increasing, in 1982 the number was 2.84 million. Cinema attendances have been falling in recent years but conversely the number of theatre visits has increased.

Tourism is becoming one of Hungary's most successful earners of hard currency. During 1982 visitors from the West increased by 17% to 2.7 million while visitors from Eastern Europe fell 43% to 7.1 million. Although the total number of visitors fell, there was an increase in export earnings in 1982 of 25% to $270 million. After deductions for costs this leaves $180 million, to make tourism the second largest earner of hard currency after agriculture. Austrians are the largest group of Western tourists, with 1.4 million visitors to Hungary in 1982.

In 1983 four priority areas were ear-marked as special development areas for tourism. These were Lake Balaton, already a favourite destination, Lake Valence, the Danube Bend and the Matra and Bülck mountains.

## Incomes, prices and consumer expenditure

Hungary's consumer price index increased by 6.9% in 1982, following increases of 9.1% and 4.6% in 1980 and 1981 respectively. The increase in 1980 was due to a price reform introduced in 1979-80 which aimed at bringing domestic and foreign prices into alignment and improving the link between producer and consumer prices.

The expectation for 1983 was for consumer prices to rise by 7.5% compared with an average rate of 4.5-5% planned for 1981-85. In September 1983 there was a round of price increases for bread (up 16%), cooking oil (20%), margarine (10%), and sugar (23%), necessitated by the poor agricultural harvests after the drought. Despite these increases consumer price

153

subsidies still remain at a high level especially on food, transport and energy.

Real wages have increased at a moderate level in recent years around the 1-2% level. In 1983 a planned cut of 4% in real wages was agreed with the IMF in return for an IMF standby loan and private consumption was expected to drop slightly in 1983 after several years of a small but steady increase.

In 1982 513,000 billion forints was spent by the Hungarian population on goods and services, with food and services accounting for the largest proportions of budgets.

**TABLE 6.15   PER CAPITA EXPENDITURE FOR PERSONAL USE IN 1981**

| Unit: % | Social groups | | | | |
|---|---|---|---|---|---|
| | **A** | **B** | **C** | **D** | **E** |
| Food | 33.3 | 34.4 | 34.3 | 27.1 | 42.1 |
| Beverages and tobacco | 9.4 | 10.2 | 9.9 | 7.1 | 10.1 |
| Clothing | 10.6 | 10.7 | 11.9 | 10.5 | 8.3 |
| Housing and maintenance | 15.9 | 18.9 | 16.5 | 16.1 | 14.8 |
| Furniture and household equipment | 8.8 | 8.9 | 9.2 | 9.4 | 8.0 |
| Health care | 2.4 | 1.8 | 1.9 | 3.1 | 3.5 |
| Transport, communications | 9.6 | 7.9 | 8.6 | 12.8 | 4.6 |
| Entertainment | 7.1 | 5.0 | 5.3 | 10.8 | 6.1 |
| Other expenditure | 2.9 | 2.2 | 2.4 | 3.1 | 2.5 |
| TOTAL | 100.0 | 100.0 | 100.0 | 100.0 | 100.0 |

**NUMBER OF HOUSEHOLD CONSUMER GOODS PER HUNDRED HOUSEHOLDS IN 1981**

| | **A** | **B** | **C** | **D** | **E** |
|---|---|---|---|---|---|
| Refrigerators | 94 | 86 | 93 | 104 | 80 |
| Washing machines | 97 | 95 | 101 | 100 | 78 |
| Vacuum cleaners | 83 | 69 | 76 | 100 | 57 |
| Passenger cars | 30 | 25 | 28 | 50 | 6 |
| Motorcycles | 26 | 37 | 48 | 18 | 7 |
| Radios | 153 | 129 | 145 | 188 | 123 |
| Television sets | 108 | 100 | 106 | 118 | 87 |

**Social groups:** A = working class; B = agricultural co-op workers; C = households with two incomes; D = white collar workers; E = social benefits dependents
Source: National Statistics

## Foreign trade and payments

Hungary's principal economic priority is to maintain its solvency by improving its balance of payments position and keeping its reputation as a reliable economic partner. Hungary is already considered to be the best choice for Western institutions lending to Eastern Europe and confirmed this position during 1983 by the following moves:

i      Repaying two loans worth $510 million to the Bank of International Settlements on time;

ii    devaluation of the forint in three stages in order to boost exports;

iii   the implementation of an austerity programme agreed with the IMF, which included a cut of 4% in real wages during 1983.

Hungary became a member of the IMF in May 1982 and of the World Bank in July 1982, and has become the heaviest borrower from the West in the Eastern Bloc. At the end of 1982 its total foreign debt to the West amounted to $8.6 billion. In 1983 the objective was for a $600 million surplus on the current account in convertible currencies to be used for principal repayments on hard-currency debts. This, however, looks unlikely to be achieved judging by trade results received so far for 1983. For the first six months of the year a foreign trade surplus of $300 million was reached (compared with a deficit for the same time in 1982). The devastating effects of the drought on 1983's harvest is estimated to have reduced export earnings in the second half of the year by about $200 million however, and the expected target is therefore unlikely to be reached.

*Foreign trade*
During 1982 over 54% of Hungary's trade was with its Comecon partners, with the Soviet Union accounting for the largest proportion. The remaining trade was divided between OECD countries (34.7%) and developing countries (10.7%).

Before analysing Hungarian trade data any further it must be pointed out that difficulties arise in the way they are presented. Imports and exports are broken down into rouble and non-rouble transactions but it is not clear whether non-rouble transactions are necessarily convertible currency transactions, and this is further complicated by the fact that a small proportion of trade with Comecon countries is conducted in convertible currencies. There is also the problem that Hungarian external trade is presented in value terms at current prices and therefore real development in foreign trade is not clear.

Hungary had a trade surplus with its Comecon partners in 1982 and 1983 and also with developing nations but trade with the developed countries in the West has been in deficit.

**TABLE 6.16   VALUE OF EXTERNAL TRADE (AT CURRENT PRICES)**

**Unit: billion forints**

|  | 1980 | 1981 | 1982 | 1983 |
|---|---|---|---|---|
| **Imports** | | | | |
| Socialist countries | 151.8 | 161.9 | 173.0 | 191.9 |
| Developed countries | 120.6 | 126.4 | 118.5 | 125.7 |
| Developing countries | 27.5 | 26.0 | 33.3 | 47.4 |
| TOTAL | 299.9 | 314.3 | 324.8 | 365.0 |
| *Of which:* | | | | |
| Settled in roubles | 136.4 | 143.7 | 158.6 | 173.9 |
| Settled in non-roubles | 163.5 | 170.6 | 166.2 | 191.1 |
| **Exports** | | | | |
| Socialist countries | 154.9 | 174.1 | 185.3 | 203.2 |
| Developed countries | 98.6 | 90.3 | 97.2 | 123.7 |
| Developing countries | 27.5 | 35.0 | 42.0 | 47.2 |
| TOTAL | 281.0 | 299.4 | 324.5 | 374.1 |
| *Of which:* | | | | |
| Settled in roubles | 120.8 | 131.6 | 141.4 | 160.1 |
| Settled in non-roubles | 160.2 | 167.8 | 183.1 | 214.0 |

Source: National Statistics

Hungary is calculated to have achieved a trade surplus in convertible currencies of $218 million in 1980, $269 million in 1981 and $737 million in 1982.

TABLE 6.17   EXTERNAL TRADE BY MAIN PARTNER COUNTRIES 1983

| | Imports | | Exports | |
|---|---|---|---|---|
| | **Billion forints** | **% of total** | **Billion forints** | **% of total** |
| Soviet Union | 95.8 | 28.6 | 108.8 | 31.6 |
| West Germany | 36.2 | 10.2 | 23.3 | 7.4 |
| East Germany | 22.2 | 6.7 | 19.9 | 5.9 |
| Czechoslovakia | 17.1 | 5.1 | 18.0 | 4.8 |
| Austria | 16.2 | 4.7 | 12.3 | 4.4 |
| Poland | 12.6 | 4.4 | 12.2 | 3.9 |
| Yugoslavia | 10.0 | 3.6 | 10.8 | 3.4 |
| Italy | 8.8 | 2.3 | 11.1 | 3.3 |
| Iran | 8.8 | 2.5 | 8.2 | 2.0 |
| U.S.A. | 7.0 | 2.6 | 5.1 | 2.0 |
| France | 7.2 | 1.9 | 4.9 | 1.5 |
| Romania | 6.4 | 1.8 | 5.1 | 1.3 |
| Switzerland | 7.1 | 2.2 | 4.3 | 1.5 |
| Iraq | 0.1 | 0.2 | 10.0 | 2.1 |
| Libya | 7.1 | 4.3 | 3.0 | 1.2 |
| Bulgaria | 4.6 | 1.6 | 5.2 | 1.8 |
| U.K. | 6.6 | 2.1 | 2.9 | 1.1 |
| Netherlands | 4.4 | 1.3 | 3.4 | 1.0 |
| Brazil | 6.3 | 2.8 | 0.4 | 0.6 |
| Sweden | 3.7 | 0.9 | 2.3 | 0.6 |
| Finland | 3.0 | 0.5 | 2.1 | 0.5 |
| Japan | 4.1 | 1.2 | 0.8 | 0.3 |
| Cuba | 2.2 | 0.2 | 2.6 | 0.8 |
| Belgium and Luxembourg | 3.3 | 1.0 | 1.5 | 0.4 |
| Algeria | | 0.1 | 1.6 | |

Source: National Statistics

Machinery and transport equipment was the largest export category in 1982, followed by semi-finished products and food, accounting for 26.9%, 16.8% and 15.5% of total exports respectively.

157

**TABLE 6.18   COMMODITY BREAKDOWN OF EXPORTS IN 1982**

|  | Billion forints | % of rouble settlements | % of non-rouble settlements | % of total exports |
|---|---|---|---|---|
| Fuels, electric energy | 19.1 | 0.8 | 9.8 | 5.9 |
| Raw materials | 15.6 | 2.2 | 6.8 | 4.8 |
| Semi-finished products | 54.6 | 10.8 | 21.5 | 16.8 |
| Spare parts | 18.1 | 9.8 | 2.3 | 5.6 |
| Machinery, transport equipment, capital goods | 87.3 | 42.4 | 14.9 | 26.9 |
| Industrial consumer goods | 49.1 | 18.6 | 12.5 | 15.1 |
| Agricultural products | 30.4 | 5.1 | 12.6 | 9.4 |
| Food products | 50.3 | 10.3 | 19.6 | 15.5 |
| TOTAL | 324.5 | 100.0 | 100.0 | 100.0 |

A further breakdown reveals that the most important single export commodity in 1982 was buses which accounted for 4.2% of the total, followed by unprocessed meat (3.7%), poultry (2.4%), rolled steel (2.3%), ready made clothes (2.3%) and wheat (2.1%).

The largest import category in 1982 was semi-finished products, followed by fuel and machinery and transport equipment. Crude petroleum was the largest single commodity imported in 1982 accounting for 11.6% of the total, followed by natural gas (3.0%), synthetic raw materials (1.9%), animal feedstuffs (1.8%) and artificial fertilizers (1.8%).

## TABLE 6.19   COMMODITY BREAKDOWN OF IMPORTS IN 1982

|  | Billion forints | % of rouble settlements | % of non-rouble settlements | % of total exports |
|---|---|---|---|---|
| Fuels, electric energy | 64.7 | 30.0 | 10.3 | 19.9 |
| Raw materials | 41.7 | 12.8 | 12.9 | 12.8 |
| Semi-finished products | 76.6 | 12.9 | 33.8 | 23.6 |
| Spare parts | 31.9 | 8.7 | 10.9 | 9.8 |
| Machinery, transport equipment, capital goods | 57.8 | 21.8 | 13.9 | 17.8 |
| Industrial consumer goods | 29.4 | 10.4 | 7.8 | 9.1 |
| Agricultural products | 5.6 | 0.3 | 3.0 | 1.7 |
| Food products | 17.1 | 3.1 | 7.4 | 5.3 |
| TOTAL | 324.8 | 100.0 | 100.0 | 100.0 |

Source: National Statistics

# Chapter Seven

# POLAND

## Introduction

Poland is the largest country in Eastern Europe (excluding the USSR) in terms of its area — 312,683 square kilometres — and the seventh largest in Europe (both East and West). During the past few years and up to the present time, Poland has rarely been out of the international news for long, being the subject of much publicity about its economic problems and its social and political unrest.

Poland differs from its partners in two very basic aspects, both most uncharacteristic for a socialist (communist) country. Under an ideology which states that all means of production are to be owned by the state for the collective good, some 70% of land is owned by private farmers, whose right to that ownership was written into the Polish constitution in 1983. The other unusual aspect of Poland is that an active and strong church is both tolerated and influential at all levels of life, and this is despite the fact that Poland is a communist, atheist state. The church is independent and operates relatively freely within the communist system.

Poland's economy, unlike that of its Comecon partners, has been declining rapidly since the late 1970s, the result of earlier expansionist policies which failed to produce the required growth. For the Communist Bloc, the decline has been unprecedented. Poland's foreign debt had grown to $25 billion  by 1983 , the highest in Comecon.

## Government

Poland's parliament, the Sejm, is the supreme organ of state. Its deputies, elected from officially-approved lists of candidates, serve for four-year terms.

The country's leader is the First Secretary of the Central Committee of the Polish United Workers' Party and Chairman of the Council of Ministers, General Wojciech Jaruzelski. He has been Head of State since October 1981.

160

The Sejm elects the government, although in terms of actual power, all major decisions are taken by the Polish United Workers' Party and the government implements those decisions. The Sejm has 460 deputies. 56.7% of the deputies belong to the Polish United Workers' Party, 24.6% belong to the United Peasants' Party, 8% belong to the Democratic Party and 10.7% are non-party. Some 23% of the deputies are women.

At a local level, there are 49 People's Councils, with 6,740 councilmen.

## The church

Poland is well known as the easternmost outpost of the Roman Catholic church, which has been an established feature of Polish life over the centuries.

The Roman Catholic church has a strong following. It is independent of the state and it has considerable status. It plays an important role in Poland's life, and often mediates in social and political problems.

All over Poland there are Catholic shrines, and the most important of these, at Czestochowa, is a focus of frequent expressions of popular feeling.

Poland has provided the first non-Italian Pope of recent times, John Paul II, whose return visits to his homeland have tried to bring closer together the dissenting parties of government and people.

## The political situation

Poland's political problems are the direct consequence of its economic problems. The over-ambitious rate of growth planned by the policy-makers of Edward Gierek's government in the early 1970s was led by imports, primarily from the West, which were expected to provide Poland with modern technologies, but the economy failed to generate the production levels and the exports which had been expected. Imports grew to such volumes that drastic cuts were imposed later in the 1970s. Investment projects were halted. Bad harvests aggravated the problems by making increased food imports necessary. The economic downturn, for many key commodities, started in 1979, well before the unrest of 1980 and 1981 and the rise of Solidarity and the free trade union movement.

161

Throughout 1980 and 1981 there were riots and strikes as food price rises were introduced. Then the movement for free trade unions arose, out of the workers' confrontation with the government and their bid to influence the economic development of the country. Solidarnosz, the Solidarity trade union, was the mass movement which emerged, and it soon had a membership of 10 million people. But a change of government, the imposition of martial law and the outlawing of Solidarity has brought about a calmer and more ordered situation.

Throughout 1981, economic output, as can be clearly seen from the tables in this chapter, slumped abysmally. In fact, the 1981 production figures are excluded from the official government statistics series which, in the 1983 edition, carry figures for 1982 and 1980 only, omitting the record of this disastrous year. The poor economic performance was aggravated by the 'free Saturdays' which Solidarity had won for the workers, giving them a five-day week.

In September 1981 Solidarity held its first (and last) party congress. It stated that the only way to economic recovery was through the acceptance and the implementation of the principle of worker self-management. It urged workers in other East European countries to set up their own independent unions. It demanded basic economic reform, free elections and the right to broadcast — this latter had been promised in the Gdansk agreement of September 1980, but had not been implemented.

In October 1981, General Jaruzelski replaced Kania as First Secretary of the Party. In December of 1981 he set up the Military Council for National Salvation, which was to run the country under twelve generals and was to put a stop to the processes which were deepening Poland's economic crisis. Martial law was declared and protestors were severely dealt with, some being shot dead. Strikes were declared illegal. Certain sectors of the economy were placed under military discipline. Solidarity leader Lech Walesa was interned. Solidarity itself was banned in October 1982. Lech Walesa was later awarded the 1983 Nobel Peace Prize, despite intensive official attempts to discredit him. Opposition to the government continued, and continues to the present through a network which operates underground, producing books, bulletins and occasional broadcasts.

The government's programme is gradually being implemented, and an amount of economic success has been achieved, with output levels improving from the second half of 1982.

162

New, government-sponsored trade unions have been set up and by late 1983 these had attracted 3.5 million members. A new political association, the Patriotic Movement for National Rebirth (PRON), has been formed and is being given a constitutional role. The church's influence is being used to promote these new forms of organisation.

Martial law was first suspended in December 1982 and then lifted in July 1983. But disturbances continue, with many clashes between police and demonstrators. These incidents are played down by the media. Repression continues to affect many people of 'suspect' views. Solidarity is still operating, despite being banned. Its supporters collect subscriptions to sustain the families of members in prison or unable to find work for political reasons. They occasionally publish and broadcast.

The government is now pursuing a more conciliatory approach. Charges against Solidarity activists awaiting trial have been reduced to lesser accusations, while some dissidents have been offered freedom if they agree to emigrate.

Food price rises which had been planned for January 1984 were withdrawn by the government following adverse reception of the proposals by the people. In an unprecedented move, the government undertook a one-month period of consultation over the proposals, which were to have raised the price of food and basic goods substantially. The lessons of 1970 and 1980 and the fall of two governments have led to a far more gradual approach to the problem of unrealistic prices. Already a Polish family spends around 50% of its income on food and drink.

## The economic situation

Around 50% of Poland's national income is provided by industry:

TABLE 7.1   NATIONAL INCOME BY ORIGIN

| Unit: % of total | 1970 | 1980 | 1982 |
|---|---|---|---|
| Industry | 44.0 | 50.9 | 49.9 |
| Construction | 11.7 | 10.0 | 10.4 |
| Agriculture and forestry | 24.9 | 14.2 | 15.7* |
| Transport and communications | 6.3 | 8.7 | |
| Trade | 11.8 | 14.0 | 24.0** |
| Other | 1.3 | 2.2 | |

* excluding forestry; ** including forestry
Source: National Statistics

Poland's disastrous economic performance in the past few years is readily apparent from the figures presented here from Poland's national statistics series (all calculated on the basis of constant prices):

**TABLE 7.2   NATIONAL INCOME**

| Previous year = 100 | 1977 | 1978 | 1979 | 1980 | 1981 | 1982 |
|---|---|---|---|---|---|---|
| Total national income | 105 | 103 | 98 | 94 | 87 | 92 |
| National income—industry | 108 | 102 | 98 | 96 | 81 | 95 |
| National income—construction | 101 | 100 | 94 | 78 | 86 | 95 |
| National income—agriculture | 99 | 108 | 92 | 82 | 109 | 91 |
| Per capita national income | 104 | 102 | 97 | 93 | 86 | 92 |

Source: National Statistics

Performance is now improving substantially. The upswing started in the second half of 1982, and in 1983 an absolute growth rate of 2.4% for the full year was achieved, the first increase in national income since 1978.

Poland's GNP, gross national product, was estimated by Western sources as $143 billion for 1981.

Poland's own national statistics calculate the country's growth on the Marxist basis of 'national income produced' or 'net material product'. Its national income in 1981 was 2.2 trillion zlotys at current prices. Poland's national income is, on average, equivalent to 83.2% of GNP as measured by the 'expenditure' method used in the West, and thus Western calculations of a country's GNP cannot be directly compared with Eastern Bloc figures of that same country's national income. 'National income produced' is the country's gross product from all material production in the national economy, *less* the material costs incurred in that production — i.e. it is net production. 'Material production' excludes non-material services, such as banking, education, health, public administration and defence. 'Material costs' cover materials including fuels, purchased power, purchased transport, repairs and other material services, also depreciation of fixed assets. Another concept used in measuring the country's economic wealth is that of 'national income distributed', which differs from 'national income produced' by the inclusion of imports. Its distribution is 89% for consumption and 11% for capital formation.

164

The present economic crisis stems from the rapid growth policy of the early 1970s, when growth levels of up to 12% per year were achieved thanks to high levels of imports, mainly from the West and funded by Western credits, and by running increasing trade deficits. Polish trade with the West grew far more rapidly than its trade in general. Imports of licences, technology and complete installations of plant for all Poland's major industries were enormous and very costly. It was planned to repay the West later with the income to be earned by the new, modern industries.

This 'new development strategy' was launched in 1972. It was a reversal of the previous policies of 20 years' standing which had aimed to cultivate local resources and skills into providing sound economic growth and to make the country independent of imported skills (these ideas had led to economic imbalances, shortages of consumer goods and popular discontent). The new development strategy aimed to industrialise and modernise in one giant step by the acquisition of superior Western technology. But the new ideas also foundered. They were halted by the economic rigidity of Poland's authoritarian system, and meanwhile the Western markets for the sophisticated products to be manufactured and exported were failing to materialise as the world recession got underway in the late 1970s.

And the Polish economy was unable to absorb the high level of Western imports. By 1980 projects valued at $16 billion were unfinished. The imported technology failed to lead to innovation within Polish industry. Meanwhile, the traditional export sectors such as coal and food were ignored in favour of new industries such as chemicals and engineering. And the implementation of Western technology led to long-term demand for more Western goods in the form of materials and components specific to those technologies, in a vicious circle increasing the import intensity of domestic production. Among the many plants involved with Western technology are Fiat Polski (with Fiat of Italy) making cars, Tewa (with Thomson of France) making semiconductors and Unitra (with Grundig of West Germany) making tape recorders — the latter has ceased production.

The rapidly growing balance of payments deficit, as export growth failed to keep pace, led to the abandoning of the new development strategy in 1975.

New economic measures were introduced, including curbs on Western imports, and an export drive was started. Growth rates had slowed as economic performance deteriorated, and became negative for the first time in 1979, declining further until 1983. Investment projects were halted as materials and energy became short — Poland was a net energy importer in 1979, having turned into a large-scale user of oil, of which little is produced domestically.

National income declined 6% in 1980, 12% in 1981, and 5.5% in 1982 when it reached its 1973 level.

During the second half of 1982, things slowly began to return to normal under the military regime and output began to recover, although inflation had risen to 100% over the year as a whole. In August 1982 manufacturing industry had its first growth since before the crisis, helped by the coal industry which was now under military discipline and back to working a six day week and extra shifts — coal output increased 16% compared with its 1981 level, reaching 189 million tonnes.

The government had not brought out a plan for 1982, but a draft forecast was eventually published giving three variants of expected performance, the most likely of which was a 3.4% decline. In the event, the decline was 5.5%. Substantial price rises were carried out early in the year, with prices for raw and intermediate materials up 80%, retail prices for food up 241% and heating up 171%, laying the basis for a sounder pricing system which was to reflect the real value of these goods in terms of supply and demand and of world prices. Increased prices permitted state subsidies to be reduced, and additional allowances to families partially compensated for the increased cost of living. But living standards continued to decline, as they had in 1981. Rationing was brought in for many consumer goods and food, and still remains in force for selected items. Savings and cash-in-hand rose substantially in 1982 as the availability of goods declined. Investments in 1982, 1 trillion zloty at current prices, were down 13.2% compared with 1981 in real terms, as the country's economic situation forced adjustments. Many projects were suspended or cancelled. However, among projects which were completed in 1982 were:

| | | |
|---|---|---|
| hard coal | — | a new mine at Bogdanka and expansions at Piast and Suszec |
| lignite | — | new mines at Belchatow and Konin |
| electric power | — | new generating units, two of 200 MW at Polaniec, one of 360 MW at Belchatow and three 170 MW turbine sets at the Zarnowiec hydroelectric power plant |

| | |
|---|---|
| chemicals | — a 180,000 tonnes per year chlorine plant and a 197,000 tonnes per year soda lye unit at Wloclawek Nitrogen Works |
| shoes | — a new factory at Bydgoszcz |
| tyres | — expansion at the Stomil Automobile Tyre Works |

In 1983 there was positive growth and national income was up nearly 6%. Industrial output growth was expected to be 4.9%, following increased investments, particularly in the sectors of fuel, power and food processing. Industrial sales were up, coal exports had improved and there was a better grain harvest, easing fodder shortages, and even a $1 billion hard currency trade surplus was expected. But all the comparisons for 1983 are against the low levels of 1982. Also, the recovery rate has been patchy, with little growth in consumer goods, and mining also performing less well than manufacturing. Inflation, although vastly reduced from 1982, was 30% compared with a target of 15%. And the 1983 achievements were at high cost in terms of working hours, and there were few benefits for the population as foreign debt repayment took priority.

For 1984, the modest growth rate was expected to continue. The government revised its targets in January 1984, from the originals issued in the autumn of 1983: national income to grow 2.6% (compared with 3.5% originally planned); industrial output to grow 4.5% (compared with 5% originally planned).

Of the many investment projects suspended in 1981 and 1982, 440 are to be resumed.

For 1985, the target is to restore the economic balance, to achieve an overall trade surplus and to reduce inflation to single figures.

167

**TABLE 7.3   PLANNED ECONOMIC GROWTH**

| (% change vs previous year) | 1983 plan | 1983 expected actual | 1984 plan | 1983-85 plan* |
|---|---|---|---|---|
| Net material product produced | 2.0-2.5 | 2.4 | 3.5** | 10-12 |
| Net material product distributed | — | 1.5 | 2.8 | 8.5-10.0 |
| Industrial output | 3.7-4.0 | 4.9 | 4.5-5.4** | 14-16 |
| Agricultural output | 1.5-2.3 | 1.5 | 1.4-2.8 | 10.0 |
| Wages | 16 | 25 | 15-17 | 53.5 |
| Prices | 15 | 25 | 15 | 35-45 |
| Exports to West | 12 | 12.5*** | 10.3-16.8 | 37.1 |
| Imports from West | 17 | 12.9*** | 2.4-10.6 | 31.8 |
| Exports to Comecon | 10 | 15.5*** | 13 | 26.4 |
| Imports from Comecon | 12 | 11.3*** | 14.5 | 28.6 |
| Trade surplus with West (billion zloty) | 107 | 135 | 181 | — |
| Trade deficit with Comecon (billion zloty) | − 80 | − 56 | — | — |

*** rate achieved in January-September; ** later revised; * for 3-year period
Source: Economist Intelligence Unit

The priorities are: to produce sufficient food for the population to preclude large-scale imports; to produce supplies of consumer goods adequate to curb inflation; to produce large quantities of high-quality goods to earn export revenues; to invest in ageing industrial plant; and to complete the many projects already begun.

Poland's economy is centrally planned and controlled and the state-owned sector dominates the country's economic life. All major enterprises (factories or groups of factories, which operate in the same way as companies in the West) are directly controlled and administered by the government. Annual and five-year plans are issued, setting the rate of growth, the level and direction of investment and sectoral priorities.

As a result of the upheavals of the past few years, the government has brought in reforms to this system which, although far from being fully implemented yet, will bring considerable benefits. The reform process is acknowledged as being a long-term programme. The state combines (large groups of enterprises) are being disbanded and enterprises can now form voluntary associations for the conduct of their business and their foreign trade operations. Profit and profitability are the new criteria, along with lower production costs and greater competitiveness. Individual enterprises are being allowed far more independence to take their own decisions on the basis of market forces. They have been given foreign trading rights and are permitted to retain part of their foreign currency earnings to purchase their own imports. Several of the official Foreign Trade Enterprises have become joint stock limited liability companies. The finances of enterprises are being tightened in an attempt to make them more responsive to cutting costs and becoming more profitable. In particular, they are being encouraged to stop paying higher wages for inferior productivity levels — charging higher prices has usually been seen as an easier way to profitability than reducing costs. Worker self-management will be brought in, as the crisis abates and the political and social situation return to normal — this will allow workers to decide on profit distribution, to formulate their own long-term plans and to appoint their own directors (except for the 'key' industries). Central controls will be loosened, and indicative planning guides will take the place of the previous command plans. The extent of all these changes has so far been very limited, but the process of normalisation will permit their implementation.

**Population and workforce**

The country consists of a large plain. 90% of the area is less than 300 metres above sea level, giving good conditions for agriculture. There are mountainous areas — Swietokrzyskie in the south of the country and Sudety and Karpaty along the border with Czechoslovakia.

Poland has 49 provinces (voivodships) and 2,365 rural communities (gmina). The main towns are:

| Town | Population at end-1981 |
|---|---|
| Warsaw (capital city) | 1,611,600 |
| Lodz | 843,000 |
| Krakow | 722,900 |
| Wroclaw | 621,900 |
| Poznan | 558,000 |
| Gdansk | 458,900 |

Continued...

| Town | Population at end-1981 |
|------|----------------------|
| Szczecin | 389,900 |
| Katowice | 363,500 |
| Bydgoszcz | 352,400 |
| Lublin | 308,800 |
| Sosnowiec | 251,900 |
| Bytom | 237,800 |
| Czestochowa | 237,700 |
| Gdynia | 237,500 |
| Bialystok | 229,700 |
| Gliwice | 202,200 |
| Zabrze | 196,800 |
| Radom | 194,400 |
| Kielce | 188,800 |
| Torun | 180,100 |

The population totalled 36.7 million in October 1983. It is expanding rapidly and is expected to grow by a further 2.3 million people by 1990. At the 1978 census, 57.5% of the population was registered as urban, 42.5% as rural; the urban population is in constant growth at the expense of the rural areas. In 1982, of a total population of 36.4 million, there were 18.7 million women and 17.7 million men. 21.5 million people were of working age (18-64 for men, 18-59 for women), 11 million men and 10.5 million women.

Both the population and the workforce are young, in contrast with several other East European (and West European) countries, which are worried about ageing populations. At the end of 1981, 50% of the total population was under 30 years. This youthfulness is an underlying cause of the social discontent. Young and newly-qualified workers had hoped to be the beneficiaries of the years of economic modernisation, but instead their frustrations at worsening living conditions, more widespread shortages of food and consumer goods and a growing housing crisis have led to the continuing unrest.

In 1982, per 1,000 head of population, there were 8.7 marriages, 1.3 divorces, 19.4 live births and 9.2 deaths. The natural population increase was 10.2 per 1,000.

Figures are given for the workforce by sector, but for the socialised sector only. The figures take no account of those in the private sector, including around 4 million engaged in private-sector agriculture. (In terms of both socialised and non-socialised economies, 26% of the active population is employed in agriculture.)

**TABLE 7.4   EMPLOYMENT IN SOCIALISED SECTOR, 1983**

**Unit: '000 workers**

| | |
|---|---:|
| Industry | 4,438 |
| Construction | 1,085 |
| Agriculture | 859 |
| Forestry | 151 |
| Transport and communications | 1,042 |
| Trade | 1,113 |
| Community services | 332 |
| Housing and non-material community services | 203 |
| Science and technology | 110 |
| Education | 845 |
| Culture and art | 82 |
| Health and welfare | 676 |
| Physical culture, tourism, recreation | 91 |
| TOTAL (including others) | 11,534 |

Source: National Statistics

Total numbers employed in both socialised and non-socialised sectors were 16.9 million in 1982.

## Manufacturing

Poland's industrial base is represented by the mining sector and heavy industry. Its manufacturing base is widely diversified, and products include locomotives, cars, ships, automotive equipment, mining machinery, construction equipment, machine tools, textiles, food. But despite heavy investment and considerable development, Poland still needs to import machinery.

Poland is the largest electricity producer in East Europe (excluding the USSR), and equal first with Czechoslovakia in terms of steel production.

171

Investments in industry will substantially increase in the late 1980s and in the 1990s.

## Machinery and equipment

This sector is of great importance in the Polish economy. Its products account for 44% of all exports, earning large sums of valuable foreign currency.

Among many well-developed branches, the manufacturers of coal-mining equipment have achieved world status, notably Kopex of Katowice, whose products are increasingly sought as an energy-conscious world returns to coal as a power source.

Shipbuilding can also be singled out as world-class, with the shipyards at Gdansk, Gdynia and Szczecin constructing the most technically complex vessels. The Szczecin yard is currently building 12 chemical carriers, while Gdynia has recently completed a series of 75,000 cubic metre capacity gas tankers for the US. The Gdansk yard has delivered several 23,000-ton container vessels to West Germany, the UK, Holland and France. Poland has also attained a high degree of specialisation in building fishing vessels, both small and of trawler-factory size. It also builds sailing yachts, most of which are delivered to Western customers.

**TABLE 7.5  OUTPUT OF MACHINERY**

|  | 1980 | 1981 | 1982 |
|---|---|---|---|
| Electric rotating machinery (million units) | 12.3 | 11.5 | 10.8 |
| Roller bearings (million units) | 124.8 | 110.0 | 105.4 |
| Metal cutting machine tools ('000 tonnes) | 37.6 | 32.1 | 33.7 |
| Metal forming machine tools ('000 tonnes) | 13.3 | 9.5 | 7.8 |
| Mining equipment ('000 tonnes) | 375.3 | 306.8 | 316.3 |
| Metallurgical equipment ('000 tonnes) | 59.9 | 44.1 | 35.5 |
| Chemical process equipment ('000 tonnes) | 74.2 | 60.1 | 52.4 |
| Construction and road building equipment ('000 tonnes) | 181.1 | 137.4 | 110.5 |
| Agricultural and forestry equipment (billion zlotys, 1982 prices) | 40.1 | 36.9 | 45.3 |

Continued...

172

**Table 7.5 continued . . .**

| | 1980 | 1981 | 1982 |
|---|---|---|---|
| Universal 2-axle agricultural tractors ('000 units) | 57.6 | 50.5 | 53.0 |
| Ploughs — tractor driven ('000 units) | 30.0 | 32.8 | — |
| Ploughs — horse drawn ('000 units) | 15.8 | 19.1 | — |
| Grain seeders — tractor driven ('000 units) | 13.4 | 12.8 | — |
| Grain seeders — horse drawn ('000 units) | 7.0 | 11.2 | — |
| Harvesters/threshers ('000 units) | 4.6 | 4.3 | — |

Source: National Statistics

**TABLE 7.6   OUTPUT OF TRANSPORT EQUIPMENT**

**Unit: '000s**

| | 1980 | 1981 | 1982 | 1983 |
|---|---|---|---|---|
| Locomotives, diesel (units) | 121 | 40 | — | — |
| Locomotives, electric (units) | 125 | 100 | — | — |
| Railway goods trucks | 15.2 | 9.1 | 6.4 | — |
| Railway passenger coaches (units) | 328 | 286 | 308 | — |
| Passenger cars | 351.1 | 239.9 | 228.3 | 270.2 |
| Fiat 125 | 61.6 | 46.8 | — | — |
| Fiat 126 | 214.0 | 150.0 | — | — |
| Polonez | 32.1 | 20.5 | — | — |
| Buses | 13.1 | 11.5 | 9.7 | — |
| Lorries and road tractors | 53.7 | 42.7 | 38.2 | — |
| Mopeds | 126.0 | 105.0 | 93.1 | — |
| Motorcycles | 94.2 | 79.2 | — | — |
| Bicycles (million units) | 1.6 | 1.3 | 1.2 | — |
| Ships of 100 dwt and over ('000 dwt) | 392.2 | 321.8 | 358.3 | — |

Source: National Statistics and Polish press for 1983

**TABLE 7.7   OUTPUT OF SPECIALISED EQUIPMENT**

|  | 1980 | 1981 | 1982 |
|---|---|---|---|
| Automated control equipment (billion zlotys, 1979 prices) | 9.3 | 8.0 | 7.7 |
| Computers and electronic data processing equipment (billion zlotys, 1979 prices) | 11.7 | 10.7 | 13.1 |
| Semiconductor elements (million units) | 262.0 | — | 178.0 |
| Transistors (million units) | — | — | 73.8 |

Source: National Statistics

## Iron and Steel

Among the major centres for steelmaking are: Warsaw and its area, and Katowice and Czestochowa and Krakow in the Upper Silesia region. At Nowa Huta outside Krakow is located one of the country's major steel plants, the Lenin works, which was completely equipped by the USSR.

**TABLE 7.8   POLAND'S IRON AND STEEL PRODUCTION**

**Unit: million tonnes**

|  | 1980 | 1981 | 1982 |
|---|---|---|---|
| Pig iron | 12.0 | 9.4 | — |
| Crude steel | 19.5 | 15.7 | 14.8 |
| Rolled products | 13.6 | 11.1 | 10.5 |
| Steel pipes | 1.1 | 1.0 | 0.9 |
| Cold rolled steel sheets | 1.6 | 1.4 | 1.3 |

Source: National Statistics

Unemployment fears abounded in 1982, as cuts in investment spending were necessitated by the worsening economic crisis, and an early retirement scheme was temporarily instituted to take up the expected labour surplus. The number of unemployed currently is small.

## Agriculture

Poland has 18.9 million hectares of agricultural land, 14.6 million of which is arable, 4 million is meadowland and pasture, and 0.3 million is orchards. Additionally, there are 8.7 million hectares of forestry land.

Socialist enterprises supplied 19.3% of total agricultural production in 1982, compared with 22% in 1980. The private sector supplies all the rest. The socialised sector consists of large state farms and a limited number of co-operatives. There are around 3.5 million private farmers.

Poland alone among Comecon countries relies on private farmers and those farmers rely to a great extent on the horse, despite the fact that Poland is an industrial country. Polish farming is not efficient, despite the advantages conferred by its geographical and climatic situation. The land is fragmented and farms are small. 30% of them are under 2 hectares in size and many farms consist of scattered plots. One farm out of eight produces only enough food for its family to live on, and Poland's agriculture achieves nothing like its full potential. Although output of many crops is at world levels and the country is a major food producer, it is forced to import food to feed its growing population. Imports of grain and feedstuffs totalled 8.2 million tonnes in 1981, compared with a reported 5.2 million tonnes in 1982.

The agricultural population is ageing, with large numbers — around one third of private farmers — being aged 60 years or over. Some 170,000-180,000 young people leave the land each year for jobs in the towns. So long term prospects are mixed. The government has not encouraged the private farmers in past years and worker numbers fell by a quarter between 1975 and 1980. But this policy has been changed and 92% of land sales in the first half of 1982 were to private farmers (in 1975 90% of land sales were to the socialised sector).

Another major problem is lack of machinery. Incomes are generally low, and since farms are small, investment is minimal and machinery is not bought. As late as the mid 1970s, only one farmer in thirteen owned a tractor, with the rest relying on horse power. Those private farmers who have machinery, together with the state sector, suffer from a lack of servicing availability for their equipment — spare parts are in short supply and the repair of agricultural machinery is normally a protracted affair. In October 1982, 250,000 of the country's stock of 650,000 tractors were reportedly out of use because there were no spare parts for them. However, the Ursus tractor plant is to expand its output to 100,000 units per year by 1989.

175

All farms are short of plant protection chemicals, while the fertiliser application rate fell to 186.2 kilogrammes per hectare in the 1980-81 season, a six-year low.

The national statistics show that total agricultural output by value was 597.9 billion zlotys in 1981 (at 1976-77 constant prices); 53% was crop output and 47% animal products. 78.6% of total output was from private farms, 16.6% from state farms, 4.3% from co-operatives and 0.5% from agricultural associations.

### TABLE 7.9  CROP OUTPUT

**Unit: million tonnes**

|  | 1981 | 1982 | 1983* |
|---|---|---|---|
| Cereals | 19.7 | 21.2 | 22.1 |
| Wheat | 4.2 | 4.5 | 5.2 |
| Rye | 6.7 | 7.8 | 8.8 |
| Oats | 2.7 | 2.6 | 2.4 |
| Barley | 3.5 | 3.5 | 3.2 |
| Potatoes | 42.6 | 32.0 | 34.5 |
| Sugar beet | 15.9 | 15.1** | 16.4 |
| Oilseeds | 0.5 | 0.4 |  |
| Tobacco | 0.1 | — |  |
| Vegetables | 4.9 | 4.2 |  |
| Cabbage | 1.6 | 1.1 |  |
| Onions | 0.4 | 0.4 |  |
| Carrots | 0.6 | 0.5 |  |
| Cucumbers | 0.5 | 0.4 |  |
| Tomatoes | 0.4 | 0.4 |  |
| Fruit | 1.4 | 2.6 |  |
| Apples | 0.8 | 1.9 |  |
| Pears | 0.1 | 0.1 |  |
| Plums ('000 tonnes) | 74.0 | 135.0 |  |
| Cherries ('000 tonnes) | 36.0 | 43.0 |  |
| Sweet cherries ('000 tonnes) | 20.0 | 28.0 |  |

* source is Polish press reports; ** the 1982 crop was smaller but of better quality, permitting a record 1.83 million tonnes sugar production with an exportable surplus
Source: National Statistics

**TABLE 7.10   OUTPUT OF ANIMAL PRODUCTS**

**Unit: million tonnes**

|  | 1981 | 1982 | 1983* |
|---|---|---|---|
| Meat** | 2.5 | 2.5 | 1.7 |
| Beef, veal | 0.5 | 0.6 | |
| Pork | 1.1 | 1.2 | |
| Poultry | 0.4 | 0.2 | |
| Cows' milk (billion litres) | 14.9 | 14.8 | |
| Hens' eggs (billion units) | 8.9 | 7.6 | |
| Sheep wool, greasy basis ('000 tonnes) | 11.2 | 11.3 | |

* source is Polish press reports; ** cool weight, excluding fats and offal
Source: National Statistics

**TABLE 7.11   LIVESTOCK NUMBERS**

**Unit: million head**

|  | June 1981 | June 1982 |
|---|---|---|
| Horses | 1.7 | 1.7 |
| Cattle | 11.8 | 11.9 |
| Cows | 5.8 | 5.8 |
| Pigs | 18.5 | 19.5 |
| Sheep | 3.9 | 3.9 |
| Poultry | 65.5 | |
| Laying hens | 61.2 | |
| Geese | 1.5 | |
| Ducks | 3.8 | |
| Turkeys | 0.5 | |

Source: National Statistics

Subsequently, livestock numbers fell sharply, with cattle numbers, in 1983, down 4.1% in the private sector and down 9.9% in the socialised sector. Pig numbers fell 23.7% and 8.8% respectively. Poultry numbers also fell. This was the result of fodder shortages, and because herds had been built up previously on fodder imports.

### TABLE 7.12 FUTURE AGRICULTURE DEVELOPMENT

|                                                          | 1982  | 1985  | 1990      |
|----------------------------------------------------------|-------|-------|-----------|
| Grain harvest (million tonnes)                           | 21.2  | 23.0  | 24.6-25.4 |
| Potato harvest (million tonnes)                          | 32.0  | 44.0  |           |
| Fertiliser consumption (kilogrammes per hectare)         | 178.0 | 205.0 | 230.0     |
| Plant protection chemicals used ('000 tonnes)            | 16.3  | 18.5  | 27.0      |
| Machinery and equipment ('000 zlotys per hectare)        | 32.0  | 52.0  |           |
| Tractors in use ('000 units)                             | 55.0  | 64.0  | 100.0     |
| Meat consumption (kilogrammes per capita)                |       | 55.5  | 58.5-62.0 |
| Milk consumption (litres per capita)                     | 255.0 | 268.0 | 285.0     |
| Fish consumption (kilogrammes per capita)                | 6.0   | 6.0   | 6.0-7.6   |
| Fats consumption (kilogrammes per capita)                | 21.6  | 22.7  | 23.6-24.7 |

Source: Economist Intelligence Unit

Meat consumption was 65.7 kilogrammes per capita in 1981, according to the national statistics. This level was expected to fall further in 1983, and will still be below the 1981 level by 1990.

Forestry output in 1981 was valued at 40.2 billion zlotys at 1977 prices.

### Mining

Poland is a leading producer of hard coal, and one of the world's largest coal exporters. Its reserves are estimated at 150 billion tonnes. New mines are being prepared and opened, and others are being expanded, but no large-scale development is planned. Output will remain steady or will rise slowly, reaching 220 million tonnes per year in the 1990s.

Coal is one of the basics of the Polish economy. Output was a record 201 million tonnes in 1979, falling in 1980 and 1981 and rising again in 1982 and in 1983 when it reached 191 million tonnes — these swings reflect the shift from 24-hour working to concessions to the workers and then to the imposition of military discipline. Coal mining is highly automated, with 97% of output produced by mechanical means.

Lignite (brown coal) mining is also important. Reserves are estimated at 900 million tonnes. Production was planned to rise 13% to 42.9 million tonnes in 1983 and to 80 million tonnes per year by 1990 and 120 million tonnes per year by the year 2000.

Poland is believed to have Europe's largest copper deposits, estimated as 2.8 billion tonnes. These reserves are located mainly in the Legnica-Glogow region, but 25% is likely to prove difficult to extract as geological conditions are adverse and seams are deep. The copper fields are extensive, and Poland may become a major world supplier. A long -term expansion programme will raise output of copper ore to 34.6 million tonnes in 1985 and 44.5 million tonnes in 1990. A new mine will open at Sieroszewice with a 5.5 million tonnes per year capacity and the existing mine at Rudna will be expanded to 12 million tonnes per year.

Other metal ores include zinc and lead, some iron and nickel and small quantities of gold. Reserves of zinc and lead ores are estimated at 350 million tonnes, and output will increase as the Trzebianka mine is expanded and modernised.

Oil reserves are estimated at 100 million tonnes. Production of oil is insignificant, only 300,000 tonnes per year, which is maintained with great difficulty. 95% of needs are imported from the USSR. Natural gas reserves are put at 730 billion cubic metres. Domestic output, around 6 billion cubic metres per year, meets 50% of requirements.

Other minerals include salt, but there are no significant reserves of phosphates, potash, aluminium oxide or apatite, and all these must be imported.

**TABLE 7.13   MINING OUTPUT**

| Unit: million tonnes | 1980 | 1981 | 1982 | 1983 |
|---|---|---|---|---|
| Hard coal | 193.1 | 163.0 | 189.3 | 191.1 |
| Brown coal | 36.9 | 35.6 | 37.7 | 42.5 |
| Coke | 19.9 | 17.9 | 17.3 | 17.1 |
| Crude oil | 0.4 | 0.3 | 0.3 | — |
| Natural gas (billion cubic metres) | 6.3 | 6.2 | 5.5 | 5.5 |
| Copper ore | 26.6 | 22.8 | 27.0* | — |
| Zinc/lead ores | 5.5 | 5.0 | — | — |
| Iron ores | 0.1 | 0.1 | — | — |

* figure is estimated and from another source
Source: National Statistics, and Polish press for 1983

## TABLE 7.14   OUTPUT OF NONFERROUS METALS

**Unit: '000 tonnes**

|  | 1980 | 1981 | 1982 |
|---|---|---|---|
| Electrolyte copper | 357.0 | 327.0 | 348.0 |
| Zinc | 217.0 | 167.0 | 165.0 |
| Lead | 82.0 | 69.0 | — |
| Aluminium | 95.1 | 66.0 | — |
| Silver (tonnes) | 766.0 | 640.0 | 655.0 |

Source: National Statistics

## Chemicals

## TABLE 7.15   OUTPUT OF CHEMICALS

**Unit: '000 tonnes**

|  | 1980 | 1981 | 1982 | 1983 |
|---|---|---|---|---|
| Sulphuric acid (million tonnes) | 3.0 | 2.8 | 2.7 | — |
| Caustic soda | 432.8 | 417.0 | 378.1 | — |
| Pesticides | 34.5 | 36.2 | 48.0 | — |
| Plastics | 666.4 | 586.9 | 551.0 | 525.4 |
| Polyvinyl chloride | 118.6 | 92.9 | 79.5 | — |
| Synthetic rubber/latex | 117.9 | 111.1 | 99.9 | — |
| Nitrogen fertilisers (million tonnes) | 1.3 | 1.3 | 1.3 | — |
| Phosphate fertilisers | 842.5 | 866.1 | 868.1 | — |
| Chemical fibres | 256.4 | 204.7 | 203.5 | — |
| Synthetic fibres | 167.6 | 139.1 | 137.2 | 157.0 |
| Pharmaceuticals (billion zlotys, 1982 prices) | 36.9 | 35.8 | 38.3 | — |
| Sulphur (million tonnes) | 5.2 | 4.8 | 4.9 | — |
| Salt (million tonnes) | 4.5 | 4.3 | — | — |
| Chlorine gas | 309.0 | 305.0 | — | — |
| Ethylene | 185.0 | 182.0 | — | — |
| Propylene | 129.0 | 117.0 | — | — |
| Organic dyes | 25.1 | 20.7 | — | — |
| Washing and cleaning products | 293.0 | 283.0 | — | 284.8 |

Source: National Statistics, and Polish press for 1983

180

One of Poland's new projects is the £200 million polyvinyl chloride plant under construction at Wloclawek. This was due to be completed in 1984 after nine years' delay and will provide capacity for 200,000 tonnes per year of PVC.

## Oil products

Processed crude oil volume was 13.4 million tonnes in 1982. There are seven oil refineries in operation (1981 data).

**TABLE 7.16   OUTPUT OF OIL PRODUCTS**

| Unit: million tonnes | 1980 | 1981 |
|---|---|---|
| Motor spirit | 3.3 | 2.8 |
| Distillate fuel oil | 5.1 | 4.3 |

Source: National Statistics

## Other manufactured goods

**TABLE 7.17   OUTPUT OF BUILDING MATERIALS**

| | 1980 | 1981 | 1982 |
|---|---|---|---|
| Cement (million tonnes) | 18.4 | 14.2 | 16.0 |
| Wall building components* | | | |
| (billion units) | 10.4 | 10.0 | 10.2 |
| Glass (million square metres) | 69.6 | 60.1 | 55.7 |

* in terms of full fired bricks
Source: National Statistics

**TABLE 7.18   OUTPUT OF WOOD PRODUCTS**

|  | 1980 | 1981 | 1982 |
|---|---|---|---|
| Hardboard (million square metres) | 115.8 | 100.6 | 112.2 |
| Furniture (billion zlotys, 1982 prices) | 96.8 | 88.5 | 87.4 |
| Cellulose ('000 tonnes) | 526.1 | 465.3 | 555.8 |
| Paper (million tonnes) | 1.0 | 0.9 | 1.0 |
| Cardboard ('000 tonnes) | 244.0 | 215.0 | — |

Source: National Statistics

**TABLE 7.19   OUTPUT OF TEXTILES AND FOOTWEAR**

|  | 1980 | 1981 | 1982 |
|---|---|---|---|
| Cotton fabric (billion metres) | 0.9 | 0.8 | 0.7 |
| Wool fabric (million metres) | 121.1 | 106.1 | 91.8 |
| Fabric for clothing manufacture — cotton (million metres) | 468.0 | 428.0 | — |
| Fabric for clothing manufacture — wool (million metres) | 68.4 | 58.2 | — |
| Knitted outerwear ('000 tonnes) | 25.9 | 21.9 | — |
| Knitted underwear ('000 tonnes) | 18.8 | 17.0 | — |
| Shoes (million pairs) | 162.3 | 144.7 | 146.1 |
| Rubber shoes (million pairs) | 21.7 | 18.4 | 18.0 |

Source: National Statistics

**TABLE 7.20   OUTPUT OF RUBBER PRODUCTS**

|  | 1980 | 1981 |
|---|---|---|
| Rubber products in total, including shoes ('000 tonnes) | 401.0 | 335.0 |
| Tyres (million units) | 6.5 | 4.8 |
| Passenger car tyres (million units) | 4.0 | 3.1 |

Source: National Statistics

## TABLE 7.21 CONSUMER GOODS PRODUCTION

**Unit: '000 units**

|  | 1980 | 1981 | 1982 | 1983 |
|---|---|---|---|---|
| Radio sets (million units) | 2.7 | 2.8 | 2.2 | 2.1 |
| Television sets | 899.8 | 764.4 | 576.0 | — |
|    Colour television sets | 147.0 | 160.0 | 145.0 | — |
| Tape recorders and dictaphones | 805.5 | 567.8 | 372.8 | — |
| Washing machines and spin dryers | 808.5 | 712.2 | 623.4 | — |
| Refrigerators and freezers | 693.6 | 553.4 | 508.7 | — |
| Electric vacuum cleaners | 961.0 | 895.0 | — | — |
| Sewing machines | 409.0 | 383.0 | 350.0 | — |

Source: National Statistics, Polish press for 1983

## TABLE 7.22 OUTPUT OF FOOD PRODUCTS

**Unit: million tonnes**

|  | 1980 | 1981 | 1982 |
|---|---|---|---|
| Meat, industrial slaughter weight | 2.5 | 1.9 | 1.9 |
|    Pork | 1.5 | 1.0 | 1.1 |
| Pork products | 0.8 | 0.7 | 0.7 |
| Fish (seafish) | 0.8 | 0.6 | 0.6 |
| Milk (billion litres) | 2.7 | 2.9 | 2.8 |
| Butter and fats ('000 tonnes) | 252.9 | 221.8 | 224.7 |
| Spirits and vodka ('000 litres) | 212.1 | 161.5 | 157.6 |
| Cigarettes (billion units) | 93.5 | 83.0 | 87.5 |
| Cereal products | 7.7 | 7.4 | — |
| Bread, excluding confectionery | 3.5 | 3.8 | — |
| Sugar | 1.1 | 1.7 | 1.8 |
| Beer (million hectolitres) | 11.2 | 10.5 | — |
| Vegetable oils ('000 tonnes) | 275.0 | 222.0 | — |
| Frozen fruit and vegetables ('000 tonnes) | 152.0 | 183.0 | — |

Source: National Statistics

## Construction

Some 85% of the country's construction activity is undertaken by socialist enterprises. The industry employed 1.3 million workers in 1981, 1.2 million of whom were in socialist enterprises.

Poland has a housing crisis. Its youthful population produces an ever-growing demand for more houses, which the construction industry cannot satisfy. Also, people migrate to the towns in large numbers, further aggravating the situation. In 1980, a bad year for the industry, only 60% of its target was achieved. Yet the long-term housing programme of 1972 had aimed to give every family its own home by 1990 at the latest, and 6.7-7.3 million dwellings were to be built over 20 years. In 1982, the industry completed 185,400 housing units, giving a usable floor area of 12.5 million square metres, while in 1983 the state sector of the construction industry completed 137,700 units, overfulfilling its target. For 1984, 130,000 units were to be constructed by the state sector, with a further 60,000 units expected from the private sector.

## Energy

While Poland exports vast quantities of coal to customers in both the Eastern Bloc and the West, it also imports large amounts of oil, to satisfy its requirements of around 16 million tonnes per year.

Its industries are energy-intensive. For every $1,000 of net industrial output, Poland uses 2.5 times more fuel than Western capitalist countries.

Fuel is short and petrol is rationed. In the 1983-84 winter season, the ration was reduced from previous levels, and selective traffic speed limits were imposed.

Solid fuel accounts for 79.7% of total commercial primary energy consumption (1981 figure).

Poland's electricity generating capacity is 26,000 MW, but only an estimated 19,200 MW are available at any one time. Electricity output was 121.9 TWh in 1980, 115.0 TWh in 1981 and 117.6 TWh in 1982.

96% of electric power is produced from coal, mainly hard coal. Lignite (brown coal) produced 25% of the country's power in 1982, and this source is to provide 40% of power in future years in order to release hard coal for export or other uses. A 4,320 MW lignite-fired power station is under construction at Belchatow — its original start-up date was 1985, but it is behind schedule and now will produce only 50% of its planned power by that date.

Poland's first nuclear power station will be built at Zarnowiec. It will be equipped with four Soviet VVER-440 reactors and with turbines and generators built in Poland. Its first unit will be operational in 1989 and its fourth in 1993.

A new electricity transmission line, bringing power from the Khmel-nitsky nuclear plant in the USSR to Rzeszow and thence to the rest of Poland via a distributor network, was planned to be completed in 1984.

**TABLE 7.23   POLAND'S ELECTRIC POWER BALANCE IN 1981**

| **Unit: TWh** | |
|---|---|
| *Supplies* | |
| Production | 115.0 |
| Imports | 4.2 |
| | |
| TOTAL SUPPLY | 119.2 |
| | |
| *Consumption* | |
| Domestic consumption | 115.0 |
|   Socialised industry | 67.4 |
|   Socialised construction | 2.5 |
|   Agriculture | 5.7 |
|   Railways | 3.9 |
|   Communal services* | 3.6 |
|   Other | 21.3 |
|     Households | 12.1 |
|   Losses in grid | 10.1 |
| Exports | 4.2 |
| | |
| TOTAL CONSUMPTION | 119.2 |

* includes urban transport, street lighting
Source: National Statistics

## Family consumption

There are continual shortages of many products in Poland, and many goods are rationed: petrol, coal, meat, butter, fats and, since June 1983, 'white goods', radios, televisions and sewing machines. When shortages occur controls are imposed and rationing is likely to remain in force although it is being eliminated where possible. There was much public discontent when rationing of butter and fats was reimposed in October 1983, following government assurances that rationing of most products would be ended (except for meat, which was to remain on ration) — this led to an official apology. Meat consumption has fallen and will continue at low levels until 1990. In place of meat, dairy products are to be promoted.

The average monthly net wage in the socialised economy was 5,789 zloty in 1980 and 11,116 zloty in 1982 (wages were slightly higher in socialised industry). This reflects the 100% inflation rate of 1982. The cost of living rose a further 30% in the first six months of 1983. Real incomes have fallen considerably over the past few years and hardship is widespread. However, there has been a substantial increase in social benefits. A recent increase in alcohol consumption is pointed to by observers as a sign of a disheartened population.

With the lack of goods to buy, personal savings rose to 1,444.7 billion zloty at the end of 1982, showing a 29.8% increase for savings held in banks and a 52.2% rise for retained cash compared with the position at the end of 1981.

**TABLE 7.24   CONSUMPTION OF GOODS AND SERVICES BY THE POPULATION**

| Unit: % of total expenditure | 1980 | 1981 |
| --- | --- | --- |
| Food | 31.1 | 32.5 |
| Alcoholic beverages | 11.7 | 9.9 |
| Non-food items and services | 57.2 | 57.6 |
|   Tobacco | 2.5 | — |
|   Clothes | 9.3 | 10.9 |
|   Housing | 12.3 | 11.6 |
|   Fuel and electricity | 1.1 | 1.0 |
|   Health and welfare services | 6.1 | 6.1 |
|   Culture and education | 10.0 | 9.7 |
|   Sports, tourism | 1.6 | 1.7 |
|   Transport and communications | 8.4 | 8.6 |

Source: National Statistics

**TABLE 7.25   PER CAPITA CONSUMPTION OF FOOD IN 1981**

**Unit: kilogrammes**

| | |
|---|---|
| Cereal products | 130.0 |
| Rice | 2.9 |
| Potatoes | 158.0 |
| Vegetables | 122.0 |
| Fruit | 32.3 |
| Meat | 65.7 |
|   Beef | 15.6 |
|   Pork | 32.1 |
|   Poultry | 11.7 |
| Fish | 7.3 |
| Fats (commercial weight) | 24.6 |
| Milk (litres) | 249.0 |
| Eggs (units) | 230 |
| Sugar | 33.4 |
| Tea (grammes) | 807.0 |
| Spirit/vodka (litres) | 4.3 |
| Beer (litres) | 28.6 |

Source: National Statistics

**TABLE 7.26   PER CAPITA CONSUMPTION OF OTHER GOODS IN 1981**

| | |
|---|---|
| Woven fabrics* | |
|   Cotton* (metres) | 22.5 |
|   Wool* (metres) | 3.1 |
|   Silk* (metres) | 5.2 |
| Footwear (pairs) | 3.9 |
| Tobacco products (kilogrammes) | 2.5 |
|   Cigarettes (units) | 2,464 |

Note: * figures are for 1980
Source: National Statistics

**TABLE 7.27   CONSUMER DURABLES OWNERSHIP IN 1981
            BY TYPE OF HOUSEHOLD**

Unit: items per 100 households

|  | Employee | Worker/<br>peasant | Peasant | Pensioner |
|---|---|---|---|---|
| Radio sets | 81.4 | 79.3 | 76.9 | 76.6 |
| Television sets | 109.9 | 102.6 | 88.1 | 91.0 |
| Washing machines/<br>  spin driers | 109.2 | 102.8 | 95.4 | 89.1 |
| Fridges and freezers | 98.0 | 84.0 | 70.3 | 76.5 |
| Vacuum cleaners | 91.5 | 53.8 | 36.4 | 65.4 |
| Electric polishers | 8.1 | 1.8 | 2.3 | 5.1 |
| Sewing machines | 54.1 | 71.3 | 67.0 | 59.9 |
| Bicycles | 87.3 | 145.5 | 124.7 | 32.2 |
| Motorcycles and scooters | 14.0 | 44.2 | 34.1 | 4.9 |
| Cars | 22.0 | 14.7 | 11.6 | 2.7 |

Source: National Statistics

## Health, education

At the end of 1982, there were 204.9 million hospital beds available, compared with 203.5 million at the end of 1981 and 200.8 million at the end of 1980. The numbers of doctors in service were respectively 66,800, 64,900 and 63,600.

At the beginning of the 1982-83 scholastic year, there were: 14,341 first-level schools with 4.5 million pupils and 245,000 teachers; 1,171 general secondary schools with 381,000 pupils and 23,000 teachers and 91 further education establishments (including 10 universities) which had 426,000 students and 54,691 teaching staff.

## Entertainment and tourism

Entertainment facilities in 1982 comprised: 2,089 cinemas (compared with 3,285 in 1970); 96 theatres; 29 concert halls; 19 opera/operetta houses.

There were also 32,900 public libraries with 7.1 million readers.

Tourism facilities include 340,000 tourist beds available. Of these, 47,000 were in hotels, 40,000 were in hostels or pensions, 41,000 were in youth shelters, and 69,000 were in guest houses. Some 3.8 million people stay at hotels each year, 1.8 million use hostels or pensions, 0.5 million use youth shelters and 0.9 million use guest houses (all 1982 figures).

## Transport and communications

In 1982 there were: 27,157 kilometres of railway (7,410 kilometres were electrified); 254,037 kilometres of road (15,000 kilometres had hard surfaces); 110,844 kilometres of bus routes; 90,560 kilometres of airline routes (this is the 1981 figure); 1,975 kilometres of pipeline; and 4,040 kilometres of inland waterway.

The transport stock comprised: 5,134 locomotives (1982); 168,663 railway goods wagons, including 97,209 coal wagons (1982); 2,634,000 passenger cars (1981); 68,000 buses (1981); 641,000 lorries (1981); 1,751,000 motorcycles and scooters (1981); 33 tugs (1982); 389 pusher tugs (1982); 333 self-propelling barges (1982); 1,191 dumb barges (1982); and 97 passenger vessels (1982); while the merchant fleet comprised 317 vessels, including 296 dry cargo vessels and 13 tankers (1982).

**TABLE 7.28   FREIGHT AND PASSENGER TRAFFIC IN 1982**

| Freight traffic* | | Passenger traffic* | |
|---|---|---|---|
| **Unit: million ton-kilometres** | | **Unit: million passenger-kilometres** | |
| Rail | 112,689 | Rail | 49,266 |
| Road | 34,024 | Road | 47,305 |
| Air | 15 | Air | 1,172 |
| Pipeline | 16,647 | Inland waterway | 70 |
| Inland waterway | 1,566 | Sea | 118 |
| Maritime shipping | 191,667 | TOTAL | 97,931 |
| TOTAL | 356,608 | | |

* socialised sector
Source: National Statistics

A 23-kilometre underground metropolitan railway is being built in Warsaw.

Poland has the fewest numbers of telephones per head of population of any European country, and there are 1.2 million subscribers waiting to be connected to the telephone system. Much central switching equipment is old and needs replacing.

## Banking

The Narodowy Bank Polski, the National Bank of Poland, is the central bank, the bank of issue and the central institute for credit, savings, clearing and foreign exchange dealings. It has 49 branch offices in the provinces, and 620 operational branch offices, national savings banks and integrated branch offices.

The Bank Handlowy w Warszawie, the Commercial Bank in Warsaw, is a joint stock company with the participation of state capital. It finances foreign transactions and renders banking services for foreign trade operations. It also finances credits for the Foreign Trade Enterprises.

The Bank Gospodarki Zywnosciowej, the Bank of Food Economy is a mixed, state/co-operative bank, which provides finance and credit services to socialised agriculture and to individual peasant farmers, as well as to the food industry, forestry and water supply sectors.

The Bank Polska Kasa Opieki is a joint stock company authorised to perform banking operations at home and abroad; it participates in operations on the international money and credit markets. It is known as Bank PKO.

The Council of Ministers has been in charge of banking operations since 1981, replacing the Ministry of Finance as the banks' final authority. A Council of Banks has been set up to co-ordinate and supervise banking activities; this council can also help in the drafting of economic plans and advise on monetary and credit policies.

New banks can now be set up, either as state banks, co-operatives, joint state/co-operative ventures or joint stock banks. Foreign banks are permitted to operate in Poland, and Polish banks can operate abroad.

## Poland's foreign debt

Poland is the largest Comecon debtor to the West. Although the external position had improved at the beginning of 1983, Poland's debt totalled $24.8 billion at that date. Western banks are continuing to reschedule Poland's debts. In August 1983 they agreed on a ten-year rescheduling period, the longest ever granted by commercial banks. $1.5 billion of principal and $1.1 billion of interest is now payable over ten years. This followed an earlier agreement in November 1982 when $2.4 billion of debt was rescheduled over seven years.

Poland also owes its Comecon partners — its debt rose to 3.7 billion roubles in 1982. The partners agreed to permit a trade deficit of 80.8 billion zlotys for 1983, but this was not reached.

## Foreign trade

In 1982, Poland achieved a trading surplus of $1 billion, the first overall foreign trade surplus in 13 years. Exports increased 12% compared with their 1981 level, in particular exports to Poland's Comecon partners rose by 23.7%, although exports to the West stagnated. Imports were reduced in 1982 (imports from Comecon rose 3.3%, but imports from the West, due to the lack of hard currency, were cut back by 26%, with imports from the developing countries down 40%). Poland's 1982 deficit with Comecon was reduced to $470 million equivalent, while the surplus with the West was $520 million with the industrialised countries and $960 million with the non-socialist developing countries.

Coal and metals are the mainstay of Polish exports. In 1982 coal exports rose 88% (compared with 1981, which was a disastrous year) to 28.5 million tonnes. Meanwhile, raw materials, semifinished goods and industrial spare parts are becoming an increasingly important part of imports, in order to maintain production levels in Polish industry.

In 1983, Poland's foreign trade surplus grew to $1.5 billion.

**TABLE 7.29   POLAND'S 1983 FOREIGN TRADE TURNOVER**

| Unit: billion zlotys | Exports | Imports | Balance |
|---|---|---|---|
| With Comecon partners | 519.1 | 560.0 | − 40.9 |
| With non-Comecon countries | 538.0 | 401.2 | + 136.8 |

Source: Economist Intelligence Unit

**TABLE 7.30   FOREIGN TRADE 1981-1983**

**Unit: billion zlotys**

|  | 1981 | 1982 | 1983* |
|---|---|---|---|
| Imports | 963.4 | 868.9 | 746.0 |
|   from socialist countries | 529.8 | 549.7 | 476.9 |
|   from non-socialist countries | 433.6 | 319.2 | 269.1 |
| Exports | 846.2 | 951.2 | 824.6 |
|   to socialist countries | 410.6 | 509.5 | 446.8 |
|   to non-socialist countries | 435.6 | 441.7 | 377.8 |
| Balance | − 117.2 | + 82.3 | + 78.7 |
|   with socialist countries | − 119.3 | − 40.2 | − 30.1 |
|   with non-socialist countries | + 2.0 | + 122.4 | + 108.7 |

Note: * January-October only
Source: National Statistics

**TABLE 7.31   FOREIGN TRADE BY AREA IN 1982**

**Unit: %**

| Imports |  | Exports |  |
|---|---|---|---|
| Imports | 100.0 | Exports | 100.0 |
| from socialist countries | 63.5 | to socialist countries | 53.6 |
| from Comecon partners | 59.2 | to Comecon partners | 50.0 |
| from non-socialist countries | 36.5 | to non-socialist countries | 46.4 |
| from developed countries | 30.7 | to developed countries | 32.6 |
| from the EEC | 18.2 | to the EEC | 21.1 |
| from developing countries | 5.8 | to developing countries | 13.8 |

Source: National Statistics

**TABLE 7.32   FOREIGN TRADE BY PRODUCT GROUP 1981-1982**

| Unit: % | 1981 | 1982 |
|---|---|---|
| **Imports** | 100.0 | 100.0 |
| Raw materials* | 10.3 | 11.8 |
| Mineral fuels and derivatives | 17.4 | 21.9 |
| Machinery and transport equipment | 28.6 | 24.4 |
| Materials and chemical products | 7.7 | 9.4 |
| Other industrial products | 15.0 | 18.4 |
| Food, beverages, tobacco | 21.0 | 14.1 |
| **Exports** | 100.0 | 100.0 |
| Raw materials* | 6.7 | 5.8 |
| Mineral fuels and derivatives | 10.5 | 15.4 |
| Machinery and transport equipment | 43.6 | 44.0 |
| Materials and chemical products | 5.1 | 4.8 |
| Other industrial products | 28.0 | 23.7 |
| Food, beverages, tobacco | 6.1 | 6.3 |

* excludes raw materials for food products
Source: National Statistics

**TABLE 7.33   SELECTED IMPORTS/EXPORTS BY PRODUCT**

| | 1980 | 1982 |
|---|---|---|
| **Imports** | | |
| Hard coal (million tonnes) | 1.0 | 1.0 |
| Crude oil (million tonnes) | 16.4 | 13.2 |
| Natural gas (billion cubic metres) | 5.3 | 5.6 |
| Oil products* (million tonnes) | 4.4 | 3.1 |
| Iron ores, crude and dressed (million tonnes) | 20.2 | 13.5 |
| Finished hot rolled products (million tonnes) | 1.0 | 1.0 |
| Passenger cars ('000 units) | 14.9 | 46.8 |
| Lorries, road tractors ('000 units) | 16.8 | 4.0 |
| Potash fertilisers (million tonnes) | 2.4 | 2.4 |
| Pharmaceutical products (billion zlotys**) | 0.9 | 18.6 |
| Wheat for consumption and fodder (million tonnes) | 3.5 | 3.6 |
| Barley for consumption and fodder (million tonnes) | 1.1 | 0.1 |
| Maize for consumption and fodder (million tonnes) | 2.5 | 0.4 |

Continued...

193

**Table 7.33 continued...**

|  | 1980 | 1982 |
|---|---|---|
| **Exports** | | |
| Hard coal (million tonnes) | 31.0 | 28.5 |
| Coke (million tonnes) | 1.8 | 1.7 |
| Oil products* (million tonnes) | 1.6 | 0.6 |
| Finished hot rolled products (million tonnes) | 1.8 | 1.4 |
| Copper ('000 tonnes) | 145.0 | 176.0 |
| Tools (billion zlotys**) | 0.4 | 5.8 |
| Metalworking machinery ('000 pieces) | 7.4 | 5.9 |
| Goods wagons and vans ('000 pieces) | 6.8 | 4.3 |
| Passenger cars ('000 pieces) | 113.0 | 67.8 |
| Buses ('000 pieces) | 6.2 | 4.8 |
| Sugar ('000 tonnes) | 24.0 | 163.0 |
| Alcoholic spirit ('000 hectolitres) | 283.0 | 226.0 |
| Footwear (million pairs) | 25.0 | 17.5 |
| Ships ('000 dwt) | 364.0 | 334.0 |

* includes synthetic liquid fuels; ** at current prices
Source: National Statistics

## TABLE 7.34   TRADE BY COUNTRY

**Unit: billion zlotys at current prices**

| Imports from | 1981 | 1982 | Exports to | 1981 | 1982 |
|---|---|---|---|---|---|
| USSR | 331.7 | 328.0 | USSR | 221.3 | 285.8 |
| West Germany | 69.9 | 59.6 | West Germany | 83.3 | 76.9 |
| East Germany | 57.2 | 58.4 | Czechoslovakia | 48.3 | 51.0 |
| Czechoslovakia | 49.1 | 50.3 | East Germany | 49.2 | 44.9 |
| France | 46.0 | 34.3 | UK | 31.7 | 34.1 |
| UK | 31.5 | 27.0 | Bulgaria | 21.1 | 29.5 |
| Hungary | 24.9 | 26.9 | Hungary | 23.3 | 28.6 |
| Canada | 19.9 | 25.2 | Romania | 18.5 | 26.2 |
| Romania | 16.3 | 23.0 | France | 23.0 | 26.0 |
| Yugoslavia | 23.6 | 18.7 | Italy | 24.3 | 24.9 |
| Brazil | 38.9 | 18.4 | Yugoslavia | 18.0 | 23.0 |
| Bulgaria | 14.9 | 18.0 | Iraq | 12.8 | 21.7 |
| Austria | 24.3 | 17.3 | Libya | 14.0 | 19.8 |

Continued...

**Table 7.34 continued...**

| Imports from | 1981 | 1982 | Exports to | 1981 | 1982 |
|---|---|---|---|---|---|
| Switzerland | 13.8 | 16.9 | USA | 26.3 | 18.7 |
| Italy | 19.3 | 14.0 | Austria | 15.0 | 15.8 |
| USA | 58.6 | 11.0 | Finland | 12.4 | 14.9 |
| Netherlands | 11.7 | 10.4 | Netherlands | 10.3 | 12.8 |
| Japan | 10.8 | 4.0 | Sweden | 13.5 | 12.0 |
| Total | | | Switzerland | 15.6 | 10.9 |
| (including others) | 963.5 | 862.0 | Belgium | 10.3 | 9.5 |
| | | | Total | | |
| | | | (including others) | 846.2 | 947.4 |

Source: Euromonitor, using Polish trade statistics

Poland is currently a limited market for the West, due to the suspension of credits by all NATO countries after martial law was declared. In early 1984, the United States eased its economic sanctions against Poland, but there is still some way to go to recover normal trading conditions.

Foreign trade has been a state monopoly of the Ministry of Foreign Trade. This ministry formulates trade policy and co-ordinates the work of all the individual organisations involved in foreign trade matters. A series of Foreign Trade Enterprises have up to now been the only entities authorised to negotiate and sign contracts with foreign companies. They have been the intermediaries between suppliers and Polish firms. But with the recent reforms, individual Polish enterprises have been given the right to undertake their own foreign trade dealings, and it is expected that this will lead to a greater development of trade.

Poland alone among Comecon countries allows subsidiaries of non-Polish companies to do business in Poland — there are 252 such foreign-owned units operating.

The Poznan International Fair is one of East Europe's major trade shows. There is an annual exhibition, held in June of each year, covering industrial and consumer goods. There are also specialised shows in October and April.

195

Two new trade and industry fairs have been operating from 1984. One is 'Simmex' — an international exhibition covering mining, energy and metallurgy, held in the steel-making centre Katowice. The other is 'Kooperacja', held in Poznan and catering for smaller companies. Medium and small light industry enterprises are important in Poland, and already this type of firm accounts for 38% of clothing output, 14.5% of chemicals and 18.2% of wood products manufacture.

# Chapter Eight

# ROMANIA

## Introduction

Romania has developed remarkably since the end of the Second World War, from being a backward, agriculturally based economy to one where industry contributes over a half of national income. The emphasis has been on the development of heavy industry, engineering, iron and steel, chemicals and petroleum refining especially, into which a high level of investment has been ploughed by the state.

Romania's President Ceausescu has ruled the country since 1965 and his leadership has been characterised by his maverick and independent stance taken towards Moscow. This is expecially the case with foreign policy as Romania has often not toed the official Warsaw Pact line. Romania has not allowed Soviet manoeuvres to take place on its soil since the 1960s, while President Ceausescu regularly entertains statesmen from many different countries and has even interceded as mediator in foreign disputes. Because of this independent attitude, Romania has been regarded favourably by Western nations and has received loans from many Western sources.

The Romanians themselves live under a strict, highly centralised and often corrupt regime however, and despite the economic achievements made during the last forty years, they have the lowest standard of living in Eastern Europe and Romania is often still classified as a 'developing' as opposed to a 'developed' country.

## Economic growth and National Income

Romania experienced rapid economic growth in the post-war period as it developed from an agriculturally based economy to an industrial one. Growth rates have settled in recent years, especially since the mid-1970s when serious problems arose in the country's external trade position. The country also had to contend with natural disasters in the form of flooding and an earthquake in 1977 and a poor harvest in 1980.

Since 1980 when an 8.8% increase in Romania's national income was planned but only 2.9% achieved, actual results have never met targets. In 1981 the plan was for an increase of 7% but the result was a 2.2% increase. 1981 was the year when the adjustment programme was implemented in order to improve the chronic balance of payments problem. The programme was helped by a three year standby credit agreed with the IMF which allowed drawings up to a total of SDR 1,102.5 million (US $1.3 billion). The objectives of the programme were to be achieved through demand management policies and structural reforms, and cutbacks in convertible currency imports had to be made in 1981 and 1982.

The policy of demand management stipulates that aggregate expenditure is only allowed to rise at rates compatible with planned rates of improvement on the current account. This implies that deceleration and negative rates of growth in investment and consumption could occur, which in fact happened in 1982 when investment fell by 2.5%. The planned target for growth that year was 5.5% but only 2.6% was achieved, not surprising in view of the decline in investment. The plan for 1983 was for an increase in national income of 5% but only 3.4% was achieved. For 1984 Romania planned a growth rate of more than 7%, which was the most ambitious of any East European country.

National wealth in Romania is calculated in terms of social product and national income. Social product is a gross measure of production and therefore involves a large amount of double-counting. National income is calculated by the production method and is the difference between gross product (social product) and gross national expenditure. In 1982 national income amounted to 628.8 billion lei or 37% of social product. The different sectors contributing towards national income in 1982 were:

| | |
|---|---|
| Industry | 55.7% |
| Construction | 7.4% |
| Agriculture | 19.4% |
| Transport and telecommunications | 6.4% |
| Other (including trade) | 10.8% |
| | |
| TOTAL | 100% |

Source: National Statistics

198

## Economic Planning

As in other communist countries economic planning is organised by the state through a series of Five Year Plans. The present Five Year Plan is different from previous ones in that lower growth rates are planned all round, e.g the planned increase in national income for 1981-85 is to total 41.1% compared with 69% for 1976-80.

Targets have been set for different sectors of the economy and investment funds for the plan have been allocated to what is considered to be necessary to achieve these targets. A sum of 1,131 billion lei has been allocated for the years 1981-85, an increase of 28.8% over previous years.

**TABLE 8.1   INVESTMENT ALLOCATION 1981-1985**

**Unit: billion lei**

| | |
|---|---|
| Industry | 642 |
| Construction | 38 |
| Agriculture | 155 |
| Transport and telecommunications | 113 |
| Science, research and development, trade, catering, tourism | 34 |
| Education, health, culture | 20 |
| Housing | 100 |
| Locally administered services | 29 |
| TOTAL | 1,131 |

Most of the growth in investment funds is to go towards the completion of previously started projects, the modernisation of productive capacity and the construction of housing. The most important ongoing project is the Danube-Black Sea Canal. Targets for various sectors of the economy have been as follows:

*Foreign trade* to grow by an impressive 75.5% during 1981-85. In view of the continuing recession in Western developed countries and the refusal of its Comecon partners to expand trade as much as the Romanians had proposed, the goal is optimistic, but it reflects the determination to reduce the country's foreign debt. Romania is banking on the better export opportunities presented when new productive capacities go into operation at the end of the Five Year Plan but outside credits, either from Western commercial banks or international sources, will be essential in providing the basis for imports of equipment for various projects and these credits are becoming more difficult to obtain than in the past.

*Industrial production* has an overall growth target of 44%. The completion of a number of investment projects is to take place during 1981-85 which will encourage rapid growth. An improvement in labour productivity is seen as a major contributor to industrial growth.

The engineering sector is planned to achieve an above average growth rate of 52.5% or 8.8% per annum. The most rapid growth will be in the construction of machine tools, for which a new ministry is to be created. The overall target is an increase of 145%, to be achieved through the construction of 12 new factories for machine tool production and the modernisation of 12 existing factories. In addition the output of auto-mated installations is to double, while that of precision instruments and electrical and optical products is to rise by over 2.5 times.

Chemicals and petrochemicals, which will absorb 16% of total invest-ment, are expected to expand by 62.7% or 10.2% per annum. Concentra-tion will be centred on the production of more sophisticated and less raw materials-intensive chemicals. The metallurgy industry is planned to increase at a slower rate of 44.7% overall.

*Agriculture* is planned to increase its output by 24.5%-27.5%, reflecting the actual growth rates of 1976-80. The success of this target is very difficult to predict because of agriculture's dependence on the climate and its vulnerability to drought and flooding. The aim is for this sector to expand export earnings as well as satisfy home demand.

*Fuels and raw materials* Total output of fuels is to increase by 33.5%, with coal experiencing the greatest leap, from 35.2 million tonnes mined in 1980 to 85.6 million tonnes planned for 1985. Oil and natural gas extrac-tion are to increase slightly. The main priority for this industry is the search for new deposits of oil, lignite and metal ores.

*Electric energy* is planned to increase by 22.3% to 82.5 billion KWh by 1985.

*Living standards* Real incomes are planned to grow by 19% in 1981-85, only half the level planned for 1976-80. In spring 1981 the President proclaimed 'a new agricultural revolution' which would improve supplies to the population. The new agricultural plan calls for annual per capita consumption of the following foodstuffs: 82.5 kg of meat and meat products; 250 litres of milk; 300 eggs; 10 kg fish; 125 kg wheat; 15 kg corn; 185 kg vegetables; 100 kg potatoes; 87 kg fruit and grapes.

This will be difficult to achieve if agriculture does not fulfill its targets, since food for export, especially to hard currency areas, will tend to have priority over supplies to the Romanian population if the foreign trade objectives are to be met.

Romania's Five Year Plan targets are notorious for being over ambitious and already it seems likely that many of the targets set for the current 1981-85 plan are unlikely to be met judging by results so far.

**TABLE 8.2   MAIN ECONOMIC INDICATORS**

Unit: % change over previous year

|  | 1982 Planned | 1982 Actual | 1983 Planned |
|---|---|---|---|
| National income | 5.5 | 2.6 | 5.0 |
| Investment | 5.0 | − 2.5 | 0.7 |
| Industrial production (gross) | 4.7 | 1.1 | 6.6 |
| Agricultural production | 6.0/7.9 | 7.5 | 5.0/5.6 |
| Retail sales, nominal | 4.6 | 12.5 | 3.0 |
| Real wages | 1.5 | − 7.4 | 4.8 |
| Exports | n/a | − 9.5 | 18.2 |
| Imports | n/a | − 24.2 | 8.0 |

**Population and workforce**

Romania's population in July 1982 amounted to 22.48 million, of which 49.3% were males and 50.7% females. The population is growing at a rate of about 0.7% per annum with 17 live births and 10 deaths per thousand. There is a relatively high percentage of ethnic minorities, the largest of which are Hungarians who account for about 8% of the population (approximately 1.8 million) followed by Germans (2% of the total) and Turks (1.6%).

The population density is 95 people per square kilometre and around half of the population lives in towns and half in rural villages. The capital, Bucharest, is the largest city, with a population of 2.21 million, followed by Prahara (852,000), Dolj (767,000), Isasi (765,000), Cluj (742,000) and Timis (711,000).

Romania's working population in 1982 amounted to 10.43 million, the largest percentage of whom work in industry, followed by agriculture, a marked contrast to the situation in 1950 when nearly three quarters of the labour force were employed in agriculture. 37% of workers are women.

**TABLE 8.3   EMPLOYMENT BY BRANCHES OF THE NATIONAL ECONOMY**

| Unit: % | 1982 | 1950 |
|---|---|---|
| Industry | 36.5 | 12.0 |
| Construction | 7.7 | 2.2 |
| Agriculture | 28.6 | 74.1 |
| Forestry | 0.4 | 0.2 |
| Transport | 6.2 | 1.9 |
| Telecommunications | 0.8 | 0.3 |
| Trade | 5.9 | 2.5 |
| Municipal services, education and arts | 4.1 | 2.3 |
| Science and scientific services | 1.1 | 0.2 |
| Public health | 2.8 | 1.1 |
| Administration | 0.6 | 1.7 |
| Other branches | 1.4 | 0.8 |
| TOTAL | 100.0 | 100.0 |

Source: National Statistics

In 1982 average monthly earnings amounted to 2,525 lei, but there were differences between various sectors, with workers in the construction industry receiving the highest remuneration.

Romanians work longer hours than any others in Eastern Europe with most people working a six-day week. In July 1982 the working week was reduced from 48 to 46 hours, and it is planned to reduce this to 44 hours in 1985.

**TABLE 8.4  AVERAGE NET REMUNERATION OF PERSONNEL BY BRANCHES OF THE NATIONAL ECONOMY**

**Unit: lei monthly 1982**

| | |
|---|---|
| Industry | 2,540 |
| Construction | 2,880 |
| Agriculture | 2,454 |
| Forestry | 2,088 |
| Transport | 2,665 |
| Telecommunications | 2,217 |
| Trade | 2,157 |
| Municipal services | 2,272 |
| Education and arts | 2,492 |
| Science and scientific services | 2,719 |
| Public health | 2,347 |
| TOTAL | 2,525 |

Source: National Statistics

## Industrial activities

During the previous Five Year Plan (1976-80) industrial production increased at an average annual rate of 9.5%, but this level has not been achieved during the current Five Year Plan. The target has been for an average increase of 7.5% per annum but in fact only a 2.6% increase was achieved in 1981 and 1.1% in 1982, the lowest increase since the war. This decline in growth can be partly attributed to the cutback in imports in 1981 and 1982 which squeezed supplies of raw materials to industry, while constraints on the use of energy also affected industrial output, especially in the ferrous metallurgy and chemical sectors.

The planned increase in gross industrial production for 1983 was 6.6% and results indicate an increase in output of 4.8%. The largest contributor to this increase was mechanical engineering which increased its output by 7% in 1982 and carried this trend over into 1983.

All industrial activity is either run by the state or by co-operatives. The total number of industrial enterprises in 1982 amounted to 1,820, employing 3.33 million people.

**TABLE 8.5   NUMBER OF ENTERPRISES AND PERSONNEL BY TYPE OF OWNERSHIP AND CATEGORY IN 1982**

|  | No. of enterprises | Personnel employed ('000) |
|---|---|---|
| State industry | 1,384 | 3,018 |
| National industry | 1,362 | 2,993 |
| Local industry | 22 | 25 |
| Co-operative industry | 436 | 311.5 |
| TOTAL | 1,820 | 3,330 |

Source: National Statistics

### Engineering

Engineering is the largest industrial sector and supplies over 75% of domestic requirements of machinery and 25% of exports. Within engineering, machine building and vehicle production are the largest branches, together contributing about 35% of total industrial output.

The machine building industry achieved a growth rate of 6.9% in 1982, well above the overall industrial production rate and has benefited from considerable investment for the expansion and modernisation of existing plant and improving the quality and technical level of products. Priorities for this sector are to expand the industry to supply up to 80-85% of the equipment and installations needed for the implementation of the present Five Year Plan and to double exports of equipment by 1985. New production facilities are being installed for the development of electronics, and electrical engineering, machine tools, precision engineering, optics, hydropower and pneumatic equipment. The country's plans for self-sufficiency in energy also mean that there is increased demand for equipment for the mining and oil industries and nuclear power stations to be manufactured.

The vehicle industry is based on the manufacture of tractors, trucks and passenger cars. At Pitesti, Dacia passenger cars have been assembled since 1968 under licensed agreement with Renault, and in 1983 the car was improved to promote exports. In a joint venture with Citroen, Oltcit cars have begun to be produced at Craiova.

The aircraft industry, which is based around Brasow and Baneasa, gained a new lease of life in 1980 with the co-production agreement with British Aerospace where BAC 1-11 jet aircraft are built under licence in Romania.

The electronics and electrical engineering industry accounts for about a quarter of total engineering output. One of the most important products made is high voltage equipment for the National Grid. The electronics sector produces the Felix C256, a third generation universal computer.

A number of sectors have been ear-marked for fast development with the engineering sector. These include fine mechanics, machine tools, advanced computers, electrical machinery, robots, electrical guidance and control equipment, heavy trucks and seagoing cargo.

**TABLE 8.6   OUTPUT OF PRINCIPAL ENGINEERING PRODUCTS 1982**

|  | Actual 1981 | Plan 1982 | Actual 1982 |
|---|---|---|---|
| Industrial machinery and equipment (billion lei) | 24.8 | 27.0 | 24.0 |
| Machine tools (billion lei) | 8.8 | — | 8.1 |
| Automation equipment and computers (billion lei) | 8.1 | 6.8 | 8.0 |
| Precision engineering, optics, hydraulic and pneumatic installations (billion lei) | 8.1 | 10 | 9.7 |
| Tractors ('000) | 74 | 85 | 80 |
| Cars ('000) | 80 | 120 | 89 |
| Bicycles ('000) | — | — | 261 |
| Seagoing ships ('000 dwt) | — | 814 | 393 |
| Household electrical apparatus and appliances (million lei) | 2.6 | 2.6 | 2.6 |
| Washing machines ('000) | — | — | 372 |
| Refrigerators ('000) | — | — | 431 |
| Vacuum cleaners ('000) | — | — | 138 |
| Radio sets ('000) | — | — | 599 |
| Television sets ('000) | — | — | 412 |

Source: National Statistics

### Chemicals

The chemical industry contributed about 8.7% of total industrial output in 1980, a decline from the 11.2% share in 1975. Petrochemicals are by far the most important individual sector within this industry, accounting for half of total chemical output. Pitesti is Romania's most important petrochemical centre, its oil refinery is one of the largest industrial enterprises in Romania and it supplies about 10% of the country's annual requirements.

The petrochemical industry grew rapidly during the late 1970s and increasing supplies of crude oil had to be bought in from abroad as domestic oil production declined. The massive increase in OPEC oil prices hit Romania's balance of payments hard and led to a slowdown in imports of crude oil and some of Romania's substantial refining capacity had to be made redundant.

More recently imports of other raw materials have been cut back and this has forced the chemical industry to reduce the production of bulk chemicals and to concentrate on more sophisticated smaller volume products. Development plans for this sector include the production of new plastics and chemical fibres and developing special materials for electronics and other high technology areas. Output of inorganic chemicals is expected to increase, together with pharmaceuticals, dyes, detergents, cosmetics and perfumes in an effort to reduce imports and increase exports. Production of fertilisers is also planned to increase to meet the needs of agriculture.

**TABLE 8.7   OUTPUT OF CERTAIN CHEMICAL PRODUCTS IN 1982**

|  | Actual 1981 | Plan 1982 | Actual 1982 |
|---|---|---|---|
| Mineral fertilisers (million tonnes) | 2.6 | 3.5 | 2.7 |
| Synthetic rubber ('000 tonnes) | — | 207 | 137.5 |
| Artificial fibres ('000 tonnes) | 205 | 226 | 224 |
| Plastic materials and synthetic resins ('000 tonnes) | n/a | — | 591 |
| Medicines (million lei) | n/a | — | 4,600 |
| Hydrochloric acid ('000 tonnes) | n/a | — | 360 |
| Soda ash ('000 tonnes) | n/a | — | 870 |
| Caustic soda ('000 tonnes) | n/a | — | 760 |

206

## Ferrous metallurgy

The iron and steel industry and iron ore extraction account for over 7% of total industrial output in Romania. The steel industry is centred around the Huendoara region of Banat near the iron ore deposits, although there are other production facilities at Resita and Galati on the Danube.

The production of steel has traditionally been given high priority and a substantial amount of investment is being channelled into the installation of new productive facilities. At Galati, one of the world's largest furnaces went into operation in 1981 and a new mill with a capacity of 4 million tonnes is being built at Calarasi, due for completion in 1985. Production of steel is planned to increase to between 25 and 27 million tonnes in 1990 compared with the 13 million tonnes produced in 1982, a disappointing year. Not only is quantity planned to increase but also quality, and Western technology has been imported to develop the production of specialised steel products at an efficient level instead of the low-grade steel produced at high cost in the past. According to the 1981-85 Five Year Plan all domestic requirements should be supplied by the metallurgical industry.

**TABLE 8.8  OUTPUT OF THE PRODUCTS OF THE METALLURGICAL INDUSTRY IN 1982**

|  | Actual 1981 | Plan 1982 | Actual 1982 |
|---|---|---|---|
| Steel (million tonnes) | 13 | 14.2 | 13 |
| Rolled steel products (million tonnes) | 9.6 | — | 9.3 |
| Steel pipes (million tonnes) | n/a | — | 1.4 |
| Crude iron ores (million tonnes) | n/a | — | 2.1 |
| Pig iron (million tonnes) | n/a | — | 8.6 |

## Other industries

The food processing industry accounts for about 13% of total industrial output and is an important earner of foreign exchange, particularly hard currency. Large canning and preserving facilities have been developed to process agricultural goods for export and there are plans to increase the output of this sector through diversification of production and the construction of storage facilities. The food industry had a good year in 1982

207

but output of the industry is very much dependent on the results of agriculture. Other important export industries include textiles, and ready made clothing, which has been a steady earner of hard currency but is now facing stiff competition from Asian producers in its traditional markets. The export of furniture to the West is also an important foreign currency earner, in 1980 Romania was the sixth largest exporter of furniture in the world.

**TABLE 8.9   OUTPUT OF CERTAIN LIGHT INDUSTRIAL PRODUCTS IN 1982**

|  | Actual 1981 | Plan 1982 | Actual 1982 |
|---|---|---|---|
| Wooden furniture (billion lei) | 15.3 | 17.1 | 16.4 |
| Woven fabrics (million sq.m) | n/a | 1,292 | 1,153 |
| Footwear (million pairs) | n/a | 122 | 107 |
| Hosiery goods ('000) | n/a | — | 336 |
| Meat and meat products ('000 tonnes) | 1.3 | 2.1 | 1.1 |
| Sugar ('000 tonnes) | 661 | 844 | 600 |
| Wine (million litres) | 1.02 | — | 1.32 |
| Beer (million litres) | 0.97 | 1.17 | 0.99 |

Source: National Statistics

**Agriculture**

Agriculture still employs a relatively high proportion of the population, just under 30% at present, although this is a marked decline from earlier years, for example 65% of the population were employed in agriculture in 1960. The proportion working on the land is expected to decline still further (only 10-15% predicted by 1990) as the exodus from the villages to the towns continues, although measures are being taken to encourage young and skilled workers to settle in rural areas. Productivity in agriculture is very low since a large proportion of the workforce are either old or very young with few skills.

Of the total amount of agricultural land in Romania (14.96 million hectares), 66% is classed as arable, 30% pastureland and meadow and 4% vineyards and orchards.

Cultivation of the land is undertaken by three different sectors, with co-operatives accounting for 60% of total agricultural land, state farms 30%

and individual farmers the remaining 10%. The co-operatives and state farms produce the bulk of the grain produced, but 50-60% of total fruit, egg and milk production and 35-45% of meat and grapes produced is from the private sector.

After two poor years of results, 1982 proved to be a good year for agriculture with increases achieved in most products. This was explained by favourable weather conditions and reforms in the wage system whereby workers are now only guaranteed about one third of their previous wage, the remainder is based on results.

The increase in output in 1982 was due largely to an increase in output of vegetables, since although cereals increased by 11.5% to 22.3 million tonnes they did not achieve the planned increase of 20%. Other products achieving significant increases were sugar beet, late potatoes, outdoor vegetables, fruit and grapes. Because of lack of fodder animal production failed to reach the 1982 target.

**TABLE 8.10   AGRICULTURAL PRODUCTION 1982**

**Unit: '000 tonnes**

| | |
|---|---:|
| Cereals | 22,334.9 |
| *of which:* | |
| Wheat and rye | 6,505.3 |
| Barley | 3,052.0 |
| Oats | 91.3 |
| Sorghum | 19.7 |
| Rice | 45.7 |
| Maize | 12,620.2 |
| Pulses | 205.5 |
| Fibre crops | 186.6 |
| Oilseed crops | 1,214.2 |
| *of which:* | |
| Sunflower seeds | 846.7 |
| Sugar beet | 6,647.3 |
| Potatoes | 5,005.6 |
| Vegetables | 4,881.4 |
| Fodder crops | 24,959.6 |
| Fruit | 1,696.3 |
| Grapes | 2,192.2 |

Source: National Statistics

**TABLE 8.11   LIVESTOCK PRODUCTION IN 1982**

| | |
|---|---:|
| Total meat ('000 tonnes live weight) | 2,230 |
| Beef | 458 |
| Pork | 1,029 |
| Poultry | 571 |
| Milk (thousand h/l) | 46,145 |
| Wool (tonnes) | 38,596 |
| Eggs (millions) | 7,155 |
| Honey (tonnes) | 16,048 |

Source: National Statistics

The results for 1983 were as high as 1982 however, although it was planned to increase by 5.1 to 5.6%, because of the severe drought which hit the country during the year.

The agricultural sector is constantly criticised by the government and the President for its failures to meet domestic demand. Because of the importance of agricultural products for export, cut-backs to the domestic market are made if harvest results are poor, and rationing has already been introduced for many foodstuffs. Romania's fluctuating and disappointing agricultural results have been attributed to a variety of reasons including the vagaries of the weather, lack of incentives, low productivity of the workforce, organisational difficulties leading to bottlenecks and shortages and the need for greater mechanisation and irrigation. In the latter case for example, the amount of land under irrigation has been around 2 million hectares for many years.

In an attempt to improve this situation a National Agricultural Programme was approved on 1 July 1983 and is planned to be introduced gradually up to the year 1990. One of the objectives is to increase the area of agricultural land from 14.96 million hectares to 15.01 million hectares by 1985 through land reclamation in the Danube delta and the increased use of natural grasslands. The amount of irrigated land is to be increased (to 5.5-6 million hectares in 1990) as is the use of soil correctives and chemical fertilisers, while prevention of soil erosion and land reclamation will also boost the area of land available. The cost of implementing these measures has been put at 100 billion lei. After similar ambitious programmes implemented in the 1970s with targets which could not be met, the same fate may fall on this programme, especially in view of the present economic situation.

Around 27% of Romania's land area is covered in forests, an area which has declined since former years. Romania has now become conscious of the economic value of its forests and in March 1983 a Council of Forestry was established which has responsibility for the afforestation and preservation of forests and maintaining the good condition of pastureland in forests for the rearing of livestock.

## Minerals

Romania possesses deposits of oil, natural gas, lignite, salt, manganese, iron ore and bauxite. There are also supplies of gold, zinc, copper, tin and uranium available in commercial quantities. These minerals have been important in helping the industrialisation process but supplies of these raw materials to industry have been increasingly difficult to guarantee as deposits become more expensive to exploit.

During the 1981-85 plan priority is being given to the development of domestic raw materials and to reducing the need for imports. New mines for the extraction of copper, iron ore, titanium, vanadium and other ores are being opened, as well as increasing development of existing mines and deposits. The objective is for self-sufficiency in non-ferrous metals by 1985, but this seems over ambitious, when in 1980 only 27% of the domestic demand for zinc, 60% of copper demand and 77% of the demand for lead was met by domestic production.

## Energy supplies

Romania has been fortunate in possessing extensive supplies of coal, oil and natural gas of its own and this has led to the pursuit of an energy policy independent of the Soviet Union, but which later created chronic difficulties for the economy.

Romanian oil production reached a peak in 1977 when 14.7 million tonnes was produced and by which time a substantial refining industry had been established. Between 1977 and 1980 imports of oil had to be increased to offset the decline in domestic supplies such that by 1980 imports of oil amounted to 16 million tonnes. Most of these imports were from OPEC countries, as Romania had cut itself off from the advantageous Comecon system whereby other Comecon countries bought oil from the Soviet Union in roubles, by refusing to join wholeheartedly the

Comecon specialisation programme in the 1960s. The OPEC oil price rises wrought havoc on Romania's external trade position and it was in the position of making a foreign exchange loss for every barrel imported, refined and re-exported. Oil imports have been cut back since 1980 and measures have been taken to help solve the problem. These include increasing domestic oil production from 11.7 million tonnes in 1982 to 13.5 million tonnes in 1983, 14 million tonnes in 1984 and 15 million tonnes in 1985. Most of this increase is from new and deeper well drilling. Drilling is being extended from 6,000 to 8,000 metres and offshore exploration is taking place in the Black Sea, which it is hoped will start commercial production in 1984-85. Another move has been to encourage conservation through higher petrol prices and limits on Sunday driving. Conservation measures are also being introduced into industry which accounts for 65% of all energy consumed in Romania. Finally oil imports will be cut, although by how much is not certain and will depend to a certain extent on world crude and product prices.

The essential aim is to reduce the amount of electricity generated by oil and gas from 50% in 1981 to 5% in 1990, and to increase supplies from other sources.

**TABLE 8.12   SOURCES OF ELECTRICITY GENERATION**

| Unit: % | | |
|---|---|---|
| | **1981** | **1990** |
| Hydroelectric | 18.0 | 23.7 |
| Nuclear | — | 21.6 |
| Coal | 25.0 | 41.2 |
| Oil/Gas | 50.0 | 5.2 |
| Solar/biomass geothermal | 1.8 | 4.3 |
| On-site industrial generation | 5.2 | 4.0 |
| TOTAL | 100.0 | 100.0 |

Source: Romanian Ministry of Power

An increase in coal production will play a crucial role if this plan is to be fulfilled. Ambitious plans have been made to increase coal production during the 1981-85 plan. A target of 87 million tonnes has been set for 1985 but this may be difficult to achieve in view of the fact that only 37.9

million tonnes was produced in 1982, although the plan was for 44 million tonnes. In order to achieve this increase in output there is to be an expansion in mechanisation and 35 new mines, both opencast and under-ground, opened between 1982 and 1985. The industry is hampered by poor conditions underground however, several serious accidents have severely hampered production, and together with pits flooding, poor equipment and too few skilled workers the targets set seem unlikely to be fulfilled.

Natural gas has been an important source of domestic fuel and in 1982 37 billion cubic metres was produced, while 1.5 billion cubic metres was imported from the Soviet Union in payment for co-operation in the construction of the Orenburg pipeline. It is expected that output of gas will decline in the future as reserves run out and coal and nuclear power become more important energy sources for power production, such that gas will be used mainly as a raw material, especially for the chemical industry.

Nuclear energy is planned to fill a large part of the gap left by oil and gas in energy production. Two Candu reactors are being built by Canada at Cernavoda, the first one of which is planned to be onstream by 1985, although the Canadians think 1988 is more probable. Eventually, Romania hopes to build more Candu type reactors by themselves and have reached an agreement with the Soviet Union for the supply of three 1,000 MW reactors. By 1990 it is hoped over one fifth of energy will be supplied by nuclear sources.

Hydroelectric power is also expected to increase its share of the total and in addition Romania is actively engaged in developing alternative energy supplies such as biomass and solar energy, in the latter case in a joint project with Bulgaria.

President Ceausescu has said he believed that Romania could be self-sufficient in energy by 1985 or shortly after. This seems highly unlikely at the present, but at least priority has now been given to Romania's energy supplies, which has been one of the more pressing problems of the economy.

**Electricity**

Nearly 69 billion KwH of electricity was generated in 1982, falling short of the target of 74.1 billion KwH planned for the year and slightly less than

213

the amount produced in 1981 of 70 billion KwH. Half of this is generated from oil and gas, and as already mentioned in the previous section it is planned to reduce Romania's dependence on these sources of fuel in favour of coal, nuclear energy, hydroelectric power and alternative energy sources.

By 1990 the plan is for 110 billion KwH to be generated, achieved through investment in thermal power stations, the introduction of new technology, the continuation of scientific research and exploration of new resources and an improvement in management in the energy sector.

During the 1981-85 plan, new power plants to increase capacity by 7,920 MW are being constructed. 2,500 MW of this will be derived from hydropower while the remaining capacity will be based on coal, bituminous shales and recycled sources. A further 9,850 MW is to be installed during the 1986-1990 Five Year Plan.

**Construction**

The construction industry has been allocated a very small percentage of investment for the 1981-85 plan, around 3% or 38 billion lei with more emphasis placed on housing than construction of capital projects. The growth in this sector is planned to be very modest with no new projects planned, only the completion of ongoing projects, with the most important being the completion of the Danube-Black Sea Canal. In comparison with sluggish home demand, Romanian construction abroad is expanding rapidly. Co-operative ventures with developing countries have been agreed and a number of important industrial and civil engineering projects have been entered into in Western Europe.

**Transport**

There has been a rapid increase in the use of road transport both for freight and passenger transport in recent years, and this is now the most popular form of transport for both types of traffic. In 1982 there were 73,363 kilometres of roads in Romania, of which 14,675 kilometres were described as motor highways and national roads. Around 479 million tonnes of freight was carried by road in 1982, nearly 60% of the total, while 72% of total passenger traffic was accounted for by road transport.

214

The amount of freight carried by rail increased up until 1980, since when there has been a slight decline. Around a third of all freight is carried by rail and just over a quarter of all passenger traffic. In 1982 Romania had 11,125 kilometres of railway track, of which 2,772 kilometres was electrified.

The amount of freight carried by water transport is about 3.9%, but this is expected to increase with the completion of the Danube-Black Sea Canal link. The Canal will handle 80 to 100 million tonnes of freight annually. This could be increased still further as a result of the recent decision by West Germany to complete the canal link between the Rhine and the Danube which should boost considerably the amount of traffic using the Danube.

Around 2% of Romania's freight is also transported via pipeline.

## Government and society

The Romanian Communist Party is the only political party in Romania. President Nicolae Ceausescu has been the party leader since 1965 during which time he has increased his own personal rule. His wife Elena Ceausescu has recently been appointed as first deputy Prime Minister in addition to her other government and party positions. The Romanian economy is run directly by the party through a highly centralized system via government ministries.

Romanian society exists under a harsh repressive regime. There is a large secret police force in addition to the corrupt civil police force.

It is difficult for most Romanians to get permission to emigrate and attempts to make this even harder were announced in January 1983 under a new decree whereby all emigrants would have to repay the cost of their education before they were allowed to leave. The figures were put at $3,700 for secondary school graduates and $3-4,000 per academic year for university graduates. This had to be paid in hard currency, and since most Romanians are not able to hold hard currency this meant that assurances had to be made by friends and relatives in the West that the money would be paid. The scheme was described in Romania merely as a means of discouraging skilled workers from emigrating which the country could ill-afford to lose, but was interpreted in the West as an infringement of human rights. The United States threatened to withdraw its 'most favoured nation' tariff treatment on Romanian goods which it was estimated would cost Romania $200 million in lost export earnings in 1983 alone. In addition relations with West Germany were strained as a result of this announcement, as there has been an unwritten agreement between the two countries that 100,000 ethnic Germans would be allowed to leave annually. A few months later Romania agreed to drop these restrictions in order to retain its tariff benefits from the US.

### Incomes, prices and consumer expenditure

In Romania's efforts to develop its economy, especially its industry, the Romanian consumer tended to be neglected when it came to policy decisions, as priority has been given to re-investment of national income in industrial projects. Romanians have the lowest standard of living in Eastern Europe, except for Albania, when measured in terms of ownership of consumer durables. They have the lowest number of passenger cars per capita and the same number of telephones overall as Bulgaria and Hungary although Romania has twice the population of these two countries. Within Romania there has been an increase in the number of consumer durables owned in recent years but the present economic plan is unlikely to provide the impetus to enable Romania to catch up with other countries.

During the 1976-80 plan, real personal incomes were expected to rise modestly by 18-20%, which would be supplemented by an increase in state contributions to pensions, children's grants, scholarships and free medical assistance. The actual results for the Five Year Plan fell short of this goal.

The target for 1981-85 has been set for an increase of 19% overall, or 3.5% per annum. The officially reported figure for 1981 was of an increase of only 2.2%. During 1982 real household incomes declined by 5.3% and real wages by 7.4% as the austerity measures of the adjustment programme agreed with the IMF began to take effect. The main reason for this drop in real incomes was a sudden and large increase in consumer prices, which was not compensated for by an increase in wages. The volume of retail sales did not fall as much as the decline in wages as consumers reduced their savings to meet their needs.

The plan for 1983 was for an increase in real terms in both earnings and household incomes, but on 1 September 1983 a pay system was introduced which could have affected the chances of this being achieved. Previously there had been a guaranteed minimum wage, a worker would definitely

216

receive 80% of his salary and the remainder would be based on productivity. Since the introduction of the new system, this guaranteed level of 80% has been abolished and all of a worker's pay will depend on the performance of the factory. This is not a relaxation by the state of its grip on industry, however, since every worker will receive a document stating what they are expected to achieve and will then have to sign an undertaking to abide by the production schedules.

This new scheme will no doubt mean that some workers will lose their jobs in uneconomic factories, but this will not lead to widespread unemployment since laid off workers are promised jobs in either a similar enterprise or a different type of enterprise within the same Ministry. The new scheme is not designed to increase labour mobility, in fact the opposite will occur. For the first five years in a new job, part of a new recruit's bonuses are compulsorily held in a savings account for them. Should employees leave before five years they forfeit the savings made plus part of their pension and also have to reimburse the firm for the cost of their training.

The main aim of the scheme is to increase labour productivity through increased incentives. Low productivity is one of the major problems affecting Romanian industry. Productivity has only increased by 2% per annum in the 1980s so far, after 6% per annum rise in the 1970s. Although there has been plenty of investment in modern machinery, factories are highly wasteful of energy and the rigidity of the highly centralized planning and management system has not helped. It is thought likely, by outside sources, that this new pay system will do little to help productivity since Romania's pricing system also needs to be reformed, but a result of the new system will be that some workers will benefit from higher pay packets but wages for many will fall.

In the five years up until 1982 consumer prices in Romania had increased at a slow rate of between 1 and 2% per annum. The adjustment programme of 1981 included an exchange rate and price reform to align Romania's prices with world market price movements so during 1981 producer prices in agriculture and industry were raised. In 1982 retail prices were increased, with food prices up by 35% and petrol by 20%. The result was an increase of 16% in the consumer price index. Other recent price rises made in order to align Romanian prices with world prices was the doubling of the price of crude oil on 1 January 1983 and a 50% increase in the price of natural gas in October 1983. This is expected to have increased the consumer price index by 5.7% in 1983.

217

**CONSUMER PRICES**

| Unit: average annual % increase | | | | |
|---|---|---|---|---|
| **1978** | **1979** | **1980** | **1981** | **1982** |
| 2.0 | 1.9 | 1.5 | 1.8 | 16.0 |

Source: International Financial Statistics (IMF)

The supply of consumer goods to the Romanian public has often been neglected and shortages of a wide range of basic food and manufactured goods are frequent. Basic food items have had to be rationed and in 1984 these rations had to be reduced still further because of the poor harvest of 1983 and the need to keep up the supply of food products for export. Meat rations were cut by 15% and flour by 13%, while milk, cooking oil and sugar supplies were also reduced, although shortages of these products already existed in many areas.

Food and beverages account for the highest percentage of household expenditure as seen in the following table:

**TABLE 8.13   CONSUMER EXPENDITURE IN 1980**

| Unit: % breakdown | |
|---|---|
| Food and beverages | 45.7 |
| Clothing and footwear | 17.6 |
| Housing: | 10.3 |
| Rent | 1.9 |
| Fuel, electricity and gas | 4.6 |
| Other expenditure | 3.8 |
| Provision of household goods, maintenance, furniture | 8.0 |
| Medicines and medical care | 0.9 |
| Transport and telecommunications | 8.7 |
| Culture and education | 5.5 |
| Other expenses | 3.3 |
| TOTAL | 100.0 |

Source: National Statistics

## Housing

Housing has been given a priority rating during the present Five Year Plan with 100 billion lei allocated for this purpose. There has been a steady increase in the number of dwellings built during the last decade, with some financed by the state and some privately. In 1981 and 1982, 325,000 new apartments and houses were built, while for 1983 the plan was for 180,000 dwellings to be built, of which 150,000 were to be built using state funds.

## Health

Health care, as in other Eastern European countries, is provided by the state. In 1982 there were 210,000 beds available for medical care (93 per 10,000 inhabitants) and there were 44,030 doctors (511 inhabitants per doctor), including 7,285 dentists.

## Education

Standards in education have improved considerably since the introduction of compulsory schooling in the late 1960s. There are 16,500 schools and educational institutions in Romania and 4.6 million pupils. During the academic year 1980-81 there were 193,000 students enrolled in 134 university level facilities, half of which were economics or technically biased.

In an attempt to increase the supply of skilled workers and technicians to industry a combination of general and vocational training is offered to students and in some cases apprenticeships are attached to secondary schools to provide skilled labour at the school-leaving age.

During the past two years there have been drastic cuts in higher education and the number of students has fallen by a quarter. The range of subjects offered has been severely cut and all humanities faculties have been abolished. It is thought that the reason for this was a short-term answer to the drastic reduction in the allocation of investment funds for education but this could well have repercussions in the future. Intense competition for investment funds in general led to the cut back in investment funds available for scientific research, education, culture, health and related fields from 5,500 million lei in 1982 to 710 million lei in 1983.


### Recreation and tourism

The establishment of sports associations in factories, villages, universities and schools since the post-war period has helped increase sporting activities in Romania, especially among the young. There are now over 7,000 sports associations with over 2 million members in Romania.

In contrast to many other countries, cinema and theatre audiences in Romania are continuing to increase, reaching their highest levels ever in 1982. This is probably because television is less widespread here than in other places. In 1982 there were 172 television subscriptions per 1,000, a steady increase since the mid-1960s when television was introduced.

The tourist industry has largely been centred around the Black Sea coast which Romania has extensively developed to cater for the package holiday industry to attract visitors from other Eastern European countries and the West. In 1981, 7 million foreign tourists visited Romania, most of whom were from Yugoslavia, Hungary, Bulgaria and Czechoslovakia. The one million Western tourists were largely from West Germany and Scandinavia. Romania is keen to encourage Western visitors to holiday there in order to increase earnings of hard currency and in July 1983 the lei was devalued against major Western currencies for tourists.

Other areas in Romania are also being developed to attract visitors, including the Carpathian mountains, Transylvania, the Danube delta and the country's spa resorts through the building of new roads, hotels and skiing facilities.


### Foreign trade and payments

Improving its external trade position has become Romania's most important economic priority, over-riding many other objectives, in order to reduce its indebtedness to the West. During 1981 and 1982 Romania enjoyed a trade surplus on its current account, a result of stringent measures taken by the authorities after the serious difficulties experienced in the years beforehand. Since the mid-1970s Romania's import bills increased alarmingly, due largely to the increase in both the amount of crude oil imported and an increase in international oil prices. By 1980 Romania's deficit on its current account was over $2.4 billion, most of which was in convertible currency, while its foreign debt had increased three and a half times between 1976 and 1980 to reach nearly $10 billion in 1980. The adjustment programme introduced at the start of 1981 and supported by a three-year standby credit agreed with the IMF in June 1981, aimed at reducing the current account deficit gradually to $1.8 billion in 1981 and $1.4 billion in 1982. A net outflow of short-term capital in 1981 of nearly $1.5 billion meant a change in plans and convertible currency imports were cut by 13%. A small trade surplus was achieved in 1981 of $100 million, although the current account balance was still in deficit albeit less than previously.

The trade surplus was increased still further in 1982 to $1.8 billion, through another reduction in imports, by 24%, although exports also fell, by 9.5%. The convertible currency trade account showed a surplus of $655 million in 1982.

**TABLE 8.14   ROMANIA'S CURRENT ACCOUNT**

| Unit: US $billion | 1978 | 1979 | 1980 | 1981 | 1982 |
|---|---|---|---|---|---|
| Exports fob | 8.02 | 9.30 | 11.02 | 12.37 | 11.56 |
| Imports fob | − 8.63 | − 10.52 | − 12.68 | − 12.26 | − 9.75 |
| Trade balance | − 0.61 | − 1.22 | − 1.66 | 0.10 | 1.8 |
| Services (net) | − 0.15 | − 0.44 | − 0.76 | − 0.94 | − 0.77 |
| Current account balance | − 0.76 | − 1.65 | − 2.42 | − 0.83 | 1.04 |

Source: International Financial Statistics (IMF)

Continued...

**Table 8.14 continued...**

**Current account, convertible currencies**

| Unit: US $billion | 1978 | 1979 | 1980 | 1981 | 1982 |
|---|---|---|---|---|---|
| Exports fob | 4.04 | 5.36 | 6.50 | 7.22 | 6.24 |
| Imports fob | − 4.63 | − 6.52 | − 8.04 | − 7.01 | − 4.71 |
| Trade balance | − 0.59 | − 1.16 | − 1.53 | 0.20 | 1.53 |
| Services (net) | − 0.19 | − 0.51 | − 0.87 | − 1.02 | − 0.87 |
| Current account balance | 0.78 | − 1.67 | − 2.40 | − 0.82 | 0.66 |

Source: International Financial Statistics (IMF)

The plan for 1983 was for a surplus of nearly $650 million in convertible currencies and for the overall trade balance to be similar to 1982's. For the first five months of 1983 it has been reported that imports were down again on 1982 and exports had increased slightly, although a number of products were still having difficulties selling on Western markets including steel, textiles, clothing and electric motors.

The deficits of earlier years led to an increase in the country's foreign indebtedness such that by the end of 1982 gross foreign debt in hard currency was $9.7 billion, although this has now been reduced gradually. During 1983 Romania managed to negotiate an agreement with 170 Western banks to reschedule 70% of the payments it was due to pay in 1983 (around $860 million).

Up until 1982 around 60% of Romania's total foreign trade tended to be with developing and developed countries in the West. With the sharp cut back in imports of convertible currencies in 1982 this proportion fell to just over half and this trend continued into 1983.

**TABLE 8.15   PRINCIPAL SOURCES AND DESTINATIONS OF IMPORTS AND EXPORTS IN 1982**

Unit: %

|  | Exports | Imports |
|---|---|---|
| USSR, Eastern Europe, China | 47.2 | 51.5 |
| Developed countries | 30.3 | 21.0 |
| Developing countries | 22.5 | 27.4 |

**TABLE 8.16   EXPORTS BY DESTINATION IN 1982**

Unit: billion lei

| | |
|---|---|
| Soviet Union | 25.8 |
| West Germany | 12.1 |
| GDR | 6.9 |
| Iran | 6.7 |
| China | 6.5 |
| Switzerland | 5.7 |
| Italy | 5.2 |
| Poland | 5.0 |
| USA | 4.9 |
| France | 4.7 |
| Czechoslovakia | 4.6 |
| Hungary | 3.7 |
| Greece | 3.3 |
| Egypt | 3.2 |
| UK | 2.9 |
| Netherlands | 2.7 |
| Bulgaria | 2.5 |

Source: National Statistics

Total exports in 1982 amounted to 151.8 billion lei, a fall of around 9% over 1981. The largest export category was machinery and transport, followed by fuel and mineral raw materials and industrial consumer goods.

**TABLE 8.17   EXPORTS BY COMMODITY GROUP**

| Unit: billion lei | 1982 | % of total |
|---|---|---|
| Machinery, equipment and transport | 46.7 | 33.0 |
| Fuel, mineral raw materials, metals | 39.5 | 24.1 |
| Chemicals, fertilisers, rubber | 15.5 | 9.9 |
| Building materials and fittings | 3.6 | 2.2 |
| Non-food raw materials and processed products not included already | 6.9 | 4.3 |
| Raw materials for foodstuff production | 4.0 | 2.4 |
| Foodstuffs | 11.0 | 7.3 |
| Industrial consumer goods | 24.7 | 16.8 |
| TOTAL | 151.8 | 100.0 |

Source: National Statistics

In 1982 total imports into Romania amounted to 124.9 billion lei, a fall of around 24% compared with 1981, which was largely in imports from convertible currency countries. Besides being the largest destination for exports, the Soviet Union is also Romania's single largest supplier of imports.

**TABLE 8.18   PRINCIPAL SOURCES OF IMPORTS IN 1982**

**Unit: billion lei**

| | |
|---|---|
| Soviet Union | 23.6 |
| GDR | 7.6 |
| Syria | 6.1 |
| West Germany | 6.1 |
| Poland | 5.2 |
| China | 5.1 |
| Iraq | 4.6 |
| Czechoslovakia | 4.5 |
| Libya | 4.3 |
| USA | 3.8 |
| UK | 3.3 |
| Hungary | 3.2 |
| Egypt | 3.2 |
| Bulgaria | 2.7 |
| Saudi Arabia | 2.6 |

Source: National Statistics

The largest single import category was fuels, mineral raw materials and metals which accounted for nearly a half of all imports in 1982 followed by machinery, equipment and transport with just over a quarter.

# Chapter Nine

# YUGOSLAVIA

## Introduction

Yugoslavia is an uncharacteristic East European Communist Bloc country, with a foot in both Eastern and Western camps. It is the most Westernised of the East European states, and is far less rigid than its fellows in its political and economic dealings. Membership of the Communist Bloc grouping Comecon (or CMEA, the Council for Mutual Economic Assistance) is at associate level only, so Yugoslavia neither benefits from all the facilities available to full members nor is bound by Comecon policies; associate status was taken up in 1964. Yugoslavia is also an associate member of the OECD, the Organisation for Economic Co-operation and Development, which is a Western-based international body.

Yugoslavia is a leader of the world's non-aligned countries. It is courted by both West and East. The pledge of further Western economic aid has been promptly countered by promises from Soviet Prime Minister Nikolai Tikhonov to raise crude oil shipments to Yugoslavia; additionally China has provided a hard currency deposit for Yugoslav use. But no political strings are accepted and independence is retained.

Yugoslavia is also uncharacteristic among Communist countries in that its government central planning system indicates what should be done, rather than directs what must be done (as happens elsewhere in the Communist world).

A high inflation rate and considerable unemployment (15% of the workforce in mid-1983) also set the country apart from its East European neighbours; this is an illustration of how its relatively open economy is affected by Western trends. The government's economic policies aim to ease these and other pressing problems.

226

## The country's composition

Yugoslavia is a socialist (communist) federal republic. Its name was officially changed in the April 1963 constitution to 'The Socialist Federal Republic of Yugoslavia', 'SFRY' (or 'SFRJ' — J for Jugoslavia). The country consists of: 6 republics — Serbia (Srbija), Croatia (Hrvatska), Bosnia-Herzegovina (Bosna i Hercegovina), Macedonia (Makedonija), Slovenia (Slovenija) and Montenegro (Crna Gora); and 2 autonomous provinces — Kosovo and Vojvodina, both attached to Serbia, which is the largest constituent republic.

Altogether there are 18 nationalities coexisting within Yugoslavia's frontiers. Unfortunately frictions exist between different regional groups, with central government stabilisation programmes sometimes going against regional interests. The present government is now working out a proper balance between the powers which are appropriate at federal and republican levels, a task neglected during the later Tito years. Regional income disparities exist. In the 'rich north', Vojvodina has a per capita gross national product which is 121% of the Yugoslov average, Croatia has 126% and Slovenia 198%. Serbia has 96% but accepts no money from the regional fund. In the 'poor south', Kosovo's per capita GNP is at the national average, Bosnia-Herzegovina's is 66%, Macedonia's is 65% and Montenegro's is 80%; all receive money from the central regional fund.

There have been sporadic eruptions of discontent in Kosovo, whose ethnic Albanian majority demands to leave Yugoslavia, claiming independent republican status; riots have been suppressed, often bloodily, but tensions still run high. The claim is unrealistic and, while the difficulties are acknowledged, the Prime Minister declares that none of the constituent nationalities sees a future for itself outside Yugoslavia. In Bosnia-Herzegovina, meanwhile, there is Moslem nationalism. Here some 40% of the republic's ethnically Slav population of 3.8 million have availed themselves of their constitutional right to declare themselves of Moslem nationality.

## The political scene

The long years of rule by President Tito, ended by his death in 1980, were followed by the splitting up of presidential power, with authority vested in an eight-man collective state presidency, which holds power for five

227

years. This collective style of leadership had been prescribed by Tito. The post of President of the Presidency rotates annually among the eight members, and the incumbent is effectively Head of State.

The Prime Minister (Head of the Federal Executive Council) is Mrs Milka Planinc, who has held this office since April 1982. Her influence has been considerable. She is Yugoslavia's 'iron lady' and her tough-line policies, with their emphasis on economic and not political measures, tackle important issues which are expected to put the country's house in order.

But central authority has been somewhat weakened since Tito's death, and increasing regionalism, already evident in Tito's lifetime, is now seen. Under the 1974 constitution all economic power is vested in the republics, leaving the federal authorities unable to impose their own programme.

In a general context, the only political party which is permitted to operate is the League of Communists of Yugoslavia (LCY). The party exerts its influence at all levels of society.

### Geography and population

Yugoslavia has 225,000 square kilometres of territory. Its land is fertile, the climate is favourable — 'mediterranean' on the coast and 'continental' inland — and it has important natural resources: rich soil, large timber reserves, coal deposits (mostly brown coal and lignite), iron and non-ferrous metal ores, non-metallic minerals and refractory materials, building stone, a large hydroelectricity potential and oil and gas. Much of the country is mountainous and not too well suited to industrial development. The main lowland area is in the north-east, in Vojvodina and north Serbia. Yugoslavia suffers from earthquakes and much damage was sustained in the 1979 Montenegro disaster. The 1963 Skopje earthquake killed over 1,000 people.

The population is growing steadily, although the rate of growth is slowing.

**TABLE 9.1   YUGOSLAV POPULATION (mid-year figures)**

| Unit: million people | 1980 | 1981 | 1982 |
|---|---|---|---|
| Birth rate per 1,000 inhabitants | 17.0 | 16.7 | — |
| Population of working age* | 14.44 | 14.50 | 14.60 |
| TOTAL POPULATION | 22.30 | 22.47 | 22.65 |

\* 15-59 years for women, 15-64 years for men
Source: National Statistics/UN

An estimate of 22.85 million is given for mid-1983, and by 1985 there will be 23.2 million Yugoslavs.

The industrial regions in the technically advanced north-west, around Ljubljana, Rijeka and Zagreb, and the north-east, around Belgrade and Novi Sad, are where the main concentrations of population are to be found.

Both the Roman Catholic and the Eastern Orthodox churches have strong followings, the Croats being predominantly Roman Catholic, and the Serbs Orthodox. There is also a sizeable Moslem population. Bosnia-Herzegovina and Serbia were for centuries part of the Ottoman Empire, which ruled over vast tracts of Southern Europe, Asia Minor and the Middle East. The Turks left a strong cultural impact, which is still seen in the more southerly parts of the country.

Serbo-Croat is the principal language of Yugoslavia. It is the first language in Serbia, Croatia, Bosnia-Herzegovina and Montenegro. Both the Latin and Cyrillic alphabets are used — Latin in Croatia, Bosnia-Herzegovina and Slovenia, and Cyrillic in Serbia, Montenegro and Macedonia. The Slovenes and the Macedonians have their own languages, in addition to speaking Serbo-Croat. These three are the official languages. Also, in Kosovo Albanian is spoken, whilst German is known by many in the north and west parts of the country.

Belgrade (Beograd) is the capital. The main cities of each constituent republic/autonomous province are listed here, with population figures and a selection of their industrial activities:

| Republic/province | City | Population | Industries |
|---|---|---|---|
| Serbia | Belgrade | 1,470,100 | machinery, printing, chemicals, drugs, textiles, foodstuffs |
| Croatia | Zagreb | 855,600 | machinery, machine tools, electrical and electronic goods, chemicals, textiles, tobacco |
| Bosnia-Herzegovina | Sarajevo | 448,500 | machinery, tobacco, textiles, wood, furniture, motor vehicles |
| Macedonia | Skopje | 504,900 | tobacco, chemicals, machinery, non-metallic mineral products |
| Slovenia | Ljubljana | 305,200 | machinery, chemicals, textiles, electrical and electronic goods |
| Montenegro | Titograd | 132,300 | aluminium smelting, agriculture |
| Vojvodina | Novi Sad | 257,700 | machinery, textiles, printing, foodstuffs, cables |
| Kosovo | Pristina | 210,000 | electric power, mining, cables, building materials |

Other major industrial centres are: Maribor — machinery, textiles, electrical equipment, foodstuffs; Nis — tobacco, machinery, textiles, rubber products; Rijeka — oil refining, shipbuilding, machinery, paper, wood; Split — shipbuilding, chemicals, building materials; Kranj — electronics, rubber goods, footwear.

## Workforce

There were 6.16 million workers in paid employment in the socialised sector in September 1983, out of the total workforce of around 14.6 million (1982 figure):

230

**TABLE 9.2 EMPLOYED WORKFORCE IN SOCIALISED SECTOR**

| Unit: '000 workers | 1981 | 1982 | Sept 1983 |
|---|---|---|---|
| *Economic activities* | | | |
| Industry and mining | 2,242 | 2,313 | 2,398 |
| Agriculture and fishing | 200 | 210 | 228 |
| Forestry | 63 | 65 | 67 |
| Water supplies | 18 | 18 | 19 |
| Construction | 622 | 612 | 598 |
| Transport and communications | 408 | 416 | 425 |
| Trade | 596 | 608 | 626 |
| Catering and tourism | 210 | 215 | 229 |
| Crafts and personal services | 172 | 177 | 183 |
| Municipal services, housing, utilities | 113 | 115 | 120 |
| Financial and other services | 204 | 209 | 217 |
| *Non-economic activities* | | | |
| Education and culture | 410 | 416 | 421 |
| Health and social services | 325 | 339 | 352 |
| Social and political organisations | 263 | 268 | 270 |
| TOTAL | 5,846 | 5,980 | 6,155 |

Source: National Statistics

Unemployment is a major problem, in sharp contrast to other communist countries, where it does not exist. In mid-1982, there were 830,000 people looking for work, and in mid-1983 there were 915,000 unemployed, representing 15% of the total workforce; 75% of those unemployed in 1983 were under 30 years old. For 1984, an increase in the unemployment figures to 1,300,000 was forecast.

## Economic organisation

Yugoslavia describes itself as a 'socialist market economy'. Its economic system is unique to itself. In the years immediately following the Second World War, a centrally-planned economy was operated, but an innovative system of self-management has been evolving ever since the 1950s.

This has sought to avoid the inefficiencies and weaknesses inherent in a centrally-administered Soviet-type economy. Yugoslavia's present system has more in common with Western economies than with East European states.

A limited amount of planning takes place, which is of an indicative type, not directive as in most of Eastern Europe. Planning is at three levels: an annual plan, called an 'Economic Resolution', a medium-term five-year plan (the current one is 1981-85), and a long-term general guide.

The discrepancy between what a plan sets as its target and what is likely to be achieved is seen in the following table:

**TABLE 9.3   ECONOMIC PERFORMANCE EXPECTED IN 1983**

| Unit: % change vs 1982 | Government's 1983 plan | OECD estimate |
|---|---|---|
| Consumer expenditure | − 6 | − 1.75 |
| General and collective consumption | 0.25 | − 0.5 |
| Fixed investment | − 20 | − 10 |
| Final domestic demand | − 10 | − 4 |
| Stockbuilding | − 1 | − 0.5 |
| Total domestic demand | − 10 | − 4.25 |
| Foreign balance | 2.75 | 2.25 |
|    Exports of goods and services | 8.75 | 2 |
|    Imports of goods and services | − 4.25 | − 7 |
| Statistical discrepancy | 7.75 | — |
| Social product* | 1 | − 1.5 |
|    Industry | 2 | − 1.25 |
| Memorandum items: | | |
|    Merchandise exports (volume) to | | |
|       convertible currency areas | 20 | 7 |
| Employment | 2 | 1.5 |
| Productivity | − 1.25 | − 3 |
| Cost of living | — | 35 |

\* also known as GMP, Gross Material Product
Source: OECD

The economy operates under a socialist self-management system, where much political and economic responsibility is devolved down through the

232

republics and districts to grass roots level. The basis of this system is the OOUR, Osnovna Organizacija Udruzenog Rada (Basic Organisation of Associated Labour). An OOUR may be one plant, or a single unit among many plants in a larger grouping. In the latter case, the factory will be a RO, Radna Organizacija (Work Organisation). A number of ROs may be merged to form a SOUR, Slozena Organizacija Udruzenog Rada (Group or Joint Organisation of Associated Labour). All industrial enterprises are socially owned (i.e. they belong to society as a whole), and are not state owned. All are managed by their workers. Each factory has its own workers' council to manage the plant, while any major decision will be taken by the whole workforce. In socialist countries, self-management enterprises never go bankrupt; when they accumulate debts, they just owe the banks. Previously, when debts reached a critical level, the slate was wiped clean by the government, but this time the country is paying the real price of borrowing at an international level.

The Yugoslavs are proud of their worker self-management system, and are constantly striving to improve, criticising its operation and making frequent changes.

### Economic progress

Yugoslavia is still a 'developing' country and is in gradual transition to 'fully developed' status; its economy is fragile. It was primarily an agrarian nation at the end of the Second World War, and since then industrialisation has been continuous.

Generally the country's economy is in poor shape. Although output of coal, electric power, iron and steel and basic chemicals was increasing during the first six months of 1983, in many other important sectors such as consumer goods, rubber products and construction, output was falling. Industrial capacity is often under-utilised, due to lack of equipment and raw materials — much of these are imported, and funds to buy them are limited. Import cuts have been a recent feature of government policies.

Yugoslavia has a large foreign debt, and its inability to keep up regular payments has drawn international attention to its economic problems. Were it not for the need for special financial provisions and conditions, Yugoslavia would have remained content to muddle through its own problems within its fragmented economy.

233

The economy is stagnating, and living standards are declining. From a growth rate of an average 6% per year in the 1970s, and 7.3% per year in the 'boom' years of 1976-1979, growth fell to only 0.3% in 1982 and no recovery is likely to have taken place in 1983 or 1984. The five-year plan has been revised and additional austerity measures have been taken.

**TABLE 9.4  PLANNED RATE OF ECONOMIC GROWTH**

Unit: % change/year

|  | 1981 plan | 1981 actual | 1982 plan | 1981-85 original | 1981-85 revised |
|---|---|---|---|---|---|
| Social product | 3.0-3.5 | 2.0 | 2.5 | 4.5 | 2.5 |
| Fixed investment | − 5.0 | n/a | − 6.0 | 1.5 | n/a |
| Industrial output | 4.0 | 4.0 | 3.5 | 5.0 | 3.4 |
| Agricultural output | 4.0 | 1.0 | 4.0 | 4.5 | 3.3 |
| Productivity | 1.3 | 1.3 | n/a | 2.0 | n/a |
| Exports of goods and services in real terms | 4.0 | 12.0 | 8.5 | 8.0 | 8.7 |
| Imports of goods and services in real terms | − 7.0 | − 5.0 | 0.0 | 1.1 | 2.4 |
| Total domestic demand | n/a | − 5.0 | − 2.0 | 2.25 | 0.5 |
| Employment (socialised sector) | 2.0 | 3.0 | 2.0 | 2.5 | 2.2 |
| Real net earnings (per employee, socialised sector) | n/a | − 5.0 | 0.0 | 2.0 | − 0.25 |

The heavy foreign debt burden is central to Yugoslavia's economic problems. Net foreign indebtedness was $18.2 billion at the end of 1982. This debt results from the rapid inflationary growth of the 1970s. In complying with the conditions requested by the International Monetary Fund which provides ongoing financial support to ease the debt burden, the Yugoslav government succeeded in greatly improving the country's export performance in the first quarter of 1983 — but at the price of squeezing internal demand.

Austerity measures include substantial price increases. The administered prices system is to be abolished, and prices will be gradually aligned with world market levels. Coal prices have been raised 25%, electricity

25%, train fares 35% and petrol 30%. Consumer credit has been tightened with new monetary policies. But the government has not been able to bring inflation under control — a 20% target for 1983 was not achieved, the yearly rate had already reached 40% in the 12 months to September 1983. Real wages fell 10% in the first quarter of 1983, following declines in previous years.

A combination of rising prices, falling wages and unemployment could lead to social unrest if the government does not slacken this pace of adjustment.

**TABLE 9.5  INDEX OF PRICE MOVEMENTS**

| Unit: December of previous year—100 | Dec 1979 | Dec 1980 | Dec 1981 | Dec 1982 |
|---|---|---|---|---|
| *Industrial products* | | | | |
| Retail prices | 123.0 | 140.9 | 141.5 | 130.0 |
| Producer prices | 115.4 | 139.6 | 137.4 | 124.7 |
| *Agricultural products* | | | | |
| Retail prices | 125.5 | 141.4 | 136.0 | 144.7 |
| Producer prices | 123.6 | 140.7 | 138.4 | 137.8 |
| Services | 123.6 | 124.1 | 127.0 | 119.7 |
| General index of retail prices | 124.1 | 139.1 | 139.3 | 130.7 |
| Cost of living | 123.1 | 137.3 | 136.2 | 132.7 |

Source: National Statistics

Already some strikes, strongly disapproved of in any communist country, have occurred. There were 174 strikes in 1982, involving 10,997 workers, mostly due to wage disagreements.

More exports to pay off debts are essential, but better export volume can only be achieved by a greater input of raw materials and intermediate goods, and these have largely to be imported. In their export drive, Yugoslav companies have, on the whole, been slow to take up the commodity credits which are increasingly available from Western governments.

Private foreign investment is actively sought by the government to enhance exports, and to acquire modern technology. Joint ventures with a foreign partner are the preferred form of direct foreign investment. The United States, West Germany and Italy are all large-scale investors in Yugoslavia.

Long term economic stabilisation is the government's aim, and its harsh new programme of price increases and cutting down on consumer demand was approved at the end of July 1983. Exports are to provide the main stimulus to the economy, since both capital investment and private consumption will fall. Self management responsibilities are to be increased. Loss-making enterprises may be closed, while greater freedom is to be given to small businesses. There were 200,000 small businesses operating in 1982, and small business currently accounts for 2.5% of GSP, gross social product (also known as GMP, gross material product). Small business is an area which is seen to have vast unused potential for economic good, and expanding it could pay big dividends. Small businesses are flexible enough to grow quickly, and could attain 15-20% of GSP. They could employ 1.5-2 million people, compared with the 500,000 they currently employ, and this would substantially ease the unemployment problem. To create a job in industry costs 1.5 million dinars, while for the same cost five jobs could be created in small business. Yugoslav workers abroad are being encouraged to return and invest their foreign exchange savings in small production and service facilities — incentives include duty free privileges up to a certain value. Estimates of nationals working abroad vary, from 450,000 to 800,000. Most of these are in West Germany.

These measures are the work of the Commission for the Problems of Economic Stabilisation, known as the Kraigher Commission — Sergei Kraigher is Slovenia's member of the collective state presidency.

Yugoslavia's GMP, gross material product, was 2,915 billion dinars in 1982. Gross material product equates with: net material product *plus* capital consumption, *less* non-productive services. The 'GMP' calculation differs from the internationally-used, Western UN/OECD 'system of national accounts' and therefore direct comparisons with other countries' data cannot be made. Yugoslavia's 'material product system' of calculating designates a large group of services as 'non-material' or 'unproductive', and these are deemed not to generate value-added but only to result in a redistribution of the value-added generated by the 'productive' industries — this is the most important difference between the two systems. The Yugoslav gross material product (also called 'social product')

236

is estimated to be about 14-15% lower than the normally-used GDP, gross domestic product. (The non-productive services are: services rendered to individuals, fees paid to self-employed professionals, and goods produced and consumed by private farmers or sold on farmers' markets.)

**TABLE 9.6   YUGOSLAVIA'S SOCIAL PRODUCT***

|  | billion dinars, current prices | billion dinars, constant** prices |
|---|---|---|
| 1978 | 901.8 | 347.8 |
| 1979 | 1,165.4 | 372.3 |
| 1980 | 1,553.1 | 380.9 |
| 1981 | 2,208.3 | 386.6 |
| 1982 | 2,924.8 | 388.2 |
| 1983 (preliminary) |  | 383.1 |

* social product = gross material product; ** using 1972 prices
Source: National Statistics

**TABLE 9.7   COMPOSITION OF SOCIAL PRODUCT IN 1982 (at 1972 prices)**

| Unit: % of total | |
|---|---|
| Agriculture, forestry, fishing | 15 |
| Manufacturing, mining | 40 |
| Building, construction | 10 |
| Transport, communications | 8 |
| Trade and tourism | 17 |
| Other (crafts, municipal services etc.) | 10 |

**TABLE 9.8   ECONOMIC RESULTS, KEY INDICATORS**

**Unit: % change vs year earlier**

|  | 1980 | 1981 | 1982 | 1983* |
|---|---|---|---|---|
| Industrial output | 4.2 | 4.3 | 0.1 | 0.0 |
| Construction (hours worked) | − 2.2 | − 4.0 | − 3.0 | − 3.0 |
| Volume retail sales | 1.0 | − 5.7 | 1.9 | − 1.0 |
| Volume retail stocks | 0.7 | − 6.9 | 5.0 | 0.0 |
| Producer prices, industrial | 27.3 | 45.1 | 25.0 | 24.2 |
| Retail prices, total | 30.4 | 47.1 | 29.5 | 31.2 |
|    Industrial goods | 31.6 | 49.3 | 28.6 | 29.3 |
|    Agricultural goods | 34.1 | 38.9 | 43.8 | 47.9 |
|    Services | 22.7 | 29.9 | 20.3 | 22.1 |
| Cost of living | 30.3 | 40.8 | 31.7 | 34.1 |
|    Food | 31.5 | 42.9 | 38.8 | 42.5 |
| Net average earnings, total | 20.5 | 33.6 | 27.4 | n/a |
|    Business | 20.9 | 35.0 | 27.4 | n/a |
|    Government | 18.9 | 27.5 | 27.9 | n/a |
| Real net average earnings, total | − 7.5 | − 5.7 | − 3.3 | n/a |
| Employment (excluding private agriculture) | 3.2 | 2.9 | 2.2 | n/a |

* first quarter only
Source: OECD

Per capita income was $2,932 in 1982, according to World Bank estimates. Foreign exchange reserves were $728 million in September 1983, and gold holdings were 1.86 million fine troy ounces at the same date.

**Manufacturing**

As already mentioned, Yugoslavia is still a 'developing' country, and it is still in the process of transition to 'developed' or 'industrialised' status. Industrial activities (manufacturing, mining, quarrying) accounted for 40% of social product in 1982, compared with 70% in East Germany, one of East Europe's more highly industrialised countries.

Yugoslavia's major manufactured products include: ships, railway wagons and locomotives, lorries, cars, electric and non-electric machinery, textiles (including synthetics), chemicals, petrochemicals, plastics, fertilisers.

Sophisticated engineering products are now produced, thanks to the development of Yugoslav industry and research, combined with the international transfer of technology.

## Metals and metal products

Steel capacity is increasing slowly and at great expense. New facilities costing £1 billion are under construction at the Zenica complex in Bosnia-Herzegovina; these should be on-stream in 1985.

The Boris Kidric Steelworks at Niksic will boost output to 450,000 tonnes of cold steel per year, and 320,000 tonnes of steel products per year when its new technology, currently being installed, is running at full capacity. An electric steel plant with continuous casting process, a blooming rolling mill and a drawing plant are only part of this firm's expansion projects; altogether it produces 250 different types of steel, and 15% of its earnings are from exports.

The Slovene Iron & Steel Works at Ljubljana produces specialist goods and high-grade steel from several different plants. Output was 800,000 tonnes of ingot steel in 1982, 39% of which was produced by the open hearth method and 61% by the electric hearth method (the latter from arc and high frequency furnaces and electroslag remelting processes).

Metalurski Kombinat Smederevo's third oxygen converter has been commissioned and the new 600,000 tonnes per year cold rolled steel expansion has started up. In a second phase, now delayed, probably to 1988, raw steel capacity will rise to 1.65 million tonnes per year. The MKS combine comprises the Smederevo Steel Works and the Heroj Srba Metal Industry, Smederevo.

Unis of Sarajevo plans a 450,000 tonnes per year coal-based Plasmared plant, using the plasma ironmaking process developed by SKF of Sweden, and a 400,000 tonnes per year steelworks.

## TABLE 9.9   YUGOSLAVIA'S IRON AND STEEL PRODUCTION

**Unit: million tonnes**

|  | 1981 | 1982 |
|---|---|---|
| White pig iron | 2.6 | 2.5 |
| Grey pig iron | 0.3 | 0.3 |
| Raw steel | 4.0 | 3.9 |
| Raw steel, convertor | 1.4 | 1.3 |
| Raw steel, SM | 1.5 | 1.5 |
| Raw steel, EL | 1.1 | 1.0 |
| Steel castings | 0.1 | 0.1 |
| Rolled products | 4.8 | 4.5 |
| Rolled sheets | 1.0 | 0.8 |
| Seamless pipes | 0.2 | 0.2 |
| Welded pipes | 0.5 | 0.5 |
| Extruded products | 0.6 | 0.5 |
| Ferroalloys | 0.3 | 0.2 |

Source: National Statistics

## TABLE 9.10   OUTPUT OF FERROUS METAL PRODUCTS

**Unit: '000 tonnes**

|  | 1981 | 1982 |
|---|---|---|
| Iron castings | 501.0 | 482.9 |
| Radiators | 58.3 | 52.8 |
| Nails | 45.6 | 50.0 |
| Metal packing containers | 135.1 | 117.8 |
| Roller bearings | 10.9 | 10.5 |
| Metal structures | 635.1 | 621.1 |
| Sewing machines ('000 units) | 127.3 | 132.8 |
| Metal utensils | 22.3 | 20.6 |
| Stoves and cookers ('000 units) | 929.2 | 940.7 |

Source: National Statistics

Copper output from the new Veliki Krivelj mine at Bor will provide sufficient ore to produce 32,000 tonnes of electrolytic copper for 30 years. Other capacity increases will boost output of many of Yugoslavia's other indigenous metals. However, 1982 production lagged behind target among many manufacturers.

**TABLE 9.11   NONFERROUS METALS PRODUCTION**

**Unit: '000 tonnes**

|  | 1981 | 1982 |
|---|---|---|
| Electrolytic copper | 132.6 | 126.9 |
| Refined lead | 86.4 | 81.3 |
| Zinc | 96.4 | 86.8 |
| Aluminium ingots | 196.8 | 246.4 |
| Antimony regulus | 2.2 | 1.9 |
| Refined silver (tonnes) | 138.0 | 104.0 |
| Bismuth (tonnes) | 102.0 | 49.0 |

Source: National Statistics

Actual and projected gold production is calculated:

**TABLE 9.12   YUGOSLAV GOLD OUTPUT**

**Unit: '000 troy ounces**

| 1981 | 140 |
|---|---|
| 1982 | 147 (estimate) |
| 1983 | 152 (projected) |
| 1984 | 159 (projected) |
| 1985 | 166 (projected) |

Source: Metal Bulletin Monthly

### TABLE 9.13   OUTPUT OF NONFERROUS METAL PRODUCTS

**Unit: '000 tonnes**

|  | 1981 | 1982 |
|---|---|---|
| Rolled aluminium products* | 152.5 | 168.3 |
| Rolled copper and copper alloy products | 118.7 | 119.1 |

* as far as known
Source: National Statistics

### TABLE 9.14   OUTPUT OF SELECTED BUILDING AND NON-METAL MINERAL PRODUCTS

|  | 1981 | 1982 |
|---|---|---|
| Cement (million tonnes) | 9.8 | 9.7 |
| Cut stone and marble (million metres$^2$) | 2.1 | 2.1 |
| Gravel and sand (million metres$^3$) | 26.6 | 24.9 |
| Lime (million tonnes) | 1.9 | 1.8 |
| Hollow brick* (million units) | 3.2 | 3.3 |
| Tiles (million pieces) | 0.4 | 0.4 |
| Asbestos cement products (million tonnes) | 0.4 | 0.4 |
| Asbestos fibre and asbestos goods ('000 tonnes) | 13.6 | 11.7 |
| Unwrought magnesite ('000 tonnes) | 300.0 | 328.0 |
| Salt (tonnes) | 418 | 428 |
| Light construction boards (million metres$^2$) | 7.8 | 6.9 |
| Roofing felt and bituminous products (million tonnes) | 0.1 | 0.1 |
| Flat glass (million effective metres$^2$) | 15.7 | 17.5 |
| Blown glass (million tonnes) | 0.4 | 0.5 |
| Refractory materials (million tonnes) | 0.7 | 0.7 |
| Ceramics, household ('000 tonnes) | 17.7 | 19.3 |
| Ceramics for construction use ('000 tonnes) | 416.5 | 407.4 |
| Porcelain, electric ('000 tonnes) | 7.8 | 7.1 |

* standard pattern
Source: National Statistics

## Machinery and equipment

One of Yugoslavia's leading manufacturers of machinery and equipment is Unis of Sarajevo (United Metal Industries — Sarajevo). This organisation manufactures 700 different products for 300 branches of technology. It has 42 factories and a further nine under construction. It employs 38,000 workers and had a $300 million turnover in 1982. Unis undertakes technical co-operation and other exchanges with 42 companies worldwide. Among its products are: cars and car parts, roller bearings, bicycles, office equipment, electronic equipment, machine tools and consumer goods.

**TABLE 9.15  YUGOSLAVIA'S MACHINERY OUTPUT**

| Unit: '000 tonnes | 1981 | 1982 |
|---|---|---|
| Construction equipment | 71.3 | 63.3 |
| Metalworking and woodworking machinery | 46.3 | 49.3 |
| Other industrial machinery | 193.4 | 204.6 |
| Agricultural machinery | 147.2 | 168.0 |
| Marine motors ('000 units) | 16.6 | 12.8 |
| Rotating machinery (million kW) | 5.4 | 4.4 |
| Transformers (million kVA) | 12.6 | 11.4 |
| Cables | 146.7 | 155.1 |
| Other electricity conductors | 32.3 | 33.3 |
| Accumulators | 72.6 | 76.3 |
| Electricity meters | 1.7 | 1.8 |

Source: National Statistics

## Advanced technology

The Nis Semiconductor Factory, known as Ei-Nis (Electronic Industries — Nis) has started up Yugoslavia's first production of integrated circuits, under licence from RCA (US), a world renowned manufacturer of these products. First-phase output from the factory is to be used for computers, professional electronics, telecommunication systems, electro-medical equipment, auto electronics and similar applications. Yugoslavia will be able to achieve world standard product quality without import dependency and the huge currency expenditures which imports entail. CMOS digital electronic circuits will be the first type of microelectronic components to be manufactured here. Some 2 million integrated circuits per year, in ceramic housing, will be the plant's initial capacity. Full capacity will be reached in 1985: 15-17 million integrated circuits per year, worth 500-600 million dinars at mid-1983 prices. 50% of output will be exported. Investments at Ei-Nis have totalled 330 million dinars to date, and a further 320 million is to be spent. The second phase of development is larger, and will be undertaken with a local partner.

**Transport equipment**

The country's main manufacturer of vehicles is Crvena Zastava, which is located in Kragujevac (Serbia). 1982 output lagged behind target, and in 1983 some 215,000 vehicles were produced, compared with an original target for the year of 270,000. Of this 1983 output, 172,300 were passenger cars (40,000 exported — many to the UK, which is Zastava's fastest-growing export market). Zastava manufactures under licence from Fiat of Italy. It was Fiat's first East European plant, and was set up 30 years ago. Output to date totals 2.5 million vehicles, 2.3 million of which are cars. The Tam organisation at Maribor (also other locations) is another transport equipment manufacturer. It produces commercial vehicles (lorries, buses and off-road vehicles, railway carriages, wagons and dollies). It also makes heating equipment — Tam supplies 60% of all Yugoslavia's central heating boilers — small machinery, tools and forgings. Its 1982 exports reached $50 million.

Shipbuilding is also important. The country's yards were fully employed during 1982, in contrast to yards in Western Europe. A $80 million contract was signed in mid-1983 to supply 20 river vessels and 4 tugboats to the USSR — Yugoslavia now has $330 million of contracts for ships from the USSR.

244

**TABLE 9.16   OUTPUT OF TRANSPORT EQUIPMENT**

**Unit: '000 units**

|                                      | 1981  | 1982  |
|--------------------------------------|-------|-------|
| Lorries                              | 17.5  | 16.6  |
| Passenger cars                       | 241.5 | 218.8 |
|   Cars for export          | 54.5  | 54.1  |
| Motors for road transport vehicles   | 260.3 | 287.0 |
| Railway freight cars                 | 2.7   | 3.0   |
| Tractors                             | 54.7  | 52.3  |
| Motorcycles and mopeds               | 74.5  | 71.7  |
| Bicycles                             | 703.1 | 692.5 |
| Dry cargo ships (million grt*)       | 8.0   | 8.2   |
| Dry cargo ships (units)              | 276   | 158   |
| Tankers (million grt*)               | 6.5   | 11.7  |
| Tankers (units)                      | 96    | 165   |

\* gross registered tons
Source: National Statistics

## Chemicals

This is an important industry, and the largest chemicals manufacturer is INA, Industrija Nafte. INA's 'Dina' petrochemical complex on the island of Krk was due to start producing in 1984, with 112,000 tonnes of low density polyethylene. Vinyl chloride monomer will also be produced here from early 1985. The Dina plant will consist of eight units. It was planned originally as a joint venture with Dow Chemicals (US), but Dow later withdrew.

**TABLE 9.17   YUGOSLAVIA'S OUTPUT OF BASIC INDUSTRIAL CHEMICALS**

**Unit: '000 tonnes**

|  | 1981 | 1982 |
|---|---|---|
| Sulphuric acid (million tonnes) | 1.3 | 1.2 |
| Nitric acid (million tonnes) | 0.8 | 0.7 |
| Ammonium nitrate | 22.3 | 30.7 |
| Caustic soda | 177.2 | 169.2 |
| Calcined soda | 147.2 | 181.9 |
| Calcium carbide | 40.4 | 39.0 |
| Phosphate fertiliser | 0.9 | 0.8 |
| Nitrogen fertiliser | 1.5 | 1.5 |
| Plastics, total | 483.4 | 408.8 |
|    PVC powder | 155.4 | 127.4 |
|    Polyethylene | 115.9 | 87.0 |
|    Polystyrene | 42.2 | 30.1 |
| Cellulose fibres | 64.1 | 66.1 |
| Synthetic fibres | 51.0 | 61.2 |

Source: National Statistics

**TABLE 9.18   OUTPUT OF CHEMICAL PRODUCTS**

**Unit: '000 tonnes**

|  | 1981 | 1982 |
|---|---|---|
| Pharmaceutical preparations | 21.8 | 21.7 |
| Soap | 32.4 | 32.0 |
| Detergents | 252.7 | 239.0 |
| Paints | 209.3 | 191.1 |
| Plastic packaging | 137.8 | 133.6 |
| Cellophane packaging | 3.9 | 3.3 |

Source: National Statistics

**TABLE 9.19   OUTPUT OF PETROLEUM PRODUCTS**

Unit: million tonnes

|                    | 1981 | 1982 |
|--------------------|------|------|
| Motor spirit       | 2.4  | 2.6  |
| Diesel fuel        | 3.1  | 3.3  |
| Fuel oil (mazout)  | 5.6  | 5.4  |
| Lube oils          | 0.4  | 0.4  |

Source: National Statistics

The country's current oil refining capacity is only partly utilised. No expansion is planned, and 1985 figures will show no change from 1983:

**TABLE 9.20   YUGOSLAV OIL REFINING CAPACITIES**

Unit: million tonnes per year

|                | 1981 | 1982 | 1983 | 1985 |
|----------------|------|------|------|------|
| Bosanski Brod  | 2.1  | 2.9  | 4.2  | 4.2  |
| Lendava        | 0.6  | 0.6  | 0.6  | 0.6  |
| Novi Sad       | 1.0  | 1.0  | 3.0  | 3.0  |
| Pancevo        | 5.5  | 5.5  | 5.5  | 5.5  |
| Rijeka         | 8.0  | 8.0  | 8.0  | 8.0  |
| Skopje         | 0.0  | 0.7  | 2.5  | 2.5  |
| Susak          | 6.7  | 6.7  | 6.7  | 6.7  |
| TOTAL          | 23.9 | 26.4 | 30.5 | 30.5 |

The Borovo Rubber and Footwear Combine, with factories at Borovo and elsewhere, is among Yugoslavia's largest industrial organisations. Every year this organisation produces: 11.5 million pairs of leather shoes; 8.6 million pairs of rubber shoes; 34,000 tonnes of tyres; 11,270 tonnes of technical rubber goods; and 6,600 tonnes of polyurethane goods.

247

### TABLE 9.21  YUGOSLAVIA'S OUTPUT OF RUBBER PRODUCTS

|                                        | 1981 | 1982 |
|----------------------------------------|------|------|
| Car tyres (million units)              | 10.5 | 9.4  |
| Bicycle tyres (million units)          | 3.9  | 4.1  |
| Technical rubber goods ('000 tonnes)   | 63.3 | 62.9 |
| Rubber footwear (million pairs)        | 17.1 | 16.8 |

Source: National Statistics

## Food, drink and tobacco

### TABLE 9.22  OUTPUT OF SELECTED PRODUCTS

| Unit: '000 tonnes                         | 1981  | 1982  |
|-------------------------------------------|-------|-------|
| Flour (million tonnes)                    | 2.3   | 2.4   |
| Bread and bakery products (million tonnes)| 1.2   | 1.3   |
| Pasta products                            | 87.2  | 90.3  |
| Fruit preparations                        | 266.2 | 384.8 |
| Canned vegetables                         | 143.8 | 163.5 |
| Fresh meat                                | 712.7 | 712.7 |
| Sausages                                  | 183.2 | 188.6 |
| Canned meat                               | 103.4 | 99.2  |
| Concentrated soup                         | 12.6  | 13.1  |
| Canned fish                               | 37.2  | 36.3  |
| Sugar                                     | 791.0 | 683.0 |
| Spirit, refined (million hectolitres)     | 45.7  | 51.0  |
| Beer (million hectolitres)                | 12.2  | 13.5  |
| Fermented tobacco                         | 59.7  | 70.2  |
| Cigarettes* (billion units)               | 63.1  | 58.2  |

* including exports, 14 billion units in 1981 and 9 billion in 1982
Source: National Statistics

## Wood, paper and allied products

Yugoslavia is the fourth largest of the non-aligned countries in the number of its paper and pulp plants. It is second (behind India) in terms of production capacity, with 1.4 million tonnes per year for paper and cardboard, and 775,000 tonnes per year for pulp. Yugoslavia is the leading non-aligned country in paper and cardboard output. It produced 1.1 million tonnes in 1982. Both production and consumption are low compared with levels in the developed countries.

The country's plentiful forests ensure adequate supplies of raw materials to all these industries. Yugoslavia is a large-scale manufacturer of furniture — the main producer company is Sipad.

**TABLE 9.23   OUTPUT OF WOOD, PAPER, FURNITURE 1981-1982**

| Unit: '000 tonnes | 1981 | 1982 |
|---|---|---|
| Sawn timber, coniferous (million metres$^3$) | 2.3 | 2.5 |
| Sawn timber, broadleaved (million metres$^3$) | 1.9 | 2.0 |
| Particle board ('000 metres$^3$) | 788.7 | 790.3 |
| Furniture ('000 suites) | 258.0 | 250.2 |
| Cellulose | 520.5 | 531.2 |
| Woodpulp | 121.3 | 128.0 |
| Newsprint | 51.7 | 28.8 |
| Writing/printing paper | 297.3 | 334.0 |
| Kraft paper | 131.2 | 127.9 |
| Cardboard | 171.9 | 173.9 |
| Paper, total | 1,151.1 | 1,144.0 |

Source: National Statistics

## Textiles, clothing and footwear

**TABLE 9.24   OUTPUT OF SELECTED CLOTHING AND FOOTWEAR PRODUCTS 1981-1982**

| | 1981 | 1982 |
|---|---|---|
| Cotton yarn* ('000 tonnes) | 117.5 | 120.8 |
| Woollen yarn* ('000 tonnes) | 56.2 | 53.0 |
| Cotton fabric* (million metres$^2$) | 376.7 | 371.6 |
| Wool fabric* (million metres$^2$) | 95.8 | 94.1 |
| Rayon fabric (million metres$^2$) | 40.8 | 36.3 |

Continued...

**Table 9.24 continued...**

|  | 1981 | 1982 |
|---|---|---|
| Readymade outerwear (million metres$^2$) | 161.9 | 169.7 |
| Knit goods ('000 tonnes) | 30.7 | 30.6 |
| Hosiery (million pairs) | 214.0 | 208.9 |
| Footwear, leather (million pairs) | 74.8 | 76.0 |
| Sole leather ('000 tonnes) | 3.4 | 3.0 |
| Upper leather (million metres$^2$) | 20.1 | 18.7 |

* includes artificial fibres
Source: National Statistics

## Consumer goods

**Table 9.25  OUTPUT OF SELECTED CONSUMER GOODS**

**Unit: '000 units**

|  | 1981 | 1982 |
|---|---|---|
| Cars | 241.5 | 218.8 |
| Telephones | 330.6 | 409.2 |
| Radios | 160.1 | 152.0 |
| Television sets | 509.5 | 489.5 |
| Light bulbs (million units) | 89.0 | 86.2 |
| Washing machines | 480.2 | 423.4 |
| Refrigerators | 684.8 | 659.3 |

Source: National Statistics

## Mining

Only about 50% of energy needs are met from domestic sources, although Yugoslavia possesses supplies of coal, natural gas and oil.

There is a plentiful supply of brown coal and lignite, and a limited amount of hard coal is available.

250

**TABLE 9.26   ESTIMATED COAL RESERVES**

| Unit: million tonnes | Coal | Brown coal | Lignite | Total | % of total |
|---|---|---|---|---|---|
| Proven | 61 | 1,278 | 13,273 | 14,612 | 65.9 |
| Probable | 17 | 335 | 1,378 | 1,730 | 7.8 |
| Potential | 37 | 845 | 4,939 | 5,281 | 26.3 |
| TOTAL | 115 | 2,458 | 19,950 | 22,163 | 100.0 |

Production was 54.6 million tonnes in 1982, satisfying 90% of domestic demand. Some 3.6 million tonnes were imported, while 700,000 tonnes were exported, giving a total supply of 57.5 million tonnes.

**TABLE 9.27   COAL OUTPUT 1980-1982**

| Unit: million tonnes | 1980 | 1981 | 1982 |
|---|---|---|---|
| Bituminous coal | 0.4 | 0.4 | 0.4 |
| Brown coal | 9.7 | 10.6 | 10.7 |
| Lignite | 37.0 | 41.0 | 43.5 |
| Total | 47.0 | 51.9 | 54.6 |

Source: National Statistics

Some 27.5 million tonnes were produced in the first six months of 1983, up 5% compared with the first six months of 1982. Output of coal will be more than trebled by the year 2000, substantially easing the country's dependence on imported energy from oil. Exploitation of coal could be increased by open-cast methods, particularly in Bosnia-Herzegovina, where reserves are suited to this method. Zenica will open a new pit, the Moscanica, which is expected to produce 1 million tonnes per year. The new pit is located on a freshly-discovered deposit of 66 million tonnes, and will be operational in 1988, at a cost of 10,000 million dinars.

The country's main reserves are located in Kosovo province and the Kolubara district of Serbia. Reserves generally are of low thermal value.

Coal is to become the major source of electricity, but this is a long-term prospect. The recent Kraigher Commission's report on economic prospects recommends increased production of dried lignite and briquettes as of particular benefit to fuel users — these have the advantage of vastly reducing carriage costs to users. The Kolubarra combine, currently under construction at a cost of 1,300 million dinars, will produce 855,000 tonnes per year of dried lignite fuel. The combine's future output has already been sold, and a second plant may be built.

**TABLE 9.28   FUTURE COAL OUTPUT**

**Unit: million tonnes**

|                 | 1985 | 1990  | 2000  | 2020   |
|-----------------|------|-------|-------|--------|
| Bituminous coal | 0.8  | 0.8   | 0.8   | 0.8    |
| Brown coal      | 13.0 | 15.0  | 22.0  | 27.00  |
| Lignite         | 68.4 | 124.0 | 217.0 | 242.0  |

Exploitation of domestic reserves of crude oil is being accelerated as can be seen in the following figures.

Output was 4.2 million tonnes in 1980; 4.4 million tonnes in 1981; 4.3 million tonnes in 1982; and will be 5.0 million tonnes in 1985 and 6.0 million tonnes in 2000.

Current output satisfies 25% of domestic demand. Reserves are located near Zagreb and in the Banat region. Hard currency to purchase the drilling equipment necessary to raise output is lacking, so growth in this sector will not be at high levels. INA, the national oil and gas company, is prospecting jointly with Agip of Italy in the Adriatic Sea, on the Mirjana 1 field. But imports will always be necessary on a large scale: crude oil imports were 10.9 million tonnes in 1980; 9.4 million tonnes in 1981; 8.5 million tonnes in 1982; and will rise to 11.0 million tonnes per year (a minimum future requirement, according to Western estimates).

Gas imports should stabilise at the level of 3 billion cubic metres per year from the USSR, plus some which may be purchased from Algeria. Output of natural gas was 1.8 billion cubic metres in 1980; 1.7 billion cubic metres in 1981; 1.7 billion cubic metres in 1982; and will be 5.0

billion cubic metres in 1985 and 8.5 billion cubic metres in 1990, as new offshore finds are exploited.

Hydroelectric power is Yugoslavia's other major energy resource. There is vast hydroelectricity potential in many of the country's mountainous regions, but drought and low water levels have affected actual output. Output was 28 TWh in 1980, 25 TWh in 1981 and 24 TWh in 1982.

## Metallurgy

Ore reserves are plentiful and varied. Iron ore production is being encouraged, to reduce the country's dependence on imported steel. Increased output from expanded mines and from newly-exploited reserves will provide Yugoslavia's steel industry with better raw material supplies. New mines include those to be opened at Omarska, and reconstruction work is being carried out at Vares. Output was 4.5 million tonnes in 1980; 4.8 million tonnes in 1981 and 5.1 million tonnes in 1982. Despite output reaching record levels, demand still far outstrips supply from domestic sources.

Yugoslavia is the second largest European producer of copper, after the USSR: output was 19.6 million tonnes in 1980; 18.3 million tonnes in 1981; and 19.7 million tonnes in 1982.

Production of copper is centred on the Bor complex in Serbia. In Macedonia, the new Bucim mine was to produce 11,200 tonnes of concentrate in 1983, adding substantially to existing capacity.

Yugoslavia's proven bauxite reserves account for 27% of all Europe's bauxite. Most is found in Bosnia-Herzegovina, and a new high-quality deposit near Pula in Croatia has been discovered — it started to produce in 1982. Output was 3.14 million tonnes in 1980; 3.25 million tonnes in 1981; 3.67 million tonnes in 1982; and will be 5.00 million tonnes in 1985 (plan).

The Dalmatia region's bauxite reserves are insufficiently viable, and the Obrovac alumina production plant is to close.

The Trepca lead/zinc complex in Kosovo is being expanded with a £300 million investment over five years, 1981-1985, and output here should reach 3.2 million tonnes by 1985 (compared with 2.8 million tonnes before). Total output of lead and zinc was 4.3 million tonnes in 1980; 4.4 million tonnes in 1981; and 4.3 million tonnes in 1982.

Yugoslavia also has other metal ore reserves. Crude antimony output was 67,000 tonnes in 1981 and 63,000 tonnes in 1982. Gold is also mined. Nickel reserves too are plentiful, and two new nickel mines near Pristina started producing in early 1983, with a combined processing capacity of 980,000 tonnes per year of ore. The Pristina reserves contain 26.7 million tonnes of ore, which has a 1.32% nickel content and a 0.07% cobalt content. The new ferronickel complex at Kavadarci near Skopje has a target to produce 21,300 tonnes per year, but this seems technically unrealistic; its 1983 target, originally 12,300 tonnes, was reduced to 10,000.

**Agriculture**

Yugoslav farmers have the benefit of good soil and a good climate, two indispensable attributes to efficient agriculture — yet production lags far behind potential. Increasing farm output is a priority target in government policies, since the country could attain much better results in this sector, and could be self-sufficient in most food products.

From being a large-scale exporter of wheat, maize, fruit, cattle and meat before the Second World War, Yugoslavia has become a net importer of many basic food requisites, including wheat, protein feed and oilseeds. In 1982, imports of agrofood products were $1.5 billion, while exports were $1.2 billion. One of the reasons for the large import dependency is Yugoslavia's 50% growth in population over the last fifty years. Nutritional patterns are changing, and while many Yugoslavs used to be undernourished, now many eat too many calories. The average diet is generally poor, with too many fats and carbohydrates and too few proteins consumed.

Some 80% of the land is privately but inefficiently farmed. Individual farms are small, being limited in size to 10 hectares of arable land plus some pasture, and they still use primitive tools and methods. The government plans more assistance for the private farmers, since they represent a sizeable part of the country's food potential. Agricultural prices are regularly increased, and output of machinery is being boosted. (In 1981, of 426,399 tractors operating in Yugoslav agriculture, the vast majority were privately owned.) The government also provides incentives for the small farmers to conclude partnerships with 'agrokombinats', the socially-owned estates, on the basis of profit and risk sharing. This will increase the small farms' efficiency and permit them to choose the organisation type best suited to their needs.

An increase in the size of small farms is likely to be permitted. In Croatia, it is planned to double the permitted acreage of lowland farms from 10 to 20 hectares, and for hill farms from 20 to 40 hectares.

Although 10 hectares is permitted, few farms actually are of maximum size. In Serbia, 3.5 hectares is the average size of farm. Rational methods are not possible on such a small scale. Besides this, a large percentage of farm workers are middle-aged or old, and there is a continuing labour shortage on the land, despite Yugoslavia's unemployment problem.

The socialised sector consists of the agrokombinats, which are large units organised on self-management principles. These farms produce 33% of Yugoslavia's food, while employing only a small percentage of the total agricultural workforce. Their share of total farm land is rising very slowly, while the private farmers' share is gradually declining. Agrokombinats often very successfully combine with the private farmers to make full use of joint machine pools and the financial facilities available to agriculture.

Crop output in 1983 was satisfactory, according to preliminary indications. The wheat crop was up and the maize crop was unchanged at its 1982 record size, despite a slightly lower acreage; maize yields were 5 tonnes per hectare in 1983, compared with 4.2-4.5 tonnes per hectare in previous years. Some crop output data for previous years is shown in the following table.

**TABLE 9.29 SELECTED DATA ON CROP PRODUCTION**

**Unit: million tonnes**

|  | 1980 | 1981 | 1982 |
| --- | --- | --- | --- |
| Wheat | 5.1 | 4.3 | 5.2 |
| Maize | 9.3 | 9.8 | 11.1 |
| Sugar beet | 5.2 | 6.2 | 5.7 |
| Meat and meat products | 1.2 | 1.3 | 1.3 |
| Apples | 0.5 | 0.5 | 0.7 |
| Plums | 0.7 | 0.8 | 1.0 |
| Grapes | 1.6 | 1.3 | 1.8 |
| Sunflower seed | 0.3 | 0.3 | 0.2 |
| Tobacco ('000 tonnes) | 59.0 | 70.0 | 77.0 |
| Soyabeans ('000 tonnes) | 34.1 | 92.3 | 197.9 |

Source: National Statistics

255

In 1984, overall agricultural output was targeted to rise 2%, with wheat output at 5.9 million tonnes, maize at 11.5 million tonnes, sugar beet at 7.8 million tonnes, tobacco at 90,000 tonnes and meat output at 1.3 million tonnes.

Yugoslavia is self-sufficient in many crops, and sometimes produces surpluses. But imports are still required of several staple foods, and even maize supplies have to be supplemented by imports despite record crops. Currently 32% of grain requirements, 48% of edible oils, 65% of fodder protein and 33% of fish for canning has to be imported.

Agriculture is a priority development sector. By the year 2000 Yugoslavia could be exporting 2 million tonnes per year of maize, 350,000 tonnes per year of beef, 150,000 tonnes per year of pork, 75,000 tonnes of lamb, 100,000 tonnes of processed meat and large quantities of wine and grapes.

**Table 9.30   AGRICULTURAL TARGETS FOR YEAR 2000**

**Unit: million tonnes**

| Crop | Target for 2000 | Output in 1980 |
|------|-----------------|----------------|
| Wheat | 7.0 | 5.2 |
| Barley | 1.5 | 0.8 |
| Maize | 20.5 | 9.3 |
| Sugar beet | 10.5 | 5.2 |
| Oilseeds and soya | 2.0 | 0.3 |
| Clover (lucerne) | 5.0 | 2.1 |

The private sector will still be operational by the year 2000, and will provide a substantial part of overall production:

**TABLE 9.31   FARM OUTPUT BY TYPE OF FARM IN YEAR 2000**

| Farm type | Wheat | Barley | Maize | Sugar beet |
|-----------|-------|--------|-------|------------|
| Social sector | 5.0 | 0.7 | 5.5 | 8.0 |
| Private sector | 2.0 | 0.8 | 15.0 | 2.5 |
| All farms | 7.0 | 1.5 | 20.5 | 10.5 |

Fertiliser needs are seen as 3 million tonnes per year by the year 2000, compared with 851,000 tonnes used in 1981.

Livestock rearing is one of farming's most important aspects, responding to the population's rising incomes and the demand for more meat.

**TABLE 9.32   LIVESTOCK NUMBERS 1981-1982**

**Unit: million head**

|         | 1981* | 1982* |
|---------|-------|-------|
| Horses  | 0.6   | 0.5   |
| Cattle  | 5.5   | 5.5   |
| Sheep   | 7.4   | 7.4   |
| Pigs    | 7.9   | 8.4   |
| Poultry | 65.1  | 67.4  |

* in January
Source: National Statistics

By the year 2000, livestock numbers are expected to have increased to: 9 million cattle; 20 million sheep and goats; 16 million pigs and 120 million hens.

Fishing is increasingly important, and fish is becoming more a regular part of the Yugoslav diet, as modern refrigeration methods become more widespread. The expansion of fisheries has, however, been much slower than planned.

**Energy**

As mentioned earlier, despite extensive indigenous resources, Yugoslavia only covers 50% of its energy needs from its own reserves, the rest being imported at great cost to the country. Energy shortages are endemic in Yugoslavia. Fuel use has been restricted in certain categories, such as the use of private cars.

**TABLE 9.33   COMMERCIAL PRIMARY ENERGY BALANCE IN 1981**

**Unit: million tonnes of coal equivalent**

| *Production* | | *Apparent consumption* | |
|---|---|---|---|
| Solid fuel | 21.8 | Solid fuel | 25.1 |
| Crude oil and n.g. liquids | 6.4 | Liquid fuel | 18.3 |
| Natural gas | 2.7 | Natural gas | 5.1 |
| Hydroelectric power | 11.0 | Hydroelectric power | 11.0 |
| Nuclear power | 0.1 | Nuclear power | 0.1 |
| Total production | 42.0 | Less net exports of electricity | − 0.3 |
| | | Total consumption | 59.4 |
| *Imports* | | | |
| Solid fuel | 3.6 | | |
| Crude petroleum | 13.6 | *Exports* | |
| Petroleum products | 1.5 | Solid fuel | 0.3 |
| Natural gas | 2.5 | Petroleum products | 0.6 |
| Electricity | 0.5 | Electricity | 0.8 |
| Total imports | 21.7 | Total exports | 1.7 |
| | | Balancing item | 2.6 |
| TOTAL SUPPLY | 63.7 | TOTAL DEMAND | 63.7 |

\* comprises output of 2 million tonnes of non-energy petroleum products (naptha, lubricants etc), unidentified changes in crude stocks and statistical discrepancies.
Source: UN Yearbook of World Energy Statistics, 1981

Energy requirements will rise steadily, according to the Kraigher Commission, to 70-73 million tonnes of coal equivalent in 1990; 102-119 million tonnes of coal equivalent in 2000; and 210-264 million tonnes of coal equivalent per year by 2020.

Electricity is primarily generated from lignite, and hydroelectric power also provides large quantities. Serbia, Bosnia-Herzegovina and sometimes Macedonia generate electricity surpluses, but shortages are widespread generally in the country. No more oil-fired power stations are being built, and there is a shortage of lignite and of hard coal for burning. The development of nuclear power has slowed down. Electricity is imported from neighbouring Austria and Italy — 1.5 TWh were imported in 1981 and 2 TWh in 1982.

**TABLE 9.34   ELECTRICITY OUTPUT BY SOURCE**

**Unit: TWh**

|                      | 1980 | 1981 | 1982 |
|----------------------|------|------|------|
| Hydroelectric power  | 28.2 | 25.1 | 23.5 |
| Thermal power        | 31.4 | 35.0 | 36.3 |
| Nuclear power        | 0.0  | 0.3  | 2.5  |
| TOTAL                | 59.6 | 60.4 | 62.3 |

Source: National Statistics

The 1984 electricity generating target was 70.3 TWh, but this is unlikely to have been reached. Hydroelectric power's performance is dependent upon weather conditions and is therefore unreliable — output was badly affected by drought in 1983. Many new power projects have been delayed. In the 1981-85 Five Year Plan period, 7,800 MW of new capacity was to have been built, but at best only 5,840 MW are likely to be completed: 2,350 MW were completed in 1981 and 1982, including the 640 MW Krsko nuclear plant; 1,640 MW were to be completed in 1983; 980 MW are likely to have been completed in 1984 and 870 MW are likely to be completed in 1985.

The nuclear power plant at Krsko in Slovenia is Yugoslavia's first. It is a pressurised water reactor, built in co-operation with Westinghouse of the USA. It took three years longer to build than planned, and entailed an 80% cost overrun. Its power output was to rise to 3.1 TWh in 1983. A second nuclear power plant is to be built at Prevlaka in Croatia, on the Sava river. This will be another PWR, and will be built jointly by the Croat and Slovene electricity generating boards, as was Krsko. There will be more nuclear power plants by 1990, and eventually some 35% of power needs will be met from this source, with a further 52% supplied by fossil fuel and the remainder by hydroelectric power.

Oil imports from the USSR are increasing, although this renders Yugoslavia more dependent on the Soviet Union. The previous ceiling on oil supplies was 4.5 million tonnes per year — this ceiling was imposed because Yugoslavia is only an affiliate member of Comecon, not a full member. But oil supplies from the USSR will now rise to 5.35 million tonnes per year, with a further 1 million probable. Yugoslavia has been

259

urged in return to sell food and other goods which normally go to the West to the USSR instead.

Natural gas imports from the USSR will also increase, from their present level of 2.5 billion cubic metres per year to 3 billion when the transcontinental pipeline being laid from West Siberia to Eastern Europe is finished. The Yugoslavs are to build their own continuation of the pipeline from Pernik in Bulgaria to Skopje in Macedonia. The Algeria-Italy undersea gas pipeline bringing Algerian gas to Southern Europe may also be used to provide 1.5 billion cubic metres a year.

Energy conservation measures have been intensified by the government, which offers considerable incentives; large-scale imports which entail increases in Yugoslavia's already very high foreign indebtedness must be curtailed. Fuel consumption in petrochemicals, agriculture and tourism was cut 50% in 1984. Total energy requirements for 1984 were estimated as: 72 TWh of electric power; 64 million tonnes of coal; 15 million tonnes of oil; 6 billion cubic metres of gas; 4 million tonnes of coking coal.

Oil imports fell 28% between 1979 and 1982, totalling 8.5 million tonnes in 1982.

## Construction

Output of the construction sector has been falling. Value, however, has risen. There has been a sharp contraction in recent orders from government and government agencies.

**TABLE 9.35  CONSTRUCTION VALUE IN THE SOCIAL SECTOR**

|  | Value of work completed* | Effective work hours (million) |
|---|---|---|
| 1978 | 161.6 | 744.0 |
| 1979 | 218.9 | 808.8 |
| 1980 | 269.3 | 798.0 |
| 1981 | 353.5 | 766.0 |
| 1982 (estimate) | 415.0 | 743.0 |

* billion dinars, at constant 1972 prices
Source: National Statistics

In 1982, 10,000 dwelling units were completed. Yugoslavia's housing stock at the end of March 1981 comprised: 6.3 million dwellings providing 372 million square metres of useful floor area, with 60.7 square metres as the average floor area per dwelling for an average 3.6 people per dwelling.

The construction sector's export orders are encouraging, particularly in the developing world. A major contractor in the field of industrial construction and civil engineering is Energoinvest of Sarajevo. This company's large staff includes 700 engineers specialising in construction problems. Energoinvest has become one of Yugoslavia's major exporters. The company undertakes contracts in the energy, mining, rail electrification and allied sectors. Among its current contracts is one recently signed with Iraq to build a $4.4 billion power transmission line.

**Transportation**

Yugoslavia is one of Europe's great transit countries. It is the natural route from Greece, Turkey and Bulgaria northwards into central and western Europe. Since Greece entered the European Economic Community, and since the signing, in July 1980, of a five-year trade agreement between Yugoslavia and the EEC, transport within Yugoslavia and the inadequacies of the Yugoslav network are standing out as being in need of improvement, modernisation and expansion. Yugoslav infrastructure is insufficient, and a source of official concern. Improvements are a government priority, and many projects are underway. A six-lane motorway is under construction, linking with Greece to the south and Austria to the north.

But the road system is a weak link in Yugoslavia's transportation. Each republic has concentrated its resources on developing its own network, with the result that the national network did not evolve in a logical fashion. Yugoslavia has 115,174 kilometres of road, of which 60,623 kilometres are macadamised.

The rail system comprises 10,000 kilometres of standard and narrow-gauge track, of which 3,000 kilometres are electrified. By the end of the Five Year Plan, in 1985 a further 3,000 kilometres will have been electrified. By this date, improved rolling stock will be operating, permitting speeds of up to 160 kilometres per hour. Railway improvements are being funded by a $110 million World Bank loan.

Inland waterways are well established, based on the Danube, Sava and Tisa rivers, which provide 1,400 miles of navigable waterway. Since transport costs on water are lower than by other means, expansion is being encouraged. A river port capable of handling 10 million tonnes per year of freight is to be built at Smederevo on the Danube. Belgrade is a major river port, and the river fleet nationally totalled 1,267 vessels in 1981.

Yugoslavia's main seaports are: Rijeka, which is undergoing a major expansion; Sibenik, where new bulk phosphate capacity is now complete; Split; Koper; Kardeljevo; Dubrovnik and Bar.

The country's merchant fleet totalled 2.5 million tonnes in 1982, and the seaports handled 29.3 million tonnes of freight. There were 87 passenger ships, 24 tankers, 336 dry cargo vessels and 13 motorised sailing vessels in service during 1982.

There are 16 international airports operating within Yugoslavia, served by JAT, Jugoslovenski Aero Transport. In 1982, 5.2 million passengers were carried and 41,255 tonnes of freight.

**Tourism**

Revenues from foreign tourists were expected to be around $1.15 billion in 1983, compared with the officially-registered $1.45 billion earned in 1982.

Yugoslavia has extensive tourist facilities, rivalling those of many established Mediterranean countries. West Germans constitute the majority of foreign visitors, 44% of all incoming tourists in 1981. Dubrovnik is the main tourist centre. This town collects 10% of all the country's tourism revenues.

The 14th Winter Olympic Games took place in Sarajevo in early 1984. It was the first winter olympics to be held in a communist country. The Olympic Organising Committee had specially built many facilities, and the most technically advanced equipment had been installed. The Games should help to establish Sarajevo as a permanent base for winter sports. It is hoped to stage world class winter sports contests here every second year.

## Education and welfare

Education in Yugoslavia is compulsory, comprehensive and lasts for eight years. In 1982 there were: 12,528 primary schools comprising 103,901 classes for 2,800,000 pupils; while in secondary schools there were 33,341 classes for 1,000,000 pupils. (Secondary school reorganisation means that numbers of schools are not available.) There are 19 Yugoslav universities.

Welfare services are extensive. In 1981 there were 265 hospitals, providing 136,820 hospital beds, and 33,514 doctors (including 18,925 specialists).

## Entertainment

Entertainment facilities include 1,278 cinemas (in 1982) with 424,000 audience capacity. Attendance, which has remained stable, averaged 3,941 visits per 1,000 inhabitants in 1982.

Television broadcasting facilities include: 8 television studios/centres; 70 transmitters; 900 repeater stations; 20,574 kW of radiated power and 20,899 total hours transmitted in 1982.

## Banking

Commercially-oriented banks have been operating since the mid 1960s, and major reorganisation has been underway since the further reform of 1977.

'Internal' banks (there were 115 in 1980) carry out internal banking functions. 'Basic' banks (there were 160 in 1980) are commercial banks operating similarly to Western commercial banks, but with a workers' council of management.

'Associated' banks (there were 9 in 1980) are formed through mergers of basic banks to pool funds for the support of major projects.

NBJ, Narodna Banka SFRJ, which is Yugoslavia's national bank, can authorise the basic banks to undertake foreign transactions on their own account, if the basic bank has the facilities to do so. NBJ operates without the strong directive powers of other national banks in East Europe.

### Consumer expenditure

Yugoslavs are fortunate in enjoying a larger range of consumer goods than is generally available in East Europe. This is the result of their more 'open' economy. The amount of consumer goods and industrial goods available in the country on a per capita basis is shown:

**TABLE 9.36   SUPPLY OF MANUFACTURED GOODS PER CAPITA IN 1982**

| | |
|---|---|
| Electric energy (kWh) | 2,928 |
| Coal (kilogrammes) | 2,630 |
| Crude oil (kg) | 587 |
| Crude steel (kg) | 176 |
| Cement (kg) | 428 |
| Sulphuric acid (kg) | 60 |
| Paper and board (kg) | 49 |
| Cotton fabric (metres$^2$) | 11 |
| Woollen fabric (metres$^2$) | 1.3 |
| Cigarettes (units) | 2,270 |
| Soap (kg) | 4 |

Source: National Statistics

**TABLE 9.37   CONSUMPTION OF FOOD PER CAPITA IN 1981**

**Unit: kilogrammes**

| | |
|---|---|
| Wheat and rye products | 152.6 |
| Maize products | 23.6 |
| Rice | 1.7 |
| Potatoes | 58.9 |
| Peas/beans/lentils | 6.4 |
| Other vegetables | 91.6 |
| Fresh fruit and grapes | 60.8 |
| Citrus fruits | 5.0 |
| Meat | 54.7 |
| Beef | 15.1 |
| Pork | 20.9 |
| Mutton | 2.4 |
| Poultry | 12.9 |
| Offal | 3.1 |
| Game | 0.3 |

Continued...

**Table 9.37 continued...**

| | |
|---|---|
| Fish | 4.3 |
| Pork lard | 10.7 |
| Olive oil | 0.2 |
| Other vegetable oil | 12.1 |
| Fresh milk (litres) | 101.1 |
| Cheese | 6.5 |
| Butter | 0.7 |
| Eggs (units) | 183 |
| Sugar | 36.1 |
| Beer (litres) | 45.8 |
| Wine (litres) | 26.9 |
| Other alcohol (litres) | 5.1 |

Source: National Statistics

## Foreign trade and external debt

Yugoslavia's world position, between East and West, is illustrated in its trading relations. Comecon purchases around 50% of Yugoslavia's exports, while Yugoslavia imports around 50% of its needs from the West.

But exports are in the process of switching from East to West — in the first 10 months of 1983, exports to the developed countries of the West rose 27.2%, while exports to Comecon countries fell 10.9% and exports to the developing world fell 4.4%. Yugoslavia's aim is to split its total trade (imports plus exports) in the following way: 40% with the industrialised West, 34% with Comecon, 26% with the developing world.

A five-year trading agreement was signed in July 1980 with the European Economic Community, and despite some initial disappointments, it is expected that trade will increase appreciably.

Yugoslavia's aim is to cut its trade deficit and gross foreign indebtedness, which has trebled since 1975 to reach $20 billion in 1982, representing 35% of national product.

**TABLE 9.38   YUGOSLAVIA'S EXTERNAL DEBT**

**Unit: US $billion**

|  | 1979 | 1980 | 1981 | 1982 |
|---|---|---|---|---|
| Total gross indebtedness | 15.00 | 18.75 | 20.00 | 20.00 |
| *less* lending | 1.25 | 1.50 | 1.75 | 1.75 |
| Total net indebtedness | 13.75 | 17.25 | 18.25 | 18.50 |
| Public total | 3.75 | 4.50 | 6.00 | 6.50 |
| IMF* | 0.50 | 0.75 | 1.25 | 1.75 |
| IBRD** | 1.25 | 1.25 | 1.50 | 1.50 |
| Other | 2.00 | 2.50 | 3.25 | 3.00 |
| Business banks | 4.75 | 6.50 | 6.50 | 6.50 |
| Interest payments | 0.75 | 1.25 | 2.00 | 2.00 |
| Capital repayments | 2.00 | 2.25 | 2.00 | 2.00 |
| Debt servicing, total | 2.75 | 3.50 | 4.00 | 4.00 |
| (as % of total current account receipts) | (20) | (20) | (21) | (24) |

\* International Monetary Fund; \*\* World Bank
Source: OECD

World banks and governments and international financial organisations have offered Yugoslavia their help, with a $4.7 billion package, comprising $600 million from an IMF standby credit arrangement; a $275 million World Bank structural adjustment loan; a $500 million short-term bridging loan from the Bank for International Settlements; $1.35 billion of financial and trade credits granted by creditor governments  and 580 commercial banks have deferred principal repayments and will maintain short-term loans at the current $1.8 billion level.

The country's trade deficit fell to $3.1 billion in 1982, compared with $7.2 billion in 1979. In the first 6 months of 1983, the overall trade deficit fell to $1.1 billion, compared with $1.7 billion in the same period of 1982; trade with the West improved, and the first 6 months' deficit with the West was $1 billion, compared with $2.3 billion in the first 6 months of 1982.

In 1983, the Yugoslavs hoped to reduce their total trade deficit to $2 billion. The current account deficit in convertible currencies should have fallen to $200-300 million, compared with $1.4 billion in 1982.

For 1984, a small current account surplus was planned by the government; to this end a system of mandatory no-interest deposits of 5,000 dinars per person is to be levied on travellers abroad (excluding nationals working abroad).

The direction of Yugoslavia's trade in 1983 can be seen in the following table:

**TABLE 9.39   EXPORTS AND IMPORTS BY DESTINATION AND SUPPLIER 1982-1983**

**Unit: billion dinar**

| | Exports | | Imports | |
|---|---|---|---|---|
| | 1982 | 1983 | 1982 | 1983 |
| USSR | 217.5 | 171.1 | 173.9 | 156.2 |
| West Germany | 41.5 | 51.2 | 107.1 | 103.0 |
| GDR | 22.6 | 24.1 | 26.2 | 26.6 |
| Italy | 41.6 | 51.1 | 56.5 | 62.1 |
| Czechoslovakia | 39.8 | 41.0 | 37.8 | 43.3 |
| Iraq | 44.6 | 28.2 | 21.9 | 44.8 |
| USA | 19.7 | 21.9 | 53.4 | 49.1 |
| Austria | 11.6 | 13.6 | 29.4 | 27.2 |
| France | 11.8 | 17.3 | 31.2 | 26.0 |
| UK | 5.4 | 9.8 | 27.8 | 15.7 |
| Iran | 12.1 | 17.4 | 14.6 | 21.6 |
| Libya | 11.3 | 14.3 | 26.0 | 20.1 |
| TOTAL (including others) | 629.1 | 628.5 | 808.3 | 770.6 |

Source: National Statistics

**TABLE 9.40   COMPOSITION OF YUGOSLAVIA'S TRADE IN 1982**

Unit: US $1 = 41.80 dinars

| by trading area | billion dinars | billion dollars | % change vs 1981 |
|---|---|---|---|
| Exports to the developed world | 120.5 | 2.9 | + 2 |
| Exports to developing countries | 89.0 | 2.1 | + 8 |
| Exports to Comecon | 218.5 | 5.2 | − 3 |
| Total exports | 428.0 | 10.2 | n/a |
| | | | |
| Imports from the developed world | 285.6 | 6.8 | − 5 |
| Imports from developing countries | 78.6 | 1.9 | − 24 |
| Imports from Comecon | 193.2 | 4.6 | − 6 |
| Total imports | 557.4 | 13.3 | − 8 |

Source: National Statistics/OECD

A breakdown by category shows that machinery and transport equipment and manufactured goods were the largest export categories in 1983 while mineral fuels and machinery and transport constituted the most important import categories in terms of same in 1983.

**TABLE 9.41   TRADE BY PRINCIPAL CATEGORY**

Unit: billion dinars

| | Exports | | Imports | |
|---|---|---|---|---|
| | 1982 | 1983 | 1982 | 1983 |
| Food | 55.4 | 60.0 | 41.5 | 36.3 |
| Beverages and tobacco | 14.1 | 13.0 | 1.1 | 1.4 |
| Crude materials exc. fuels | 29.4 | 29.6 | 88.4 | 83.2 |
| Mineral fuels, lubricants and related minerals | 11.5 | 15.5 | 217.6 | 209.5 |
| Chemicals | 67.0 | 60.9 | 97.7 | 111.5 |

Continued...

| Table 9.41 continued... | Exports | | Imports | |
|---|---|---|---|---|
| | **1982** | **1983** | **1982** | **1983** |
| Manufactured goods | 137.7 | 147.1 | 119.9 | 116.9 |
| Iron and steel | 15.9 | 17.3 | 48.1 | 42.4 |
| Non-ferrous metals | 24.7 | 32.0 | 14.9 | 14.8 |
| Metal manufactures | 28.6 | 29.9 | 13.9 | 12.9 |
| Textile yarns and fabrics | 28.1 | 25.5 | 18.4 | 21.4 |
| Machinery and transport equipment | 196.3 | 196.3 | 217.4 | 185.0 |
| Non-electric | 71.8 | 72.7 | 126.1 | 109.4 |
| Electric | 61.5 | 63.5 | 37.7 | 39.0 |
| Transport | 63.0 | 60.1 | 53.6 | 36.5 |
| Miscellaneous manufactured goods | 115.1 | 103.7 | 21.3 | 20.7 |
| TOTAL | 629.1 | 628.5 | 808.3 | 770.6 |

Source: National Statistics

The organisation of foreign trade is regulated by the government. Yugoslav economic organisations wishing to undertake foreign trade must register with the local court. This is permitted if the organisation has adequate financial resources and staff qualified to carry out foreign exchange operations.

Co-operation between Yugoslav and foreign firms is widespread. The Yugoslav partner in a joint venture will produce components equal to at least 15% of the value of the final product. In 1983, the regulations governing foreign companies operating in Yugoslavia were eased.

Licensing agreements with foreign companies are numerous. They cover patents, industrial models, trademarks and technical expertise. Some granted licences include:

cigarette manufacture by a local company, Duvanska Industrija Vranje, which will produce 'Winston' and 'Camel' cigarettes under agreement with RJ Reynolds of the US;

jeans manufacture by Varteks, a Yugoslav producer which will make 1 million pairs of jeans per year for 5 years, under agreement with Levi Strauss (US).

There are good prospects for overseas products within Yugoslavia. Electric power equipment, mining and extraction machinery, telecommunications equipment, computers and peripherals, analytic and scientific instruments and textile equipment are in great demand, to serve several priority sectors within the Yugoslav economy. The government is concentrating on the construction of more thermal electric power facilities for its non-nuclear energy needs, while in the mining sector many new deposits have been identified but not yet exploited. Since the oil crisis, domestic coal reserves have become more important in the national energy plans, and feature prominently in the 1981-85 Five-Year Plan.

The Yugoslavs are keen to extend trading links with existing and potential partners. Help and support is available from their worldwide network of embassies and commercial departments.

# Chapter Ten

# OUTLOOK

## Introduction

This chapter will attempt to forecast the prospects for Soviet and East European development over the next decade concentrating on the problems of economic growth and prospects for East-West trade.

The development of East-West trade will be subject to a number of political factors which are difficult to predict at this stage and it may be useful to indicate the background to some of these problems.

Although attention is largely focussed on the relations between the US and the USSR it was shown in Chapter 2, that direct trade links between the two superpowers were not of great importance. According to US figures, US exports to the USSR in 1979 (taking the last year before trade was affected by the US partial grain embargo) amounted to $3.6 billion which was almost entirely composed of foodstuffs, while US imports from the USSR were only $0.9 billion. Neither is US trade with other countries of the region of great significance. US exports to the region as a whole (including Yugoslavia) in the same year only amounted to $6.4 billion out of a total of $47 billion by the OECD countries as a whole, while imports from the region were only $2.4 billion out of OECD imports of $40 billion. Over half of US exports to East European countries were foodstuffs.

Thus, despite US technological supremacy over the USSR and Eastern Europe in a number of industrial fields, technology trade between the US and the region is of relatively little significance. Many of President Reagan's advisers believe that technology originating in the US is utilised in the region and that it may be utilised in the military sector. Some of this is of course acquired by covert means unrelated to legal trade flows. In addition, however, it is also argued that US technology originally transferred to other sectors of the world through the normal trade channels of technology transfer may then be transferred to the USSR and Eastern Europe by means of trade in machinery and equipment. The US administration has clearly indicated its intention to restrict or prevent technology being transferred in this fashion, and this will clearly affect the nature of East-West trade for the foreseeable future.

Some other political factors that are frequently ignored but may be of some significance in affecting the climate of East-West relations and East-West trade may be briefly indicated in these introductory comments. Two changes in the Soviet leadership in as many years, and the recent US Presidential elections tend to concentrate attention on the leaders of the two superpowers in determining the state of East-West relations. Two factors on the Soviet and East European side may be worth noticing.

Firstly it is apparent that there has been a substantial deterioration in East-West relations in the early 1980s. The degree to which this deterioration has affected the outlook and career prospects of administrators and officials in institutions concerned with economic relations, and how enduring such changes may be, is far more difficult to assess.

Secondly the age structure of East European party leaders, particularly in the Balkan states where personal influence of the party leader has been strongest, indicates the strong probability of significant leadership changes during the remainder of this decade.

## Prospects for growth: quantitative assessments

It is normally considered that central planners are capable of maintaining a high level of demand and that factors affecting the supply of inputs to the economy are more important than demand factors in determining the level of output in centrally planned economies. Consequently most attempts to forecast the growth of output in Soviet and East German economies use a production-function approach, in which an attempt is made to estimate the rate of growth of inputs to the economies (normally including just labour and capital, but sometimes including an estimate of natural resources), secondly to evaluate their contribution to economic development (i.e. to attach weights to the specific factors of production) and finally to attempt to evaluate the expected rate of 'technical progress'.

It was argued in Chapter 1 that the rate of growth of labour productivity in the USSR and Eastern Europe has not been significantly different from that of Western Europe when a fairly long time horizon is considered and that observed differences in industrial growth rates could be largely attributed to the higher rate of growth of the industrial labour force and the growth of capital stock (productive machinery and equipment etc.). Furthermore economic growth has slowed substantially since 1978 and the incremental capital-output ratio (the amount of new capital required to produce a given volume of output) has been increasing (implying a deterioration of economic performance).

This chapter will attempt to assess the prospects for economic growth in the countries of the region by indicating the principal factors that will affect the size of the industrial labour force and the size of the capital stock. The need to utilise more costly sources of energy (which will involve increased capital expenditure per unit of output) will also be examined. Finally an assessment of the external factors that may affect how these policies will be implemented will be provided, together with an indication of how this may affect trade prospects with the region.

In arriving at these assessments I have been considerably influenced by papers presented to the annual colloquium on Soviet and East European economic prospects organised by the Economics Directorate of NATO. The papers are not classified and are subsequently published. I have in particular been influenced by papers presented by Daniel Bond (1982) and Jan Vanous (1983) of Wharton Econometric Associates of Washington DC. In addition to their econometric analyses both the above are highly respected analysts of Soviet and East European economic affairs and my debt to them is as much one of approach as data utilisation as I have attempted to reassess and re-estimate some of their conclusions in the light of events that have occurred since those papers were written.

**The growth of the population and labour force**

Population growth is still highest in Poland and Romania but is negative in Hungary and virtually stationary in the GDR. The birthrate in Romania has fallen substantially in the early 1980s (no data have been published for 1983) and population growth can largely be attributed to an ageing population. President Ceausescu has announced draconian measures to stimulate the birth rate in 1984 including stiffer penalties for abortion (contraceptives are not freely available) and compulsory monthly tests on women as a condition for eligibility for any form of health care. In most countries of the region the proportion of the full time labour force accounted for by women is high by West European standards and there is little scope for further rapid increases in the labour force by increasing the employment of women.

273

The growth rates of the labour force are subject to considerable annual variation, although some clear trends can be identified.

The growth rate of the industrial labour force has been highest in the less developed economies of Bulgaria and Romania and the non-Russian regions of the USSR, but by 1983 total labour force growth in the state and co-operative sectors (excluding collective farmers and the private sector) was everywhere below 1% per annum (no data are available for Romania). Furthermore in each country of the region the proportion of the labour force employed in the non-productive sectors (services, education, health, housing, etc) increased between 1980 and 1983 at the expense of the sectors producing material output.

The fall in labourforce growth in Hungary may be partially explained by the growth of private sector employment, but it is apparent that the rate of growth of employment in the sectors producing material output will be very low throughout the region for the remainder of the decade. Even in Romania the total labour force is only expected to grow by 2.5-3.6% over the entire next Five Year Plan period. Any growth in material output (and East European growth statistics only include material output) will therefore require a substantial increase in labour productivity in the material sectors of the economy.

**TABLE 10.1   THE GROWTH OF THE LABOUR FORCE AND THE POPULATION IN 1983**

| Unit: % | | Annual labour force growth | | | |
|---|---|---|---|---|---|
| | **Total** | **Prod** | **Non-prod** | **Ind** | **Con** |
| Bulgaria | 0.5 | 0.4 | 0.8 | 0.7 | 1.4 |
| Czechoslovakia | 0.6 | 0.5 | 0.8 | 0.5 | 0.1 |
| GDR | 0.5 | 0.2 | 1.6 | 0.5 | −0.1 |
| Poland | 0.1 | −1.1 | 2.4 | −1.0 | −1.8 |
| Hungary | −2.3 | −2.5 | −2.0 | −4.0 | −4.1 |
| Romania | 1.6 | 1.5 | 1.9 | 2.1 | 0.4 |
| USSR | 0.8 | 0.6 | 1.2 | 0.6 | 1.4 |

Prod = productive sector; Non-prod = non productive; Ind = industry; Con = construction

Continued...

**Table 10.1 continued...**

| | Population Growth (per 1,000) | Women in workforce % of workforce |
|---|---|---|
| Bulgaria | 2.3 | 49.3 |
| Czechoslovakia | 2.8 | 46.8 |
| GDR | 0.7 | 50.3 |
| Poland | 10.2 | 43.7 |
| Hungary | − 2.0 | 45.1 |
| Romania | 5.3 | 38.2 |
| USSR | 2.8 | 51.1 |

Sources and methods: all figures estimated from CMEA statistical handbooks.
Labour force data refer to the state and co-operative sectors only.

Furthermore, the rate of growth of the industrial labour force is declining in each country of the region, with the effect that in the more industrialised economies where the move away from employment in agriculture and forestry has ceased (i.e. all countries except Bulgaria and Romania) the industrial labour force is growing more slowly than the total labour force.

Finally another striking feature is that in each country except Bulgaria and the USSR the labour force in construction actually declined from 1980 to 1983. The reasons for this are largely linked to the fall in net material product growth and are analysed in the section on investment.

A further factor which will affect the number of man-hours supplied in the economy is the length of the working week. Thus any growth in the labour force and in the industrial labour force in particular may be offset by reductions in the number of hours worked, and in particular by a reduction in Saturday working. This factor has been particularly notice-able in Poland and may help also to explain the attempts to increase the size of the labour force in the productive sector. Several countries in the region have been forced to delay measures to shorten the working week.

## Qualitative factors affecting labour productivity

The quality of work actually performed in the workplace is likely to be as critical as the number of man-hours worked (or stated to be worked) in a number of countries of the region in the immediate future. Again Poland and Romania are likely to be the two economies most affected by this. One major factor, largely beyond the control of the workers themselves, is likely to be the amount of time spent in enforced idleness because of the lack of availability of inputs. This may arise from two factors. Firstly it may be expected that bottlenecks arising from planning failures may intensify unless there is an improvement in the organisation of planning techniques. Supply planning could be improved by increased usage of relatively unsophisticated computers. It is likely however that this will be a critical area of future Western controls on exports to communist countries. More critically shortages in supplies of raw materials, components and crucial energy may occur as a result of balance of payments constraints. These problems may therefore be less critical in countries that have less severe balance of payments problems, notably Czechoslovakia, Bulgaria, the USSR and the GDR. Poland and Romania are again likely to be the hardest affected. Poland experienced considerable power shortages and electricity cuts even before the current set of problems and Romania has introduced draconian measures to curtail energy consumption, including bans on heating in apartments and an instruction that domestic household electricity consumption must be halved, a regulation that is enforced by party activists. (These problems became acute in January 1985 with the extreme cold weather.)

These constraints on domestic consumption, together with the endemic consumer shortages that are reported in those countries are also likely to affect labour discipline and work incentives. Firstly the effect of monetary incentives on work discipline and productivity is of course considerably reduced if there is little to spend earnings on, or they cannot be used if obtained. Romania for example has increased the supply of white goods to the population as domestic foodstuff supply has dwindled. The constraints on domestic electricity consumption of course makes them virtually unusable. In addition the need to queue for basic staple commodities, possibly for hours, is effectively a hidden form of work and contributes to absenteeism. Finally the whole problem of shortages saps morale, breeds cynicism, and contributes to low productivity.

## Prospects for growth of the capital stock

Changes in the capital stock are largely determined by the volume of new investment brought into service in a given period minus the volume of capital taken out of service. The critical variable that planners can affect is the volume of new investment undertaken in the non-military sector of the economy. The situation facing the majority of East European countries at the beginning of the 1980s is that the volume of new investment is actually declining, although this does not necessarily imply that the stock of capital is being reduced, provided retired capital is still smaller than new investment. A continuation of this trend would of course imply an increase in the age of capital in use throughout Eastern Europe. Furthermore, as much of the reduction in new investment involves cut backs in investment of machinery and equipment imported from the West, the problem has considerable importance for exporters, particularly in Western Europe.

The growth of new investment in the economies will be critically affected by the following variables:

a)   The growth of domestic material output (net material product). Critically however this will depend not just on actual physical output in the economy (NMP produced) but the amount that remains available for distribution in the domestic economy after resource flows connected with foreign trade and, where applicable, foreign investment have been netted off. The latter concept is normally referred to as net material product (NMP) utilized and is normally measured in East European economies in domestic (constant) prices. The use of domestic constant prices means that a deterioration in the terms of trade which would require an economy to export more domestic output to achieve a given volume of imports would be reflected in a reduction in NMP utilised relative to NMP produced. If, however, the deterioration in the terms of trade purely resulted in an equivalent balance of payments deficit (however financed) the ratio of NMP utilised to NMP produced would remain unchanged. The fall in ratio of NMP utilised to NMP produced has become critical for the East European economies in the early 1980s and may continue to pose problems for the remainder of the decade.

b)   The pressure to maintain (or not to reduce too drastically) consumption levels.

c)   The demand for defence expenditure.

### Net Material Product utilised

From 1971-1975 foreign borrowing allowed NMP utilised to grow faster than NMP produced for each CMEA country except the GDR and the USSR. In the second half of the 1970s the initial reduction in rate of new borrowing from the West and the need to run balance of trade surpluses to repay existing loans resulted in this process being reversed and NMP utilised has grown more slowly than NMP produced, with the problem becoming particularly acute in the early 1980s. The problem has also been complicated by the gradual increase in the price of Soviet oil exported to Eastern Europe. In the mid-1970s the USSR ran substantial trade surpluses with East European nations (i.e. East Europe was not required to increase its exports to pay for the increased price of Soviet oil) but in 1978, and again in 1982 and 1983, the USSR substantially increased the real volume of its imports of machinery and equipment from Eastern Europe.

Estimates of the comparative rates of growth of NMP utilised to NMP produced from 1975-1982 for all the CMEA countries are shown in Table 10.2. They indicate that for Bulgaria, Czechoslovakia, Hungary and Romania, the ratio of NMP utilised to NMP produced had fallen below 90% in 1982 in comparison with 1975 while it has remained approximately constant in only the USSR. The greater part of this reduction in the ratio took place in 1981 and 1982 and preliminary data suggests it continued in 1983. As a result NMP utilised actually fell between 1980 and 1982 by 23% in Poland, 7% in Czechoslovakia, 6% in Romania and 2% in Hungary. The constancy of the Polish ratio reflects the drastic reduction in NMP produced and the ratio of NMP utilised to NMP produced has been largely maintained by balance of trade deficits with the CMEA countries, particularly the USSR, while the repayment of Western deficits has not commenced. Similarly, Hungary's avoidance of a more rapid reduction in NMP utilised in the 1980s largely reflects continued large deficits in visible trade with the West in 1981 and 1982.

**TABLE 10.2 AVAILABILITY OF NET MATERIAL PRODUCT FOR UTILISATION IN 1982**

| | Growth NMP 1975 = 100 | | | Growth NMP utilised 1980 = 100 | NMP utilised in investment 1980 = 100 |
| --- | --- | --- | --- | --- | --- |
| | prod | utilised | ratio | | |
| Bulgaria | 147 | 123 | 84 | 110 | 114 |
| Czechoslovakia | 119 | 105 | 88 | 95 | 75 |
| Hungary | 123 | 108 | 88 | 98 | 79 |
| GDR | 129 | 117 | 91 | 98 | 82 |
| Poland | 85 | 82 | 96 | 80 | − 60 |
| Romania | 147 | 126 | 86 | 94 | 76 |
| USSR | 130 | 132 | 101 | 107 | 117 |

Sources: Estimated from CMEA statistics, and plan fulfilment data.

The constancy of the Soviet figures partly reflects the lower proportion of foreign trade but also shows that the USSR has used its oil wealth initially to eliminate the need for new borrowing and subsequently start to repay debt to the West and increase the volume of arms supplies to the Third World. While the real value of imports and exports from non-socialist countries has grown about equally, there have been some gains in trade with East European countries, partially offset by a transfer of resources to developing countries.

**Investment**

Faced with an actual reduction in the resources available for distribution in the domestic economy, central planners have been, and will continue to be, faced with some awkward decisions to make concerning the distribution of those resources between investment and consumption. The available evidence indicates that despite the high priority attached to investment per se, it is also to a considerable extent used as a residual factor when NMP utilised oscillates. In the early 1970s when foreign borrowing was accelerating and NMP utilised grew faster than NMP produced, the East European countries (with the exception of the GDR) maintained the rate of growth of consumption (including social consumption) below the rate of growth of NMP produced and channelled the increase in available resources into investment. Similarly, in the period from 1976-80, when the need to repay loans and the terms of

279

trade inside CMEA moved against the East European nations with the result that NMP utilised grew more slowly than NMP produced, planners in all countries maintained the rate of growth of consumption above that of NMP produced and reduced the rate of growth of investment. The cutbacks in investment growth and ultimately in investment itself have grown more severe as the pressures themselves have been increased, and inevitably even the official statistics have supported anecdotal evidence which indicates that there has been a drastic reduction in the growth of personal consumption, or even a decline in personal consumption.

Data on actual levels of investment and capital formation in Soviet and East European economies are again subject to a number of statistical and conceptual problems which make accurate comparisons between countries and between years impossible and even approximations are hazardous. Plan data are normally presented in constant prices, while initial figures for fulfilment are frequently given in current prices. Price changes in the machinery sectors have been considerable in most countries in the 1980s resulting in problems of interpretation. Data are sometimes republished in constant prices or in terms of 'physical volume' but the methods of deflation are suspect and vary considerably from country to country.

Different measures are also used and are frequently difficult to reconcile. The most straightforward measure is capital outlay (gross fixed capital formation) or the sum of new (gross) investment undertaken in the economy in any given year. This is the indicator which is probably subject to the most annual variation. As the rate of growth of investment has been fairly high until comparatively recently and there has been a marked reluctance to close down obsolete plant, the growth of the capital stock has remained positive even when the new investment has been negative. This factor is likely to continue through the mid 1980s.

An additional measure is the proportion of net material product utilised which is distributed towards the 'accumulation fund', the latter being broadly defined as 'net investment plus stock changes'. This measure also includes investment for military purposes and depreciation is probably undervalued. However, combining the proportion of NMP utilised allocated to accumulation with estimates of the growth of NMP utilised an approximate measure of the growth of net investment in the economy can be arrived at.

Some of these estimates for the Soviet and East European economies are also shown in Table 10.2.

280

Despite the reservations about the actual measures, some clearly definable trends can be discerned throughout the region.

a)  The planned rate of growth of investment throughout the region (including the USSR) will be considerably lower than previously and the ratio of investment to NMP produced will decline in each country of the region.

b)  The proportion of NMP utilised devoted to investment declined in each country of the region between 1975 and 1982. The growth of net investment in each country, except Bulgaria and the USSR, was negative in both 1981 and 1982. Investment was negative in Bulgaria in 1982 and the firm growth in investment in the USSR in 1982 followed negative growth in 1979 and 1980. The largest falls in investment were registered by Poland and Romania, although the quality of the data means these estimates should be treated with extreme caution.

The unavoidable conclusion is that external pressures have forced the East European countries to curtail their rate of domestic investment below the levels originally planned, which were in themselves lower than those attained previously. The degree of cutbacks appears to be greatest in those countries that are most severely affected by balance of payments pressures, although Czechoslovakia does not fit this general pattern. It may well be that the Czech leadership are more nervous of possible public reaction to cuts in living standards.

The evidence of declining growth of investment is also coupled with evidence of a lower ability of investment to stimulate economic growth. In each country of the area the incremental-capital-output ratio (the amount of new investment required to generate a given increase in NMP produced) has been declining and by implication is planned to decline further in the 1980s. If this is combined with the decline in capital growth itself, the expected growth rate will be slower still.

## External factors affecting growth prospects in the 1980s

The initial reduction in imports from the West and the move towards trade surpluses was largely imposed on the East European economies by the loss of confidence of the Western banking community in the credit-worthiness of the region as a whole, following Poland's need for debt rescheduling. Western bank confidence has been largely restored by the demonstrated ability of the more centralised economies to restrain import demand in the early 1980s and Western banks would probably be willing to increase their total lending to the USSR, Bulgaria, Czechoslovakia and probably the GDR on purely commercial grounds. Hungary's higher export volume to GNP and more sophisticated banking system and personnel have also helped to maintain the confidence of Western commercial banks despite higher levels of indebtedness. In 1983 the USSR, GDR, Hungary and Czechoslovakia did undertake some new medium term borrowing in Western markets although this was less than their repayments of maturing debt and consortium loans to the USSR in 1983 were oversubscribed. Only Yugoslavia, Poland and Romania still present problems and Poland and Romania have concentrated their repayments efforts on commercial banks, placing lower priority on repaying suppliers credits and foreign government loans. Any further lending to Poland in the short term will probably be concentrated on efforts to assist Poland to refinance debt or to pay for imports associated with export industries. Romania appears to have embarked on a more rapid rate of debt repayment than would appear necessary or even economically sensible, in order to achieve Ceausescu's stated target of eliminating foreign debt by the end of 1988. This target has been largely inspired by the desire to eliminate interest charges and to prevent IMF interference in Romania's domestic policies. Romania has not taken up the final credit tranche made available to it by the IMF in 1984 and though it may be sound policy to reduce crude oil imports, it does appear that the burden of adjustment borne by the domestic population when food is being exported to earn hard currency may be greater than is strictly necessary.

It appears, therefore, that with the exception of Poland and Yugoslavia, the major constraint to increased Western credit availability is the attitude of the East European Governments themselves. The majority of countries were considerably damaged by rising Western interest rates in the 1980s which, by reducing hard currency availability required a reduction in imports of machinery, components and raw materials, and thereby reduced the level of NMP utilised and required them to cut back domestic investment rates. Although the more centralised economies were the most effective in making this readjustment and are therefore the most attractive to Western banks, it is precisely those economies that consider the maintenance of a continued high rate of domestic investment, unhindered by market fluctuations, to be their major economic achievement. Furthermore those economies have proved to be less successful in assimilating and diffusing Western technology throughout their economies. They may therefore prove to be considerably reluctant to re-embark on a policy of new borrowing.

If this assessment is correct the improvement in economic performance in 1983 reflected in higher growth rates and a reduction in indebtedness should not be regarded so much as a turning point in East European economic policy, but a continuation of the strategy pursued in 1981 and 1982, in which the pattern has been one of attempting to restore equilibrium in the economy by transferring excess demand from the foreign sector (by cutting imports) to the domestic sector, firstly by cutting investment and then consumption. Different countries are at different stages of this process, with Bulgaria, Czechoslovakia and the GDR the nearest to completion before a new equilibrium pattern of development may be pursued. At the other extreme, Poland was the most severely affected and still has the most difficult readjustments to make which may still prove difficult in view of the less quiescent nature of its workforce. Romania comes next in terms of seriousness of the problem and appears to be pursuing an over-rapid rate of restoration of equilibrium. Finally, Hungary really only commenced the external readjustment process with any severity in 1983.

## Changes in interest rates

Any increase in world interest rates would of course increase the interest payments on outstanding debt to be made by the East European countries and would therefore reduce the amount of hard currency available for imports. As this would also result in a reduction of GNP utilised to GNP produced which would lead to a probable reduction in investment rates, the most likely target for a reduction in imports would be machinery. Furthermore, if increased interest rates in the West reduced growth in the West, this might be expected to reduce Western demand for imports, including those from East Europe. Similarly, any increase in interest rates would considerably strengthen the political impetus to reduce trade links with the West.

It is difficult to say whether a reduction in world interest rates would have entirely opposite effects, but might just result in speeding up the repayment of outstanding debt.

## Changes in world oil prices

The initial effect of any sustained fall in world oil prices would appear in the first instance to improve the economic outlook of the East European countries that are net energy importers and to worsen the position of the USSR as a major net oil exporter.

Although the Soviet terms of trade with the West (and indirectly with Eastern Europe) will be adversely affected by the current fall in world oil prices, it is possible that they will transfer these costs to Eastern Europe. When faced with oil prices that were lower than initially expected in 1982, the USSR reacted by increasing the volume of oil sold to the West to maintain hard currency earnings and cutting supplies to Eastern Europe. At the 39th CMEA Session in Havana in November 1984, the USSR announced that it would continue to supply oil to Eastern Europe, but did not specify the quantities concerned. Any further cutbacks in Soviet deliveries to Eastern Europe would require those countries to divert their hard currency earnings towards importing oil from the Middle East and could lead to a further reduction in imports from the West.

## Short term forecasts

Plan data indicating the annual average rate of growth of net material product (produced) and gross industrial output established in the five year plans for 1981-5 are shown in Table 10.3 together with provisional estimates of the average annual rates of growth actually achieved in the first three years of the plan period. In all countries industrial output is below the growth rate planned, while only in Bulgaria is NMP produced higher than the plan targets. The shortfall is probably greatest in Romania, where the initial plan targets can only be described as highly optimistic, while GNP growth was lowest in Czechoslovakia.

**TABLE 10.3   PLANNED AND ACTUAL GROWTH RATES IN CURRENT FIVE YEAR PLAN (1981-1985)**

**Unit: annual average**

| | Net Material Product | | Gross Industrial Output | |
|---|---|---|---|---|
| | Plan | Actual | Plan | Actual |
| Bulgaria | 3.7 | 4.0 | 5.1 | 4.4 |
| Czechoslovakia | 2.7-3.0 | 0.7 | 3.4-3.7 | 2.0 |
| Hungary | 2.7-3.2 | 1.8 | 3.5-4.0 | 2.0 |
| GDR | 5.1-5.4 | 4.1 | 5.1 | 4.0 |
| Romania | 6.7-7.4 | 2.8 | 7.6 | 2.8 |
| USSR | 3.4-3.7 | 3.7 | 4.7 | 3.5 |

Notes: Plan = targets specified in five-year plans; most annual plans have been subsequently revised downwards; Actual = average growth rate over 1981-83.
Source: CMEA statistics; data on plan fulfilment. Plan targets.

In constructing production functions to estimate growth rates for the CMEA-six as a whole (including Poland) for 1981-5, Daniel Bond (NATO 1982) estimated that the capital stock would grow by 1.9% per annum and that labour supply would grow by 0.6%. As a result he estimated that GNP (according to Western definitions and therefore including services) would grow by 1.9% per annum and that industrial output would grow by 2.2%. Consumption was estimated to grow by 2.1% per annum. His estimates anticipated a higher availability of Western credit than ultimately proved to be the case, reflected in a higher level of indebtedness in 1985 than now appears probable. He did however note that growth would be critically affected by a reduction in credit availability and argued that a fall in hard-currency imports of around 30% over the period would result in approximately 15% of industrial capacity remaining under-utilised in 1985 which he estimated would in turn be equivalent to 1% less growth than expected per annum. On this basis GNP would only grow by about 1% per annum over the period. Bond does not think that the worsening of East European economic performance in 1978-80 heralds a new trend of poor performance, but should be regarded as 'short term aberrations from a more gradual downward sloping trend of slower growth rates'.

Bond also estimates that the labour supply in the USSR will grow by 0.4% per annum over the period and that capital stock will grow by 2.0%

per annum, resulting in an industrial growth rate of 2.7% per annum and of GNP of 2.6% per annum. Bond's calculations are of different statistical concepts than those published in CMEA data and cannot be strictly compared with the data in Table 10.3.

The predictions he makes for Soviet growth rates however are not dissimilar from those of other Western attempts to re-estimate Soviet growth and appear reasonably accurate. With hindsight the predictions of aggregate economic performance in the CMEA-six appear to be slightly more optimistic than achievements in the period from 1981-3 when Polish performance is included. Thus net material product produced actually fell for the six as a whole in 1981 and 1982 largely as a result of the approximately 10% average annual fall in Polish output.

In general, however, there is much to commend in this analysis. The credit squeeze in the first three years of the plan may have been tighter than initially expected as a result of which investment has actually declined and capital stock has grown more slowly than anticipated. This has resulted in the period of abnormally poor performance being continued longer than initially expected and it is unlikely that the growth rate initially forecast will be attained. Furthermore the cutbacks in investment will jeopardise future economic growth, both by affecting the size of the productive base and by increasing the age of capital which could in turn damage export prospects. Bearing these reservations in mind, Jan Vanous of the Wharton Econometric Associates has recently revised their estimates of East European economic growth in the medium term to around 1.5-2.5% pa.

## The longer run prospects

### *Major determinants*

In the longer run the most critical factors affecting Soviet and East European economic prospects and East-West trade will probably be

a) energy supplies;

b) political attitudes towards East-West relations on both sides.

The problem of energy supplies will be critical both for the size and potential structure of East-West trade. It was shown in Chapter 2 that energy supplies now account for over 80% of Soviet exports to Western Europe, of which oil is currently the most important. Soviet energy supplies to Eastern Europe also substantially reduce the need for those countries to obtain supplies from the Middle East, thereby releasing some hard currency for imports from the West. A reduction in Soviet output, involving a reduction in supplies to either Eastern or Western Europe must be expected to drastically reduce the region's hard currency earnings and therefore, unless substantial volumes of new credit are made available and accepted, will substantially reduce CMEA imports from the West. The development of energy supplies will be of considerable importance in the coming decade or so and investment in both expanding energy development, in substitution between different types of energy supply and energy conservation measures, together with measures to improve the transport network, will be accorded high priority in the next plan period.

It is this development that offers the greatest area of potential for an expansion of Western exports to the region. There is also, however, considerable political controversy between Western Europe and the USA concerning the desirability of such co-operation, with the USA arguing that such development involves a risk of Western Europe becoming so dependent on Soviet supplies that their political independence could be weakened. Furthermore co-operation in energy development may mean (and does involve Canadian and Romanian) co-operation in the nuclear sector, while the technology used in certain projects (e.g welding of alloys) may be adaptable for military purposes. There is also considerable evidence of Soviet and East European disillusionment with co-operation with the West which may well result in a reduced level of economic ties regardless of Western attitudes.

## Soviet energy supplies to Eastern Europe in the future

The East European countries consume approximately twice as much energy per unit of GNP as the EEC nations. This can in part be attributed to the energy-intensive structure of industrial output and in part to wastage and inefficiency in consumption. Until the second half of the 1960s the East European countries were far more dependent on coal as a source of primary energy than the West European economies but started to alter the structure of domestic consumption to include a greater proportion of oil and gas in primary energy consumption in the early 1970s. Although this policy was to prove unfortunate after the OPEC price increases it was continued throughout the 1970s, while energy consumption in total also increased.

As a result energy consumption per unit of GNP increased in each East European country from 1975-80 and the proportion of that consumption that was met by oil and gas also increased in each country, resulting in increased demand for imports.

In all cases except Romania this increased demand was principally met by Soviet supplies, thereby reducing Soviet availability for export. Between 1970 and 1975 East European energy consumption grew by 94 million tonnes of standard fuel equivalent (mtsfe), while domestic production only increased by 46 mtsfe. Net imports of energy grew by 48 mtsfe of which 42 mtsfe were supplied by the USSR. From 1975-80 East European consumption grew by 125 mtsfe, while domestic production only grew by 79 mtsfe requiring an increase in net imports of 46 mtsfe. In practice Soviet exports to Eastern Europe actually increased by 57 mtsfe over this period as the East European countries substituted Soviet oil for Middle Eastern supplies.

A critical problem will be the extent to which the USSR will be able to continue to meet East European demands and the terms on which it will do so. Daniel Bond (NATO 1982) estimated that East European consumption growth would slow down considerably between 1980 and 1985 and would only increase by 37 mtsfe, of which 30 mtsfe would be met by increased East European output, requiring an increase in net imports of only 7 mtsfe. He also expected Soviet exports to Eastern Europe to increase by 19 mtsfe, thereby further reducing East European dependence on non-Soviet oil.

In the event East European energy consumption has grown substantially more slowly than in previous years in 1980-83, largely as a result of the slowdown in NMP growth (although this is itself partly caused by lack of energy availability).

Most Western analysts of Soviet energy production predict that Soviet primary energy production will grow substantially less quickly than domestic consumption throughout the rest of this decade resulting in a reduced availability for export and providing the Soviet leadership with some awkward decisions concerning whom to supply. There is however some considerable disagreement about how serious the problem will become, with some authorities arguing that there would be little or no availability for export to the West if the USSR were to meet all of East European increases in demand.

It is anticipated that the problem may be less severe in the next decade when new gas fields in particular may be brought into service which could restore the Soviet Union's position as a substantial net energy exporter by the end of that decade. Soviet data submitted to the European Commission for Europe present more optimistic forecasts of Soviet production possibilities up to 1990, but their lower estimates also indicate a slightly reduced export availability in 1990.

There are indications that this might result in reduced energy exports to Eastern Europe. It was shown earlier that faced with a hard-currency cash-flow problem in 1982 the USSR cut back its exports to Eastern Europe and increased deliveries to the West. Furthermore the USSR appears to be revising its estimates of future East European energy consumption downwards in the light of estimates that higher levels of consumption would place considerable strain on Soviet capacity. In the late 1970s Soviet energy experts forecast that East European energy consumption would reach 1000 mtsfe by 1990, this figure has subsequently been revised downwards to 800 mtsfe initially and then to 725-760 mtsfe. (Actual consumption in 1980 was 636 mtsfe.) The USSR appears to be providing a firm indication to Eastern Europe that they must cut their growth of domestic energy consumption.

### Soviet policy towards East European co-operation in the development of Soviet energy resources for bloc consumption in the 1980s

The USSR has given priority emphasis in the early 1980s to the development of a joint energy policy which would encourage the substitution of oil in electricity production by other primary energy sources including nuclear power, hydroelectric power and low quality coal and lignite while simultaneously limiting the growth of demand. As a result the East European economies are being encouraged to develop whatever resources they can find within their own borders. Should they find domestic development excessively costly they will of course have a greater incentive to co-operate in joint CMEA ventures to develop Soviet supplies for bloc use, or to cut back domestic consumption. More specifically Soviet policy towards a joint energy policy for the CMEA includes:

a) reducing the energy-intensity and raw material cost of East European and Soviet industry;

b) rationalising the structure of bloc industry and locating energy and raw material intensive industries closer to sources of supply (i.e. inside the USSR);

c) encouraging the East European countries to bear a greater share of the cost of development and transportation of Soviet resources for bloc consumption:

 i) directly by stimulating joint investment projects (eg. joint prospecting, pipeline and railroad construction) whereby the participants' capital costs will be repaid in the form of products resulting from the project and/or

 ii) indirectly, by increasing the price of Soviet raw materials which would require the East European countries to export more machinery and foodstuffs to pay for imports, thereby releasing Soviet domestic resources for energy development;

d) making a more rational appraisal of the costs of development of bloc energy resources and encouraging a greater volume of imports from outside the region;

e) seeking alternative sources of primary energy and electricity by developing nuclear and hydroelectric power, low quality coals etc.

**Can CMEA develop energy resources without Western co-operation?**

It was demonstrated in the introduction to Chapter 1 that in practice the largest CMEA joint-venture to date had involved significant quantities of Western inputs, and that an expansion of intra-CMEA trade could also involve an expansion of East-West trade. The most likely effect of an attempt to develop CMEA energy resources for bloc consumption is to lead to a change in the structure of East European imports from the West. The leading Soviet specialist on CMEA affairs argued in 1983 that the East European countries and the USSR imported too many commodities that could be produced domestically pointing to machinery and equipment, metal products and foodstuffs. Wasteful purchases could be eliminated with improved CMEA co-operation and long term dependence could be limited by buying single items and licences for development in CMEA rather than complete installations. Thus the longer term East-West trade relationship would involve joint CMEA development of Western processes to meet CMEA needs.

It is highly probable that if there is a general reduction in East European imports from the West (or no sustained improvement from their current low levels) that the East European countries will concentrate their purchases on items related to CMEA energy policy in particular. Thus a reduction in the energy-intensity of East European industry will require an alteration in the structure of industrial output which could in particular place greater emphasis on microelectronics, involving co-operation with Western firms. Investment in energy-saving machinery and equipment is likely to reinforce the demand for computer monitoring systems, while attempts to economise on manpower will increase the demand for robotics.

Similarly the development of joint construction projects, particularly gas pipelines, the development of nuclear power, even increasing the volume of East European exports to the USSR for use in such diverse CMEA integration projects as car production or the transformation of natural gas into animal feedstocks will require initial capital imports from the West.

## Will the West co-operate in CMEA development?

The critical question remains of whether it is in the West's interests to co-operate in CMEA ventures and if not how can a policy designed to prevent such co-operation be implemented? Philip Hanson (NATO 1983) argues that two principal reasons are often advanced for preventing the sale of specific items to the region. The first is political — to express disapproval of specific policies and to attempt to bring about a change in those policies. The rationale of President Carter's grain embargo was essentially to express disapproval at the Soviet invasion of Afghanistan.

More critical in the current context is the second reason — the preservation of military security, and although there may be greater agreement in the West on the desirability of such a goal there is far less agreement on the policies to be pursued to achieve such a goal. At one end of the spectrum it may be argued that any export that contributes to Soviet and East European economic welfare, including grain, permits resources to be released for use in the military sector and therefore enhances Soviet military power. At the other end of the spectrum it can be argued that only items that clearly enhance Soviet military technology and that cannot be produced in the bloc due to technological inability and cannot be obtained from third parties are worth the difficulties involved in mounting an embargo.

CoCom (see Chapter 1) is largely concerned with preventing the sale of items that fall into the second category, although as noted in this chapter the current US administration does not perceive the range of products currently embargoed to be sufficiently embracing. The critical area is the dual-use items that are sold for civilian purposes but may have a military application. US officials argue that unlike the civilian sector, the Soviet military sector is capable of adapting peaceful civilian processes for military purposes just as rapidly as the US and the export of dual-use technology may lead to Soviet superiority in certain military items.

Unfortunately such dual-use items, particularly in the field of micro-electronics, robotics, lasers and integrated circuits are likely to constitute a high proportion of Soviet and East European demand from Western Europe and Japan in the immediate future and questions of what to embargo are likely to be of crucial importance. As the US may seek to outlaw companies dealing in such items, if not embargoed by CoCom, from dealing with the USA, many businesses are going to have to think very carefully before entering the CMEA market.

### East-West co-operation in energy supplies and interdependence

If, as expected, the giant Samotlor oilfield in West Siberia is about to decline from its peak output and smaller oilfields cannot increase their output to compensate, the major prospects for Soviet energy policy in the medium term will depend on the substitution of oil by natural gas.

Soviet gas reserves are estimated at about 40% of the world's reserves or equivalent to about 70 years supply. The major obstacle to the devel-oment of this sector lies in the transportation of gas to the market which will require co-operation in pipeline development. Natural gas exports involve a number of physical problems that critically affect the supplier/customer relationship which in these circumstances are also of crucial political importance. Exports of crude oil, delivered by tanker involve little or no physical interdependence as importers and exporters can switch suppliers and customers at very short notice. Traditionally the

USSR has varied its crude oil sales according to its hard currency requirements. Gas shipments by tanker are costly and uneconomic compared to delivery by pipeline. The latter, however, involves large sums of capital expenditure and a long term relationship in which suppliers and customers enter into contractual obligations to deliver and receive fixed volumes and involve therefore a far greater degree of long term interdependence. The US administration has again expressed its concerns about West European dependence on Soviet natural gas supplies and has attempted to prevent the sale of compressor stations for use in gas pipeline construction, either produced under American licence or by West European subsidiaries of US companies.

Many West Europeans, however, see the longer run implications of such interdependence as positively beneficial envisaging a situation in which the USSR supplies Eastern Europe with energy, exporting some of its surplus for hard currency, much of which will be utilised to purchase grain from the American continent which could in turn be used to alleviate Latin American indebtedness. The circle could be completed by US purchases from Japan and Europe. Although the scheme appears utopian it would only involve marginal trade shifts from current levels.

Although this may be the most rational economic future for the region it would require considerable political changes that do not appear to be on the short-term agenda.

**Summary and conclusions**

1)  All the countries of the region have been forced to readjust to the lack of Western credit which has required them to cut back imports in 1981, 1982 and 1983 to bring about balance of trade surpluses to enable the repayment of outstanding debt. The reduction in external debt has been most noticeable throughout the region, except Yugoslavia in 1983. The external position of Yugoslavia, Poland and to a lesser extent Romania may continue to cause some concern for the next few years. It is also too early to give Hungary a clean bill of health. Each of the above countries would probably be better placed to repay long-term loans if new short-term credits are provided to facilitate the purchase of specific essential imports.

The more centralised economies, the USSR, the GDR, Bulgaria and Czechoslovakia offer little grounds for concern at current levels of indebtedness.

Imports from the West are unlikely to be able to expand substantially without a reduction in interest rates and in the rate of repayment of outstanding debt, which could involve more short-term credit.

Albania's trade with the West is insignificant and is unlikely to expand drastically without a change in leadership, although an export drive has recently been mounted.

2)  The need to generate balance of trade surpluses has led to a reduction in resources available for distribution in the domestic economy. In most cases this has resulted in cuts in the level of new investment in the 1980s. Only Bulgaria and the USSR had a higher level of new investment in 1983 than in 1980. Similarly the number of people employed in the construction industry has declined in every country except Bulgaria and the USSR.

3)  Soviet and East European investment in the remainder of the decade will have to give priority to securing balance in the supply and demand for energy, which may involve a further diversion of resources from investment in industrial plant and equipment. The need to utilise lower quality and higher cost sources of energy will also result in higher capital-output ratios.

4)  Widespread cuts in domestic investment in the early 1980s which were most severe in Poland, Hungary, Romania and Czechoslovakia are also likely to affect those countries' ability to produce commodities that will be competitive in the West, thereby further limiting their ability to generate foreign currency and making an increase in the volume of imports less likely.

5)  The demand for imports from the West that can be financed is likely to be concentrated on equipment for increasing energy production and energy saving. In particular large-diameter pipelines offer a market to West European steel industries.

Other priorities are likely to include microelectronics, communications equipment, integrated circuits and items for their production,

294

industrial robots, specialised steels and alloys. The USA will probably step up its attempts to restrict the export of these items from Western Europe.

The USSR will continue to import grains but will attempt to reduce its dependence on imported animal feedstocks, including maize. Where possible it will divert its purchasing power away from the USA towards Latin America and Canada.

In the longer term Soviet purchasing power will largely depend on its ability to substitute natural gas for oil in its exports to the West. Its major alternative source of hard-currency earnings may prove to be arms sales.

6) Public reaction throughout the bloc to austerity measures has been far more muted than that in Latin America. This conclusion holds good for Poland also. The widespread economic hardship currently being experienced in Romania may provide an interesting test of this argument.

# FACT FILE

# FACT FILE TABLES

## TABLE 1   DISTRIBUTION OF THE POPULATION

|  | Total population (million) | Area '000 km² | Density persons per km² | % urban |
|---|---|---|---|---|
| Bulgaria | 8.93 | 110.9 | 81 | 64 |
| Czechoslovakia | 15.44 | 127.8 | 121 | 64 |
| GDR | 16.70 | 108.3 | 154 | 77 |
| Hungary | 10.68 | 93.0 | 115 | 55 |
| Poland | 36.45 | 312.7 | 117 | 58 |
| Romania | 22.48 | 237.5 | 95 | 51 |
| Yugoslavia | 22.42 | 256.0 | 88 | 44 |

## TABLE 2   VITAL STATISTICS 1983

|  | Birth rate | Death rate | Infant mortality rate | Life expectancy male, years | Life expectancy female, years |
|---|---|---|---|---|---|
| Bulgaria | 13.6 | 11.4 | 16.8 | 69.9 | 74.9 |
| Czechoslovakia | 14.8 | 12.1 | 15.6 | 68.0 | 75.0 |
| GDR | 12.5 | 13.7 | 12.0 | 69.2 | 74.9 |
| Hungary | 11.9 | 13.9 | 19.0 | 66.1 | 73.7 |
| Poland | 19.7 | 9.6 | 19.2 | 67.0 | 75.0 |
| Romania | 17.4 | 9.7 | 26.0 | 67.5 | 72.5 |
| Yugoslavia | 16.4 | 8.5 | 29.0 | 69.0 | 74.5 |

rates per 1,000

**TABLE 3     TRENDS IN SIZE OF THE POPULATION**

**Unit: millions**

|                | 1955  | 1965  | 1970  | 1975  | 1980  | 1983  |
|----------------|-------|-------|-------|-------|-------|-------|
| Bulgaria       | 7.50  | 8.20  | 8.49  | 8.72  | 8.88  | 8.96  |
| Czechoslovakia | 13.16 | 14.19 | 14.35 | 14.86 | 15.30 | 15.43 |
| GDR            | 17.94 | 17.02 | 17.06 | 16.85 | 16.74 | 16.68 |
| Hungary        | 9.80  | 10.16 | 10.32 | 10.54 | 10.71 | 10.70 |
| Poland         | 27.28 | 31.50 | 32.53 | 34.02 | 35.27 | 36.45 |
| Romania        | 17.33 | 19.03 | 20.25 | 21.25 | 22.27 | 22.55 |
| Yugoslavia     | 17.52 | 19.32 | 20.37 | 21.37 | 22.30 | 22.80 |

**TABLE 4   TRENDS IN VALUE OF GDP**

**Unit: $ billion at current prices**

|                | 1979 | 1980 | 1981 | 1982 | 1983 |
|----------------|------|------|------|------|------|
| Bulgaria       | 19.2 | 20.8 | 24.1 | 26.8 | 25.9 |
| Czechoslovakia | 38.2 | 40.4 | 42.0 | 43.8 | 43.0 |
| GDR            | 75.9 | 79.0 | 84.5 | 89.8 | 91.5 |
| Hungary        | 19.1 | 22.4 | 22.7 | 21.4 | 19.9 |
| Poland         | 56.5 | 58.3 | 60.0 | 63.0 | 62.6 |
| Romania        | 33.2 | 38.4 | 41.3 | 42.8 | 43.2 |
| Yugoslavia     | 61.6 | 63.1 | 63.4 | 57.7 | 58.2 |

Source: IMF/OECD/World Bank/National Statistics

**TABLE 5   EMPLOYMENT BY TYPE OF ACTIVITY**

**Percentage breakdown**

| | Agriculture | Manufacturing & mining | Construction |
|---|---|---|---|
| Bulgaria | 27.8 | 32.3 | 8.0 |
| Czechoslovakia | 14.0 | 37.7 | 9.6 |
| GDR | 10.7 | 41.2 | 7.0 |
| Hungary | 21.8 | 33.3 | 7.5 |
| Poland | 31.4 | 29.4 | 7.2 |
| Romania | 29.3 | 36.1 | 7.7 |
| Yugoslavia | 4.9 | 40.9 | 10.8 |

| | Services & finance | Transport & communications | Others |
|---|---|---|---|
| Bulgaria | 24.0 | 7.0 | 0.9 |
| Czechoslovakia | 30.6 | 6.6 | 1.5 |
| GDR | 33.7 | 7.4 | |
| Hungary | 29.5 | 7.9 | |
| Poland | 23.9 | 7.6 | 0.5 |
| Romania | 18.4 | 7.1 | |
| Yugoslavia | 35.7 | 7.7 | |

Source: ILO/Statistical Offices

## TABLE 6 AVERAGE WAGES BY MANUFACTURING SECTOR

**Unit: $ per hour**

| | Food, beverages tobacco | Chemicals | Textiles | Transport |
|---|---|---|---|---|
| Bulgaria* | 1.29 | 1.56 | 1.28 | |
| Czechoslovakia* | 1.25 | 1.41 | 1.46 | 1.48 |
| Hungary | 0.58 | 0.62 | 0.54 | 0.62 |
| Poland* | 1.31 | 1.45 | 1.26 | 1.40 |
| Romania** | 0.50 | 0.58 | 0.51 | |
| Yugoslavia | 0.59 | 0.68 | 0.51 | 0.67 |

| | Printing, publishing | Iron, steel | Electrical machinery |
|---|---|---|---|
| Bulgaria* | 1.47 | 1.87 | |
| Czechoslovakia* | 1.28 | 1.71 | 1.22 |
| Hungary | 0.60 | 0.69 | 0.56 |
| Poland* | 1.30 | 1.77 | 1.25 |
| Romania** | 0.53 | 0.70 | |
| Yugoslavia | 0.67 | 0.66 | 0.62 |

Source: ILO
Notes: * 1981 figures; ** 1979 figures

302

## TABLE 7    CEREAL PRODUCTION IN 1983

Unit: '000 metric tonnes

|  | All cereals | Wheat | Barley | Maize | Potatoes |
|---|---|---|---|---|---|
| Bulgaria | 7,899 | 3,600 | 1,046 | 3,101 | 428 |
| Czechoslovakia | 11,061 | 5,820 | 3,600 | 710 | 3,105 |
| GDR | 10,035 | 3,470 | 3,900 | 4 | 7,500 |
| Hungary | 13,800 | 5,980 | 1,012 | 6,455 | 1,506 |
| Poland | 22,099 | 5,165 | 3,262 | 70 | 34,473 |
| Romania | 19,195 | 5,000 | 2,500 | 11,500 | 6,100 |
| Yugoslavia | 17,295 | 5,524 | 661 | 10,719 | 2,580 |

Source: FAO Production Yearbook

## TABLE 8    AGRICULTURAL PRODUCTION IN 1983

Unit: '000 metric tonnes

|  | Meat | Fresh cow's milk | Cheese | Eggs | Butter |
|---|---|---|---|---|---|
| Bulgaria | 767 | 1,996 | 134 | 146 | 24 |
| Czechoslovakia | 1,462 | 6,496 | 188 | 261 | 149 |
| GDR | 1,838 | 7,471 | 225 | 336 | 265 |
| Hungary | 1,711 | 861 | 47 | 215 | 33 |
| Poland | 2,436 | 11,041 | 328 | 423 | 261 |
| Romania | 1,696 | 3,134 | 123 | 348 | 47 |
| Yugoslavia | 1,521 | 1,384 | 44 | 239 | 9 |

Source: FAO

**TABLE 9   PRODUCTION OF ENERGY IN 1982**

| | Total energy production m. tonnes of coal equivalent | Coal '000 tonnes | Lignite, brown coal '000 tonnes | Crude petroleum '000 tonnes | Natural gas terajoules |
|---|---|---|---|---|---|
| Bulgaria | 18.44 | 241 | 31,941 | 300 | 2,849 |
| Czechoslovakia | 66.27 | 27,436 | 97,097 | 89 | 22,750 |
| GDR | 89.86 | — | 276,038 | 55 | 117,000 |
| Hungary | 22.93 | 3,039 | 23,040 | 2,027 | 257,198 |
| Poland | 171.08 | 189,314 | 37,649 | 241 | 167,152 |
| Romania | 89.27 | 7,200 | 30,700 | 11,742 | 1,640,000 |
| Yugoslavia | 35.01 | 388 | 54,276 | 4,340 | 54,162 |

Source: UN Yearbook of World Energy Statistics

**TABLE 10   INDUSTRIAL OUTPUT OF METAL PRODUCTS 1983**

| | Pig iron million tonnes | Crude steel million tonnes | Aluminium '000 tonnes | Smelter copper '000 tonnes | Refined copper '000 tonnes |
|---|---|---|---|---|---|
| Bulgaria | 1.7 | 2.9 | | 60.0 | 62.0 |
| Czechoslovakia | 9.5 | 15.1 | 34.5 | 10.0 | 25.0 |
| GDR | 2.2 | 7.2 | 57.0 | 17.0 | 50.0 |
| Hungary | 2.0 | 3.7 | 74.0 | 0.6 | 12.9 |
| Poland | 9.3 | 16.4 | 44.4 | 320.0 | 360.1 |
| Romania | 8.9 | 13.5 | 223.3 | 40.2 | 47.0 |
| Yugoslavia | 2.8 | 4.1 | 258.2 | 119.3 | 123.7 |

Source: International Iron & Steel Institute/World Metal Statistics

## TABLE 11   PRODUCTION OF TRANSPORT EQUIPMENT 1983

**Unit: '000**

|  | Passenger cars | Commercial vehicles | Motor cycles, scooters | Mopeds |
|---|---|---|---|---|
| Bulgaria |  | 2.3 |  |  |
| Czechoslovakia | 177.6 | 85.2 | 137.0 | 135.0* |
| GDR | 188.4 | 39.6 | 83.8 |  |
| Hungary |  | 13.2 | 1* |  |
| Poland | 270.0 | 51.3 | 55.0 | 107.0 |
| Romania | 160.0 |  |  |  |
| Yugoslavia | 210.1 | 37.9 | 72.0* | 703.0** |

Source: Statistical Office/International Road Federation/OECD/UN
Notes: * 1982 figure; ** 1981 figure

## TABLE 12   PRODUCTION OF CHEMICALS

**Unit: '000 tonnes**

|  | Sulphuric acid 1983 | Hydro-chloric acid 1982 | Nitric acid 1982 | Nitrogen-ous fertilisers 1982/83 | Phosphate fertilisers 1982/83 |
|---|---|---|---|---|---|
| Bulgaria | 847 | 17 | 970 | 758 | 239 |
| Czechoslovakia | 1,322 | 70 | — | 656 | 335 |
| GDR | 935 | 106 | — | 948 | 286 |
| Hungary | 606 | 31 | 1,150 | 671 | 224 |
| Poland | 2,781 | 69 | 2,000 | 1,298 | 868 |
| Romania | 1,783 | 115 | — | 2,008 | 750 |
| Yugoslavia | 976 | 87* | 729 | 402 | 378 |

Source: FAO Fertiliser Yearbook/UN Review of Chemical Industry
Note: * 1981 figure

## TABLE 13   RATES OF EXCHANGE 1982-84

|  | Currency unit per US $ | | | Currency unit per £ sterling | | |
|---|---|---|---|---|---|---|
|  | 1982 | 1983 | 1984* | 1982 | 1983 | 1984* |
| Bulgaria (lev)** | 0.9 | 1.0 | 1.0 | 1.6 | 1.4 | 1.3 |
| Czechoslovakia (kcs) | 12.4 | 12.9 | 12.7 | 17.9 | 18.9 | 14.9 |
| GDR (mark) | 2.5 | 2.7 | 3.0 | 3.8 | 3.9 | 3.6 |
| Hungary (forint) | 36.6 | 42.7 | 50.9 | 63.4 | 67.0 | 56.2 |
| Poland (zloty)** | 88.0 | 95.0 | 125.6 | 139.5 | 131.7 | 152.0 |
| Romania (lek) | 4.5 | 4.5 | 4.4 | 18.8 | 19.5 | 18.8 |
| Yugoslavia (dinar) | 50.3 | 92.8 | 200.8 | 101.1 | 163.2 | 305.0 |

Source: IMF/UN/Financial Times
Notes: * Dec. 1984; ** end of period

## TABLE 14   BALANCE OF TRADE IN 1983

|  | $ million | | Visible balance | Exports as a percentage of imports |
|---|---|---|---|---|
|  | Imports | Exports | | |
| Bulgaria | 11,625 | 11,370 | − 255 | 97.8 |
| Czechoslovakia | 15,800 | 16,507 | + 707 | 104.5 |
| GDR | 21,524 | 23,793 | + 2,269 | 110.5 |
| Hungary | 8,303 | 8,696 | + 393 | 104.7 |
| Poland | 9,931 | 10,951 | + 1,020 | 110.3 |
| Romania | 6,918 | 9,382 | + 2,464 | 135.6 |
| Yugoslavia | 11,104 | 9,038 | − 2,066 | 81.4 |

Source: UN/IMF

## TABLE 15   EXPORTS OF BASIC COMMODITIES 1982

**Percentage breakdown**

|  | Food & beverages | Fuels & raw materials | Chemicals | Basic manufactures |
|---|---|---|---|---|
| Bulgaria | 16.8 | 18.8 | 4.3 | 1.7 |
| Czechoslovakia** | 3.8 | 9.4 | 5.9 | 17.7 |
| GDR** | 6.1 | 11.8 | 11.4 | * |
| Hungary | 22.6 | 10.7 | 10.2 | 12.0 |
| Poland | 7.1 | 17.1 | 9.0 | 7.9 |
| Romania** |  |  | 0.3 | 7.0 |
| Yugoslavia | 11.2 | 6.7 | 10.5 | 22.0 |

|  | Machinery & transport equipment | Miscellaneous manufactured goods | Others |
|---|---|---|---|
| Bulgaria | 46.9 | 9.4 | 2.1 |
| Czechoslovakia** | 51.7 | 11.4 | 0.1 |
| GDR** | 55.8 | 14.9 | — |
| Hungary | 31.5 | 10.6 | 2.4 |
| Poland | 43.8 | 7.3 | 7.8 |
| Romania** | 9.9 | 1.7 | 81.1 |
| Yugoslavia | 31.1 | 18.1 | 0.4 |

Source: Yearbook of International Trade Statistics
Notes: * included in food and beverages; ** 1981 figures

## TABLE 16   IMPORTS OF BASIC COMMODITIES 1982

**Percentage breakdown**

| | Food & beverages | Fuels & raw materials | Chemicals | Basic manufactures |
|---|---|---|---|---|
| Bulgaria | 2.6 | 50.8 | 5.5 | 4.8 |
| Czechoslovakia | 8.4 | 33.6 | 7.4 | 10.2 |
| GDR | 19.4 | 32.8 | 9.4 | * |
| Hungary | 6.6 | 27.8 | 13.6 | 16.7 |
| Poland | 16.6 | 24.0 | 14.6 | 10.3 |
| Romania** | | | 0.5 | 0.3 |
| Yugoslavia | 5.0 | 36.4 | 12.4 | 15.1 |

| | Machinery & transport equipment | Miscellaneous manufactured goods | Others |
|---|---|---|---|
| Bulgaria | 33.9 | 2.2 | 0.2 |
| Czechoslovakia | 34.8 | 3.8 | 1.8 |
| GDR | 33.1 | 5.3 | — |
| Hungary | 28.9 | 5.5 | 0.9 |
| Poland | 27.1 | 4.6 | 2.8 |
| Romania** | 8.0 | — | 91.2 |
| Yugoslavia | 27.8 | 2.7 | 0.6 |

Source: Yearbook of International Trade Statistics
Notes: * included in food and beverages; ** 1981 figures

308

## TABLE 17   INDEX OF CONSUMER PRICES 1979-1983

| 1970 = 100 | 1979 | 1980 | 1981 | 1982 | 1983 |
|---|---|---|---|---|---|
| Bulgaria | 107.7 | 122.9 | 123.3 | 106.4* | |
| Czechoslovakia | 108.6 | 111.8 | 112.7 | 110.8 | |
| GDR | 98.5 | 98.9 | 99.1 | | |
| Hungary | 142.4 | 155.4 | 162.5 | 173.7 | 186.4 |
| Poland | 143.6 | 157.1 | 190.4 | 243.4 | 294.5 |
| Romania** | 98.5 | 100.0 | 102.2 | 119.5 | 125.7 |
| Yugoslavia | 428.5 | 558.7 | 787.4 | 1,100.0 | 1,474.5 |

Source: ILO
Notes * rebased on that year; ** 1980 = 100

## TABLE 18   TRENDS IN TOTAL CONSUMER EXPENDITURE 1979-1983

| | 1979 | 1980 | 1981 | 1982 | 1983 |
|---|---|---|---|---|---|
| Bulgaria (billion leva) | 9.4 | 10.2 | 10.8 | 11.5 | 12.1 |
| Czechoslovakia (billion koruny) | 304.6 | 315.0 | 324.0 | 344.8 | 357.4 |
| GDR (billion marks) | 114.8 | 118.6 | 130.6 | 157.7 | 169.2 |
| Hungary (billion forints) | 399.6 | 441.2 | 477.7 | 513.1 | 551.6 |
| Poland* (billion złoty) | 1,475.0 | 1,668.4 | 2,029.5 | 3,459.5 | 4,329.2 |
| Romania (million lei) | 315.3 | 341.7 | 369.9 | 457.3 | 512.5 |
| Yugoslavia (billion dinars) | 623.4 | 822.9 | 1,148.2 | 1,518.7 | 1,959.2 |

Source: National Accounts/Euromonitor/OECD
Note: * figures are for net material product-personal consumption only

**TABLE 19  TRENDS IN TOTAL RETAIL SALES 1979-1982**

|  | 1979 | 1980 | 1981 | 1982 |
|---|---|---|---|---|
| Bulgaria |  |  |  |  |
| (billion leva) | 10 | 12 | 13 | 13 |
| Czechoslovakia |  |  |  |  |
| (billion koruny) | 250 | 255 | 261 | 268 |
| GDR (billion marks) | 96 | 100 | 103 | 104 |
| Hungary (billion forints) | 313 | 342 | 381 | 411 |
| Poland   (billion zloty) | 1,235 | 1,334 | 1,511 | 2,690 |
| Romania (million lei) | 198 | 213 | 223 | 251 |
| Yugoslavia |  |  |  |  |
| (billion dinars) | 524 | 698 | 974 | 1,286 |

Source: Retail Trade International/National Statistics

**TABLE 20  COMMUNICATIONS AND MASS MEDIA 1982**

|  | Telvisions per 1,000 people | Radios per 1,000 people | No of daily newspapers | Circulation per 1,000 |
|---|---|---|---|---|
| Bulgaria | 190 | 189 | 12 | 234 |
| Czechoslovakia | 280 | 291 | 30 | 304 |
| GDR | 356 | 349 | 39 | 517 |
| Hungary | 265 | 267 | 27 | 242 |
| Poland | 334 | 441 | 44 | 237 |
| Romania | 270 | 330 | 35 | 181 |
| Yugoslavia | 199 | 212 | 27 | 103 |

Source: UNESCO/Statistical Office

310

# Bulgaria

# Czechoslovakia

# East Germany

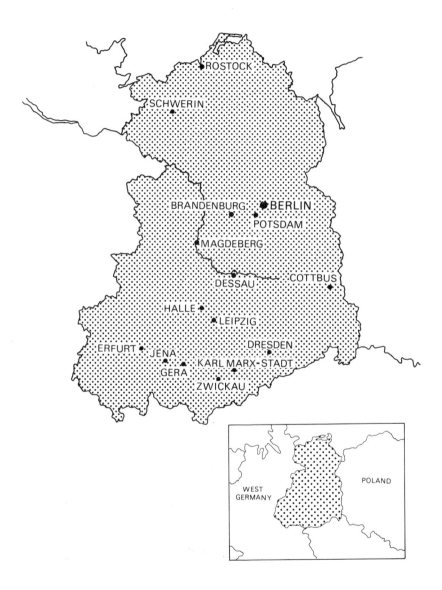

# Hungary

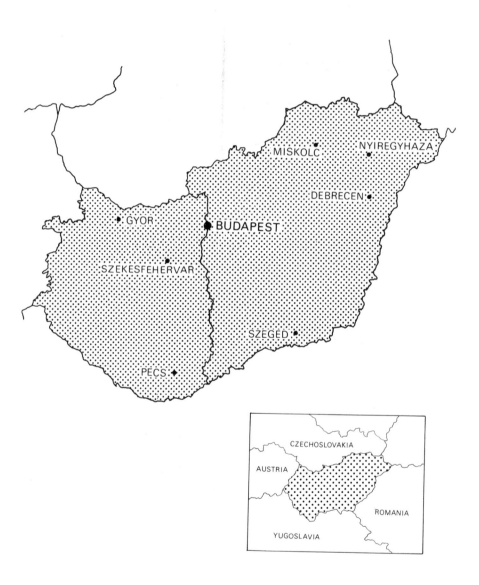

# Poland

# Romania

# Yugoslavia

# LIST OF TABLES

Continued...

Continued...

Continued...

Continued...

Continued...

Continued...

324

**Eastern Europe Outlook**